THE
MIRACLES
OF
Saint Anthony Mary Claret

"You shall be holy unto me, because I the Lord am holy, and I have separated you from other people, that you should be mine."
—Leviticus 20:26

Saint Anthony Mary Claret (1809-1871) as Archbishop of Santiago, Cuba.

THE
MIRACLES
OF
Saint Anthony Mary Claret
—Archbishop and Founder—

by

Fr. Juan Echevarria, C.M.F., Ph.D.

Translated by Sister Mary Gonzaga
Of The Congregation of the Sisters of Divine Providence

*"The spirit of the Lord is upon me, because
the Lord hath anointed me: he hath sent me to
preach to the meek, to heal the contrite of heart,
and to preach a release to the captives, and
deliverance to them that are shut up."*
—Isaias 61:1

TAN BOOKS AND PUBLISHERS, INC.
Rockford, Illinois 61105

IMPRIMI POTEST: Adm. Rev. Justus Sedano, C.M.F.
Sup. Provincialis

NIHIL OBSTAT: Adm. Rev. Msgr. J. J. Clifford, S.T.L., J.C.L.
Censor Deputatus

IMPRIMATUR: ✠ Joannes Josephus Cantwell
Archiepiscopus Angelorum
Die 15, Decembris 1937

Originally published by the Claretian Major Seminary, Compton, California in 1938 under the title *Reminiscences of Blessed Anthony Mary Claret*. Reprinted in 1992 by TAN Books and Publishers, Inc. under the present title.

Library of Congress Catalog Card No.: 92-61033

ISBN: 0-89555-473-9

TAN BOOKS AND PUBLISHERS, INC.
P.O. Box 424
Rockford, Illinois 61105
1992

"You are the salt of the earth. But if the salt lose its savor, wherewith shall it be salted? It is good for nothing any more but to be cast out, and to be trodden on by men. You are the light of the world. A city seated on a mountain cannot be hid. Neither do men light a candle and put it under a bushel, but upon a candlestick, that it may shine to all that are in the house. So let your light shine before men, that they may see your good works, and glorify your Father who is in heaven."

—*Matthew* 5:13-16

PUBLISHER'S PREFACE

We are very pleased to present *The Miracles of St. Anthony Mary Claret*, which was originally published in 1938 by the Claretian Major Seminary at Compton, California under the title *Reminiscences of St. Anthony Mary Claret*. This book is actually a chronological biography of the Saint, presented in the form of a series of short anecdotes about many of his more famous miracles and the unusual events of his life.

This book is obviously not intended to be a complete and thoroughgoing life of St. Anthony Mary, but rather it is an attempt to demonstrate his warmth and humanity, on the one hand, and the scope and impact of his life, on the other.

We have chosen to retitle this book *The Miracles of St. Anthony Mary Claret* to give it more appeal and to communicate more effectively the fact that—since the first publication of this book—he has been canonized by the Church (1950). We are definitely unabashed and unapologetic about the fact that St. Anthony Mary Claret was a miracle-worker. From perusing numerous Saints' lives, it is our conviction that, if one digs very deeply into the life of any given Saint, he will find there elements of the miraculous, to a greater or lesser degree, depending on the person. Consequently, why should we not let people know right from the start what they will be encountering in this book?

The main question readers can legitimately ask is, "Why *three* books on St. Anthony Mary Claret?" Since we have already republished Fanchon Royer's masterful and highly moving *The Life of St. Anthony Mary Claret*, plus the powerful *Autobiography of St. Anthony Mary Claret*, why do we issue yet another? Do these books not duplicate each other?

To an extent, they do. Obviously, the Saint led only one life, and there is bound to be duplication in these three narratives. Nonetheless, St. Anthony Mary Claret is such an important Saint for us today that as much as possible needs to be known about him. Most importantly, his life is a blazing example to our poor, sin-beleaguered age of the importance and seriousness of the Catholic Faith. If one man would consume himself so completely in spreading and making better known that Faith, there must be something in Catholicism to look at most seriously. For why else would a priest, for example, in just 35 years preach some 25,000 sermons—that averages almost 2 per day, for each day of his priesthood. And why would he curtail his sleep, sometimes to only one hour a night, in order to write 144 books and pamphlets in that same time span? He must have been about something very serious, something which well deserves our attention.

But perhaps even more important is the example he has given for priests and those other apostles of Christ who have dedicated their lives to spreading the Catholic Faith and making it better known. What a stupendous example he has given of how much just one person can achieve when on fire with the love of God! A person can hardly imagine the Apostles themselves more in love with Christ or more dedicated to His work.

Each of the three books on St. Anthony Mary Claret reveals a different facet of his personality and his apostolate. The *Autobiography* shows his life and his work as he saw it, from inside, revealing what motivated him, as he personally stated it; yet it is perforce too modest regarding his miracles and zeal. *The Life* puts it all into perspective and tells basically everything. But *The Miracles* emphasizes his command and power over people and events—often almost as if he did not want it or intend it.

Each book, therefore, has its own message, for each gives its own special insights into the life and work of a man singularly appointed by God to do great things for the Church and to serve as seemingly an unparalleled example to our soft and comfort-oriented age as to what one person can really accomplish when driven by the love of God, the salvation of souls and the welfare of Holy Mother the Church.

May the reissuance of this present book of miracles from the life of St. Anthony Mary Claret serve to inspire Catholic people everywhere and to instill in our young people especially the desire to dedicate their lives to God and to the service of His holy religion.

Thomas A. Nelson, August 11, 1992
Feast of St. Philomena, Virgin and Martyr.

PROLOGUE
HISTORICAL SOURCES

The life of Blessed Anthony Claret is a wheat-field, wide in extension, laden with grain, sprinkled with drops of blood from his moral martyrdom.

Historians and critics, pedagogues and ascetics, orators and psychologists have made their harvest in these wheat-fields of gold. We have gathered loose wheat-stalks from the heaps that have been dispersed and have formed them in a Claretian sheaf. This sheaf of golden white wheat is called REMINISCENCES of Blessed Anthony Mary Claret, Archbishop and Founder.

This book has the character of an ordinary biography. The life of Father Claret, so profoundly popular in his time in all its moral greatness, has not as yet entered into the consciousness of our generation.

Remnants of the calumnies are still afloat in the air. Defamatory writings remain in the libraries. Recollections of scandal which impiety provoked in order to destroy the apostolate of that enlightened man, are stored in memories as *Supervivencias morbosas.*

The life and virtues of Father Claret must, therefore, be published on an organized plan. Our means of diffusion is to speak of Blessed Anthony to the people in a language which they understand best, in the form of brief history, in interesting episodes, in charming anecdotes, which touch the spirit and surprise it.

*   *   *

Masterly works are the historic foundation, but their necessary complement for popular propaganda are books of rapid circulation which carry the message of ideas to the multitudes.

They are like rills of running water that spread fertility in the fields, their sources nurtured by great masses of snow which rest upon the mountain peaks. For this reason these pages have an absolute objective reality.

They do not bear in their indexes nor in their notes the spectacular apparatus of an easy criticism. They are, however, built upon visualized documents. In the architectural frame of the historian we have placed, with calculated sobriety, some carved adornments.

There existed pieces of colored enamel, and we have worked them into one piece causing the whole to shine as one great mosaic.

*   *   *

The historic sources which we have used as tools in arranging these REMINISCENCES into a picture gallery have principally been the following:

The Autobiography of Blessed Claret, with critical notes of Very Rev. Juan Postius, C.M.F.

The Resumé of the Admirable Life of His Excellency, Sr. D. Antonio Claret y Clara, by Very Rev. Jaime Clotet, a work of extraordinary merit for its order, clarity, criticism and its abundance of notes and documents.

The Life of Archbishop Sr. Claret, by the illustrious Sr. D. Francisco de Paula Aguilar, Bishop of Segorbe.

The Life of Venerable Antonio Claret, by Rev. Jacinto Blanch, C.M.F., and finally, the Informative and Apostolic processes of Vich, Madrid, and Tarragona.

These are the principal quarries from which we have hewn the blocks of historical material to form this essay of notes. There remains, however, in the depth of the quarry an abundance of stone of better quality. And, if God should bless this work with its acceptance by the public, we will add, in the second edition, new life-pictures which will reflect the many-sided personality of Blessed Father Claret.

Let these REMINISCENCES suffice for today. May they be a small remembrance of his Beatification.

JUAN ECHEVARRIA, C.M.F.

Madrid, 25th of February, 1934, Day of the Beatification of Antonio Maria Claret.

TABLE OF CONTENTS

xi

St. Anthony Mary Claret's vision of the Blessed Virgin Mary with
the Christ Child on Christmas night, 1864.

THE MIRACLES OF
SAINT ANTHONY MARY CLARET
Archbishop and Founder
by
FR. JUAN ECHEVARRIA
Missionary Son of the Heart of Mary

I

THE VILLAGE OF SALLENT
BIRTH OF ANTHONY—UNDYING FAME OF SALLENT
HOPES OF HIS SONS

Blessed Anthony Mary Claret was born in the town of Sallent on December 24, 1807. Pope Pius VII ruled the destinies of the Church at that time; King Charles IV occupied the Spanish throne. Anthony Claret, our Father, was to be, as time went on, the great apostle and wise counsellor of both Church and Throne in the midst of the revolution which would break out, volcano-like, in the XIX century.

Sallent is a picturesque village of Spain, in the principality of Catalonia, in the province of Barcelona, and in the diocese of Vich. It has some five thousand inhabitants and is situated on the banks of the turbulent river, Llobregat. Its principal industry is the manufacture of textile goods.

Sallent, in spite of its material progress, would today have shared the fate of so many similar progressive towns—historical obscurity—had not a child been born there, a child with a predestined mission, who was to become a Priest, an Apostle, a Founder, an Archbishop, a Confessor of princes and kings, and above all, a Saint. This child stamped the *cross of glory* on Sallent, his native town, so that it now shines in a golden frame on the immense map of Spain.

People give their heroes life-blood, language, character,

1

geniality, impulse; but heroes, on the other hand, bestow immortal history upon their people.

* * *

All that is good and great seems to be making progress in the village of Sallent with triumphant display; Faith, customs, wealth, culture, and citizenship. One would say that the Beatified extended over it his wide, purple archiepiscopal mantle as a panoply of protection.

Sallent is today not even a shadow of what it will be tomorrow. The presentiments of our heart tell us so. We find there an humble and saintly little house, as holy and humble as the house of Nazareth. It is the house in which our Blessed Father, Anthony, was born. His order has acquired this house, which we, his sons, venerate as a relic. We have converted the lower floor into a church and the upper floor into an oratory. At some future time nearby buildings having been torn down and space sufficient having been left for the purpose, we shall erect a Basilica in honor of Blessed Anthony Mary Claret, similar to the one built in Assisi in honor of St. Francis and the one in Loyola in honor of St. Ignatius. This cradle of our Father will be the center of religious pilgrimages, the official house of spiritual exercises, and the international home of the Sons of the Heart of Mary.

For this reason Sallent is for us a symbol, an appeal, and a hope.

II

THE THOUGHT OF ETERNITY

The Childhood of Anthony—His Preoccupation
The Pendulum of Eternity—Smiles and Tears
Seeds of the Apostolate

John Claret and Josepha Clara, the parents of Blessed
Anthony Mary, were blessed with eleven children. The fifth of
the boys, the Beatified, on the day of his baptism on December
25, 1807, was given the name Anthony, Adjutorio, and John.

On account of his great devotion to the Blessed Virgin he
himself added the sweet name of Mary on the day of his Episcopal consecration.

The character of children is usually wanting in reflection.
This, however, was not the case in the childhood of Blessed
Anthony Mary. Grace prevented the impulses of nature in him,
and put into his thoughts and acts maturity, profundity, and
constancy.

Anthony was five years old—an age of instinct and not of
reason; an age of spontaneous impetuousness and not of reflex
conscience; an age of ingenious mirth and not of deep preoccupation of conscience. Even in this infantile age, terrible problems of eternity agitated and disquieted his spirit.

At night, his mother, after putting him to bed with the greatest care, signed his forehead with the sign of the cross, and
recommending him to his Guardian Angel, kissed him and
returned to her occupations. As the child did not fall asleep
the mother visited him from time to time to watch him. On
seeing that he was not asleep, she worried as only mothers can
worry. Why did the child not sleep? What was he thinking
of? What were his feelings? "Eternity, eternity! Always,
always! Never, never!" These were his thoughts and sentiments.

* * *

Days upon days blended and mounted up in his imagination; months upon months, years upon years, centuries upon

centuries. Finally he heard, like a sad and distant echo the word: "Eternity, eternity!"

He imagined enormous distances, horizons without limits, immensities without end and without comprehension. Finally, there in the midst of the shadows, at the motion of a pendulum which came and went into the depths of eternity, he listened to the words: "Always, always!"

Then the child looking heavenward and thinking of the eternity of the blessed, smiled, but later wept. He wept bitter tears; he wept with a trembling heart, amid unrestrained groans and sighs; he wept because he thought of the pains suffered by the damned.

"What! I asked myself then," Blessed Anthony wrote later in his autobiography, which, through obedience, he had to publish, "will the pains of the damned never cease? Will they have to suffer incessantly? Yes, always, always! This thought caused me great sorrow, because I am naturally compassionate. It made a deep impression upon me, be it because I conceived it early, or because of the many times I thought of it; but it is certain that nothing was more vivid to my mind. This same idea has made, makes, and will make me work, as long as I live, for the conversion of poor sinners, to procure their conversion by preaching, hearing confessions, and by means of books, pictures, pamphlets, and familiar conversation."

Thus far the words of Blessed Anthony. Can one then wonder at the sacrifices of his apostolate? His writings concerning eternity issue from his thoughts of eternity.

Let us sow the seed of high ideas and holy impressions in infancy, so that the seedling of childhood may bring forth the fruit of greatness and heroism in manhood.

THE VALUE OF CHARITY

The Man and the Saint—Popular Alarm
The Child and the Grandfather
Recollection of Benediction

One must form the man and the saint conjointly. One must prepare nature with habits of honesty, of truthfulness, of respect, and of fidelity, so that the splendid architecture of grace may rest upon these natural virtues. Would it not be sad to see a Christian seemingly practise the virtues of a saint and lack the duties of a man. All of these virtues Anthony's parents tried to inculcate into his soul. One of them, namely, respect, veneration, and helpfulness to decrepit old age, shines with brilliancy in the following incident of his childhood.

The heel of the invader trampled sacrilegiously upon the soil of the country, and the War of Independence broke out furiously in Spain, like a national fire. This war, like all wars, had its martyrs and its traitors; principally because of it, foreign dominion extended over the peninsula. But who knew the results of the first battles? Who knew of the advance of the enemy? Alarm, uncertainty, and sinister presage reigned everywhere. The terrifying rumors reached Sallent that Manresa was a prey to flames, that the village of Callers was a heap of ruins, and that the neighboring people had fled from their homes to hide in the fields and in the mountains. Was it true? The people believed it.

At night this news was brought to Sallent. The half-moon shone brightly on high: the stars trembled; the barking of the dogs was heard in the distance. All was in solitude. Suddenly the silence of the night was broken, and the mystery of the shadows was revealed. The people of Sallent dashed wildly, disorderly, and confusedly into the streets; with the light of their improvised lanterns they fled. But whither? To the fields, to the mountains, to the forests. And why? Because they believed that that very night foreign hordes would set fire to their town, and the inhabitants be shot down.

*   *   *

A child suddenly appeared in the middle of the street, which was overflowing with a motley crowd. A child, with serenity and tenderness, led an old man by the hand. "Do not fear, grandfather," said the child, "I will accompany you to safety." And the old man exclaimed: "God bless you, my son. None of my old friends and companions wished to help me. Only you, my son. God bless you."

The aged man wept bitterly. The child prayed. At their side two Guardian Angels, that of the child and that of the old man, joined their snow-white wings to form a triumphal arch over them.

What happened next? Nothing. Sallent was not attacked by the French troops; an invisible force directed them toward the North. Calm ensued among the fugitives, and they returned to their homes. After these hours of terror and anguish, only one recollection pervaded the atmosphere of Sallent, the remembrance of the child who, without fear of danger, while all the rest fled, accompanied an aged invalid through the streets. What was the name of that child? "Anthony Claret."

His biographers add that since that day his companions venerated him, his elders blessed him, and the mothers of the town reverently envied him.

IV
PREDICTIONS OF AN APOSTLE
The Centers of Formation—Finding of the Money
The Child Co-adjutor

The three great centers of moral formation are the home, the school, and the parish. The three educators who, with official character must work on the intelligence and the heart of the child, are the father, the teacher, and the parish priest.

John Claret was the father of Antonio; Antonio Pascual was his teacher; and Dr. Jose Amigo was the parish priest. These three, respectively, made little Anthony a good son, a good pupil, and a good parishoner. It is documentally evident that John Claret, feeling the responsibility of Christian paternity, taught his children to invoke God and to pronounce the sweet names of Jesus and Mary. He explained the rudiments of Christian doctrine. He urged them to learn their morning and night prayers, and grace before and after meals. He read spiritual books, such as formed his modest library, to them. On feast days he accompanied them to the parochial Mass and to other religious functions.

Anthony profited so greatly by all these instructions that, more than once, on request of his brothers, he improvised a pulpit in the home, from which he repeated the teachings he had received. These lessons sank so deeply into his conscience and influenced his moral conduct in such a way that, one day, passing along the street, he saw a coin of insignificant value, and picking it up, he examined it, and believing that perhaps it had fallen from a window, he called at the neighboring house and left it there.

* * *

His teacher, Don Antonio Pascual, a religious and extremely active man, affirms that Anthony never missed class, always brought well-learned lessons, and surpassed the other pupils, particularly in the study of Catechism and Sacred History. He was often placed in the teacher's chair to explain the lessons to the class. His parish priest, Don Jose Amigo, declares that he always saw something extraordinary in Anthony. When he found that the child could recite the rosary and that he could enunciate the different mysteries, he made little Anthony his coadjutor of the parish.

Every Sunday afternoon Anthony led the prayers and the rosary from the altar steps. Could all these public infantile actions of the future Apostle of Spain mean nothing to the observing spirit?

Though still quite young, he appears, in the family, as a preacher to his brothers; in the school, a preacher to his schoolmates; and in the parish, a preacher to the parishioners. These are the first signs of an ecclesiastical vocation. They are splendid indications of the great Missionary of the XIX century.

HIS FIRST COMMUNION

His Attraction to the Tabernacle—The Two Booklets
The Great Day—The Resolution

Jesus, our Sacramental Lord, is seated on the throne of the Tabernacle, wrapped in mysteries; a host of angels, veiling their faces with their wings as a sign of reverence, is forming a guard of honor. In Heaven Jesus has the angels, but while He lives among us in the Holy Tabernacle, He wishes that children, the angels of earth, keep Him company and attend Him. To-day, in the days of His Eucharistic Life, as yesterday, in the days of His mortal life, our sweet Savior exclaims: "Let the little children come unto Me."

From his most tender years, Anthony felt this allurement of the August Prisoner of the altar, and for this reason the church was his center of attraction and the paradise of his spiritual delights.

Sometimes, on leaving the school, he fled from the games of his companions to hasten to the foot of the altar. He remained on his knees, immovable, with his little hands joined and his eyes fixed on the Tabernacle, giving Jesus the simple confidence of his heart. What was he telling Him?

When on Sunday mornings, and above all, on the great feasts and at Paschal time, he saw so many persons kneeling at the foot of the altar, communicating fervently, and then returning to their places recollectedly, like a rosary of Eucharistic hearts, the soul of Anthony, a prey to holy envy, trembled with emotion, and tears fell stealthily. What were his emotions?

When casually a little book entitled "Finezas de Jesús Sacramentado," the pages of which are saturated with Eucharistic aroma, fell into his hands, and he afterwards read another book, also highly spiritual, he ingeniously meditated on the pages of these two books and surrendered himself to their holy suggestive influence. What was he thinking of?

Our Blessed Father later expressed, in his autobiography, something of what he then thought, felt, and said. "Oh, with what pleasure," he wrote, "and with what profit to my soul, I read those books. Having read some pages, I closed the book, pressed it to my heart and raising to Heaven my eyes overflowing with tears, I said: "O Lord! What good things am I ignorant of. O, my God! O, my Love! Would that I had always loved Thee!"

His confessor believed that he was now prepared to make his First Communion. His teachers and his parents judged likewise. At the age of ten—an age then considered very early for this transcendental act—he received the Bread of Angels for the first time. Jesus made an exchange of Tabernacles; he left the tabernacle of the altar, radiant with gold, and entered into the tabernacle of that heart, radiant with virtue. What emotion of joy and fulness of happiness did little Anthony then experience. "I cannot explain," he wrote in his autobiography, "what happened within me the day on which I had the incomparable happiness of receiving, for the first time, my loving Sacramental Lord into my heart."

It is evident that, as practical fruit, he deposited that very day the following bouquet of resolutions at the foot of the altar:

I will receive Holy Communion frequently.

I will visit the Blessed Sacrament whenever I can.

I will attend the instructions given on Sunday in the church, and will recite the rosary there.

What did Jesus give him as a First Communion gift in exchange for these generous resolutions? The most precious of graces, the grace to fulfill them with perseverance and with love.

Is not this model of First Communion a contrast with so many First Communions of our day, in which the attire of the body and scenic effect at the altar are given more attention than the adornment of the soul and the fervor of the prayers?

THE PILGRIMAGE TO FUSIMANYA
"COME, ANTHONY"—THE SHOP-ORATORY—THE SANCTUARY OF FUSIMANYA—TWO PILGRIMS

The heart of Anthony was a beautiful golden ring in which God had set a diamond from Heaven—the love of the Blessed Virgin.

"Mother," says the man of every age, invoking in his sorrow the one who gave him his natural life. "Mother," says the Christian in every crisis of his spiritual life, invoking the sweet co-redemptrix, who ·is the channel through which all graces come to us. The relation between son and mother is, in human life, something consubstantial and necessary. For this reason, devotion to the Blessed Virgin is an essential attribute in the life of the practical Catholic.

Anthony used to play with children of his own age on a plaza in Sallent, very near the parish church. Often he suddenly heard a mysterious interior voice saying, "Come, Anthony." Then with the haste and the docility of another Samuel he replied, "I am coming, Mother." Leaving his games and companions he entered the church, knelt at the foot of Our Lady's altar, and there spent his hours of recreation in sweet colloquies with his Mother.

His father was a weaver by profession. In his shop were several men who worked under him in the manufacture of cotton textiles. Seeing the seriousness of Anthony's conduct, and the dexterity and the skill which his son showed at the task, he placed him in charge of the shop and made him overseer of the men. He soon won the good-will of all. Taking advantage of the moral ascendency which he had acquired over them, he permitted himself to remind them of some maxims bearing upon a Christian life, such as the precepts of confession, of annual Communion, of Sunday Mass and feast days of obligation. On seeing that the simple laborers listened to his counsels

so willingly, he took another step on the road to spiritual conquest. He invited them to recite the rosary with him every day
while they worked in the shop. They accepted the invitation,
and this practice converted the factory into a public oratory
where fervent prayers to Our Lady flowed from the lips of
Anthony and the workmen.

*   *   *

Not far from Sallent, about a league and a half, is a shrine
called "Nuestra Señora de Fusimanya," "Our Lady of Fusimanya." Access to this hermitage is very difficult. In order to
reach it, it is necessary to climb a steep path, a series of mountains, some bare and craggy, others covered with oak trees and
pines, in a leafy forest. But nothing could lessen the fervor of
Anthony's love for the Blessed Virgin. In spite of all these
obstacles and sacrifices, he often went, in company with his
sister, Rosa, to the shrine of Fusimanya. On contemplating
the shrine of Our Lady in the valley below from a nearby
mountain, he felt the joy of a son when catching a glimpse of
his mother, whom he is about to see after a long absence. He
often wept tenderly and broke out into affectionate exclamations. Rosa and he, taking their rosary, recited it piously while
they prostrated themselves at the feet of Our Lady. Later,
Father Claret visited the shrine many times, as he had done in
childhood.

Today the sons of Sallent do not wish to forget the example
of their illustrious predecessor. They organize, with growing
enthusiasm, pious pilrimages to the shrine of Fusimanya. They
are planning to erect a tablet and to place upon it the following
inscription: "Blessed Anthony Claret came here often on holy
pilgrimage."

VII

THE FIRST TRIALS

The Two Temptations—"Forward, My Son"
Here Comes the Saint—Vigilance

His face grew pale; his eyes looked, but he did not see. A strange tremor agitated his body. Amid tears and sobs he exclaimed: "What will become of me? I wish never to offend Thee, my God; rather let me die than sin."

His parents regarded him with grief, his companions looked upon him with pity and asked themselves, "What can be the matter?" God was trying to strengthen him. It is the top of the oak that receives the first sudden attack of the hurricane. It is the hour of temptation. But what temptation? The most horrible of all, that of blasphemy, and even against the most loved object of his heart, the Blessed Virgin. He knelt down in the church and there the temptation assailed him strongest. He raised his eyes anxiously toward the image of Mary, and a confusion of heretical and obscene words rushed to his lips. In tears he approached his confessor, who paid no attention to what the child was saying. Thus his affliction increased.

"It was the greatest affliction that I have ever suffered in my life," Blessed Anthony wrote later referring to this temptation. He struggled and suffered, and at last he conquered gloriously; and this same suggestion of the demon never assailed him again.

*   *   *

The frustrated enemy fled for some time from the youth, who showed valor and dexterity in battles with the spirit; but he again turned against him more furiously and cruel than ever, with a temptation which Anthony would never have expected—hatred towards his mother. Nothing could frighten the heart of a good son more. This was the trial to which God subjected him now, in order to refine his virtue and to form in him the most advantageous of the sciences, experience. But Anthony, taught by his first temptation and accustomed to the moral struggle, soon conquered the new enemy. His confessor, on learning the means of which he had availed himself, means which he had not learned except from God, said to him with paternal accents, "Go forward, my son! God is guiding you; correspond with His grace."

*　　　*　　　*

This victory over the temptations gave new impetus to his spiritual life; it caused him to increase his prayers and devotions. His fame for sanctity became more public and outstanding.

"Here comes the saint," the workmen said when he came to the shop. One day, as he drew near a group of fellow-workmen who were enjoying familiar recreation, he noticed that his presence displeased them. One of them, more daring than the rest, said resolutely: "Say, Anthony, do not come here. Go away. Leave us because we wish to speak of bad things." "Thank you for your advice," responded Anthony. He never again joined those companions.

Later on, these youths regretted their conduct toward him, and wishing to try the firmness of his resolution to abandon them forever, invited him to lunch. Anthony thanked them for the invitation, but declined it. They insisted and Anthony replied: "I will think it over. Tomorrow I will give you my answer." This sufficed for his former friends to claim a triumph. "We have conquered," they said to one another. "Tomorrow Anthony will dine with us, and then we shall make amends." The fixed day came, but Anthony had disappeared from the house. His companions did not know his whereabouts. "Who had conquered?"

These first temptations awakened in his heart the sentiment of humility. These first deceptions of the friendship of the world rooted in him the holy habit of vigilance.

VIII
THE FACTORY AT BARCELONA
His Attraction for Work—Consultation of Conscience
Padre Amigo—His Slight Faults

The Civil War had ceased; at its cessation spirits recovered serenity, and people developed their initiatives to work to advantage.

In the year 1825, on completing his seventeenth year, Anthony left Sallent, accompanied by his brother, John, in order to establish themselves in the "City of the Counts."

Barcelona, the queen of the Mediterranean, restfully faces the sea. The "Tibidabo" and the "Montjuich" stand, like sentinels as if to guard it. Barcelona is the great city of the principality. It has wide streets, sumptuous buildings, and there is always a bustling crowd. What did the young Sallentino say when he, for the first time, beheld the brilliant spectacle and the large number of inhabitants?

Anthony had but one passion, the passion for work. He went to a factory and matriculated into a designing class sponsored by the Board of Trade. Here he won the first prizes. It was not long before he became foreman of the shop. He won this position by his genius and his exemplary conduct. Proof of his dexterity and ability are two magnificent models which the young man, on resuming his ecclesiastical studies, gave to Don Cristobal Bofill, manufacturer at Vich. One consisted of seventy-five pages with 823 patterns of woolen cloth, and the other consisted of twelve pages with four hundred patterns of cotton cloth, all his own invention and make.

"The sole object of my desires was manufacturing," Blessed Anthony wrote in his autobiography, referring to this period of his life. "My attachment to it was a delirium. My thoughts were continuously absorbed in machines and looms, in putting them together and taking them apart, so that I could think of nothing else.

15

"What great patience Thou hadst with me when I had forgotten Thee, O my God! The Gospel maxim, 'thorns have suffocated the good wheat' was fulfilled in me at that time.

*   *   *

Anthony attended the church of the Fathers of the Oratory on Sundays and Feast Days during his stay in Barcelona. On seeing many people absorbed for so long a time in exercises of piety, the doubt assailed him that perhaps he was not fulfilling the precept of keeping holy the Feast Days. Anxiety followed doubt; torment followed anxiety. In order to quiet his troubled conscience, he immediately went to the sacristy and spoke to Brother March, a lay-brother of the Oratory of St. Philip Neri, who presented him to Father Amigo, with whom Anthony had the following conference:

"Father, I hear Mass on Sundays and Feasts of obligation: I confess and communicate frequently; I recite the rosary every day. In the afternoons of Feast Days, however, instead of giving myself over to dangerous diversions with my friends I devote myself to drawing and to solving problems at home. I could come, as others do, to the devotions in the church and remain there, as they do, but I do not do it. Father, have I fulfilled the precept of sanctifying the Feast Days?"

Father Amigo, agreeably surprised by the sincerity of that acknowledgment which supposed a great delicacy of conscience, replied: "Yes, my son, you have complied fully with the precept; you employ your time well. God bless you."

Blessed Father Claret, when older and full of fervor exclaimed with sorrow: "That was the period of my tepidity. O, my Jesus! O, my mother! How great was your patience with this poor creature!"

As the rays of the sun penetrate through a crack of a dark room and reveal an infinity of atoms and of dust, so the Saints by the rays of grace find in their consciences a multitude of imperfections and of sins. The retina of the eyes of the worldly is not disposed to receive the vision of this microscopic world of slight faults.

IX

THE PRODIGY OF THE WAVES
The Beach of Barceloneta—The Surging Waves
The Invocation of the Virgin—Salvation
Story Told by Anthony

An immense crystal mirror presents itself to view. It is the sea. Its deep waters assume suavity in the reflection of the blue skies. The sun's rays spread a conflagration of glory over the water. Its waves, agitated by the breezes, break over the sand and spread a mantle of lace work.

In his hours of rest Anthony delighted in contemplating this spectacle. In the summer time, when his health began to fail through excess of work, he went to the beach frequently to breathe the fresh air and thus to restore his strength.

One day, as at other times, he went, accompanied by some friends, to wade in the water at Barceloneta, a solitary and abandoned beach, which now attracts crowds because of the marvelous transformation made by engineers. Anthony had seated himself there when suddenly a terrific wave took hold of him and dragged him into the sea, submerging him into the agitated waters. His companions, on seeing it, wept and cried for help. Unable to give him assistance, they ran home hurriedly to tell of the tragedy. Anthony, struggling in mid-sea with the tempest, remained serene amid grave dangers. While the waves were tossing him on high and submerging him, Anthony, from the depth of his heart, cried to Our Lady, "Holy Mother, help me!" Instantly a wave seemed to carry him in its arms. Without any effort on his part, he floated on the water. Soon after, without knowing how, he found himself safe on shore. His face was calm; his clothing dry. He did not doubt but that it was a miraculous intervention of Our Lady, whom he had invoked in the hour of danger.

17

The storm at sea continued. The waves rose mountain-high and opened again, forming deep abysses; striking furiously they threw a water-spout into space. Anthony then understood his imminent danger. He began to weep. He wept because he thought of his unpreparedness to die, and exclaimed amid sobs: "O, my God! What would have been my fate, the fate of my soul if I had been drowned now! Thanks to thee, Holy Virgin, my Mother, for having saved me. I will try to live better and be more fervent in the future." He looked about but saw no one. His companions had fled in consternation. Anthony, finding himself alone, went to his rooming-house. On seeing him, his friends who had supposed that he was already a corpse in mid-ocean, were amazed, especially at seeing him tranquil. They cried out: "A miracle! This is a great miracle!" They questioned him, but he was silent.

After a lapse of years, Anthony, with supreme simplicity, wrote in his autobiography: "Since I did not know how to swim, I was on the point of drowning. The thought of invoking the Blessed Virgin came to me. I did the best I could, and without knowing how, I found myself instantly on shore. I became frightened when I thought of the imminent danger of death through which I had passed and how Our Lady had delivered me."

X

DANGERS AND SAD HAPPENINGS
THE CHASTE JOSEPH—THE INFIDELITY OF A COMPANION
THE CALL OF GOD

Anthony made rapid progress in the manufacture of textiles; but God did not wish him to be a weaver, but a priest. For this reason he called him, step by step, from the workshop to the sanctuary of retirement and prayer. What inspirations of grace impelled his heart? They were varied and opportune. Let us consult his autobiography: "The Mother of God delivered me from danger pertaining to my soul, in a manner similar to that in which the Lord freed the chaste Joseph. In Barcelona there was a countryman of mine whom I visited from time to time. Being then a young man, and making good wages, I do not mean to say that I dressed luxuriously, but with a certain care, perhaps too much so. God knows whether I shall not have to give an account of this on judgment day!

"I presented myself one day at the house of this friend and asked for him. The young lady of the house bade me await his speedy return. In the meantime I noticed that she was setting a snare for me. Having invoked the Blessed Virgin, I escaped from her sight. I left the house hurriedly, never to return."

This instance showed him the danger to which chastity is exposed in the world.

*   *   *

At another time, he entered into partnership with a young man of his own age, and both bought lottery tickets. The lottery ticket prize was twenty-four thousand *duros*. His unfaithful companion, after having received that amount, told him that he had lost the winning ticket. This act, after having placed the young man on the road to robbery, caused him to begin drawing money on different persons and robbing people of jewelry and other valuables until he was detected and condemned to two years imprisonment. This occurence produced a deep impression upon Anthony, which he afterwards expressed in the following words:

"I cannot explain the blow which this happening dealt me, not so much for the loss which I sustained, although it was quite large, as for the loss of my good name. I said to myself: 'What will people say? They will believe that I have been an accomplice in his games and thefts.' A companion in prison! I was so ashamed that I did not dare to go out into the street, imagining that all my acquaintances would look at me and speak of the subject."

Proof of this deep impression which had been made upon Anthony is found in the words of the saintly Father Clotet written in his Memoirs:

"When a missionary, he himself referred to the deep sorrow which the conduct and well-merited punishment of his companion produced in him. He told it with such an energetic tone of voice that it was evident that after so many years the impression had not left his mind. His reputation, however, was so good that no one suspected, nor could suspect, that he was an accomplice of the misdemeanors of that unfortunate young man."

These dangers and deceptions moved the spirit of Anthony deeply, yet they were the means of grace to a higher life. Business no longer attracted him with the usual force. The world was losing ground in his heart, and God was conquering it. The hour of his supreme decision soon arrived. This hour of struggle and of triumph, of violent uprooting and of loving submission, is the most interesting point in the lives of the saints!

XI
THE HOUR OF GOD
EAGERNESS FOR BUSINESS—THE LOOMS OF FANCY
Quid prodest?—THE ADVICE OF FATHER AMIGO
MORAL CRISIS—RESOLUTION

"And you, what will you be?" his parents asked him when he was a child. Anthony always answered: "I wish to be a priest."

"Well, if you wish to be a priest," said his father, "you must learn Latin." He then placed him under the tutorship of Don Juan Riera, a virtuous priest who lived at Sallent at the time. But in a short time this priest died, and Anthony had to suspend the study of the language, much to his regret.

Transferred now to Barcelona and entangled in the business of manufacturing, he seemed not to feel the same impulses of his first vocation. But God touched his heart anew, and Anthony faithfully followed the call of grace.

* * *

Let us read the story which he himself gives in his autobiography:

"Who would have said so? The attachments that I had to the things pertaining to my work were precisely the means God employed to tear me away from it.

"In the last days of the third year of my stay in Barcelona, while assisting at Mass, I had great difficulty in banishing the thoughts that assailed me. Although I enjoyed thoughts of my art, I wished that they would not come to me during Holy Mass and my other prayers. I wished to be occupied only with what I was doing, therefore, I tried to avert these distractions. But in vain. I could not curb my imagination; its rapid movements, like a wheel, impelled by a superior force, could not be stopped suddenly. Besides, new ideas and discoveries came vividly to my mind. During Mass I had more machines in my head than

21

there were saints on the altar. In the midst of this aggregate of
fantasms I remembered to have read in childhood that maxim
of the Gospel which says: 'what will it avail a man if he gain
the whole world and lose his soul!' The remembrance of this
sentence made a deep impression. It was an arrow that wounded
me. Suddenly changed, like Saul on the way to Damascus, I
began deliberating what I should do. I could not decide, and
lacking an Ananias, who would guide me in this new state of
my soul, I directed myself to St. Philip Neri, or rather to the
Fathers of the Oratory. While walking through the corridors,
I saw an open door where I asked permission to enter. There
I found an humble lay-brother, called Brother Paul, to whom
I told the object of my visit and the resolution I had taken.
Having listened to me with much charity and patience, he said
to me humbly: 'I am a poor lay-brother, who cannot give you
advice, but I will accompany you to a wise and virtuous Father.'
He conducted me to Father Amigo, who, having listened to me,
approved of my resolution of abandoning the world, and
advised me to resume the study of Latin."

* * *

Anthony's spirit was now serene. He immediately resumed
the study of the Humanities under the direction of Don Francisco Mas y Artigas. He succeeded in learning Latin in nine
months so that he could speak it correctly and fluently. His
application to study, for the purpose of abandoning the world,
grew to such an extent that, while weaving, he had the book
before him, preparing his lesson.

God's hour had arrived. His heart was uprooted from the
business world. He now wished to undertake only a supreme
business, the business of salvation.

XII

A PROVIDENTIAL INTERVIEW

Words of Praise—"Be a Good Seminarian"
Don Fortunato Bres—His Spiritual Director
His Mode of Life

"Sir, I know a young man, a native of Sallent, who is a model of virtue, very fond of study and of matters pertaining to the Church. I believe that he will be a good priest." Thus spoke Don Mariano Casajuana, the administrator of the properties and the domain of the Bishop of Sallent.

The Bishop, who was Don Paul de Jesus Corcuera, responded:

"Tell him to come to the palace, for I wish to know him."

Don Mariano immediately informed Anthony's parents of the Bishop of Vich's desire. They, filled with hope and joy, wrote to their son who was still in Barcelona, advising him to come to have an interview with the Bishop as soon as possible.

Anthony was not pleased with this news because his extraordinary fervor and his loathing of the world had already inclined him to become a religious priest. He consulted Father Canti, a priest of the Oratory, who told him resolutely: "Go to Vich." Anthony obeyed, and in the year 1829, on the Feast of St. Michael, the Archangel, a date never to be forgotten, he arrived at Vich, accompanied by his family. The Bishop received him cordially. Much to the surprise of the youth, the Bishop immediately assured him of his acceptance, saying: "My son, you are admitted into my seminary. Be a good seminarian."

Don Fortunato Bres, chaplain and steward of the palace, then interviewed him. He, also, charmed with the virtues and manners of the youth, said: "Come to my house; I wish to keep you with me while you are a seminarian; you will be like a brother and a member of the family to us."

Anthony saw in all this the hand of God which opened the road to a priestly career. He remained in Vich and resolved to increase in fervor in his new life as a seminarian.

*   *   *

The first step Anthony took towards the goal was to choose a spiritual director. He selected Father Bach, Superior of the Oratory of St. Philip Neri, a wise and virtuous priest who lived at Vich, devoted to the direction of souls. He submitted his new mode of life for the approbation of his new director. Having obtained his approval, he fulfilled it with minutest exactitude. He arose at four o'clock in the morning and made an hour's mental prayer. He served or piously assisted at Holy Mass; then studied until eight. With greatest modesty he went to class where he took notes of all important points in his courses. After class he visited the Blessed Sacrament and then began to study anew. Spiritual reading, a review of his lessons, assistance at class, visits to the Blessed Sacrament and to Our Lady, study, the recitation of the rosary, general and particular examinations of conscience, and good works filled the remaining hours of the afternoon and night.

His companions were often surprised at finding him on his knees before a crucifix in his cell. He daily prayed before an image of Our Lady of the Angels, which Don Fortunato venerated in a little tower in the garden. With the permission of his director he took the discipline on Monday, Wednesday, and Friday; on Tuesday and Saturday he wore the cilicium (bristle girdle worn in penance). These were, in general, the methods and rules which Anthony followed while a seminarian, according to his companions and his first biographers.

His soul seemed to be at the height of happiness. Nevertheless, one idea, one desire, one anxiety preoccupied his mind day and night. He thought God was calling him to the cloister, and for that reason he wished to join a religious Order.

ROAD TO THE CARTHUSIAN MONASTERY

THINK IT OVER WELL—SPIRITUAL CONSULTATION—EN ROUTE
PERPLEXITIES—THE VOICE OF ILLNESS—THE RETURN

"Weary of the world, I determined to leave it and to become a religious of the Carthusian Order. This was the end and
object of all my desires. Before, however, carrying out my
plan, I thought it my duty to communicate with my father. I
did this at the first occasion that presented itself when he came
to Barcelona on business. His affliction was great when I told
him of my intention. He made known to me the flattering hopes
he had placed in me, the great achievements he and I could
attain in manufactory. His grief increased when I told him that
I wished to be a Carthusian monk, but since he was a good
Christian, he soon resigned himself to the Holy Will of God."

"I do not wish to oppose your vocation," he said. "God
deliver me! Think it over well. Recommend the act to God
and consult your spiritual director. If he tells you that it is
the will of God, follow it, then all will be well. I will respect
and adore God's will, although I shall feel it keenly."

Anthony wrote these golden words in his autobiography,
and they give us the keynote of his spiritual life in Barcelona,
and the secret of his activities in the seminary, emphasizing in
proper time the profound Christianity of his father, who with
such strength and resignation gave up to God the best loved of
his sons, the hope of the family, and the support of his business.

Who would have suspected the heroism of that young manufacturer, pious and jovial, who, among patterns and looms,
seemed to dream only of the advancement of his industry? Who
would have believed that he cherished the resolution to separate
himself from the world, he who was so studious, and so com-
municatively holy that in this atmosphere he seemed to be in
a paradise of hidden delights and abundant aspirations? Never-

theless, one central idea prevailed and animated his studies and prayers, the idea of being a Carthusian.

*   *   *

Now that he had his father's permission, he needed to obtain the leave of his confessor. The latter was the Reverend Bach, of the Oratory of St. Philip Neri. When Father Bach heard of the young seminarian's plan he was at first somewhat perplexed. He asked for some time to recommend so grave and transcendental a subject to God. After consideration, seeing that the impulse of grace, far from diminishing, rather augmented in the heart of Anthony, he approved of his vocation, although rather reluctantly. He, however, wrote to the Rev. Fr. Prior of the Carthusian Monastery of Montealegro. Upon the praises and recommendation he made of the virtues of the new aspirant, Anthony was admitted amid the rejoicing of the community.

But who can fathom the plans of Providence? Did God wish the manufacturer of yesterday and the seminarian of to-day to be a Carthusian? Did God intend, perhaps, to inspire him with these earnest desires for retirement and austerity to separate his spirit and his heart from things of the world; and, in the solitude of the interior of a Carthusian monastery, amid forgetfulness and renunciation, to form the future great apostle of God and of souls?

The hour of parting came. Upon bended knee, Anthony asked Father Bach's last blessing. The good Father was moved. He blessed and embraced him, and giving him two letters of recommendation, one for Father Prior and the other for a Priest, an old acquaintance and friend of his, he bade him adieu.

*   *   *

Anthony left Vich early in the morning. A dense cloud, foreboding a storm, floated in the east. But what did a natural storm mean to him who had the calm of a good conscience within? "Farewell, vanities of the world!" he exclaimed in his interior. "Farewell, friends and family! God alone! When shall I enjoy thee, blessed peace of the monastery, so terrifying to the world, but so sweet and happy to my soul." Thus he spoke in intimate soliloquies as he went along the road to Barcelona. Suddenly a cruel question crossed his mind, "Who knows if God is really calling me to the Carthusian monastery?" He rejected the doubt as he would a diabolical suggestion; soon another question assailed him: "Who knows if your health will be able to stand the rigors of the Carthusian Order?"

He struggles to suffocate these fears in his interior, but a third question came to augment his fears: "Why did your confessor hesitate in approving your religious vocation?"

Anthony's spirit was deeply troubled; nevertheless, he continued on his road to the Monastery valiantly. He was near the Monastery of Montealegro when suddenly a terrible storm arose. The rain fell in torrents around him. This, together with the fatigue of the day, the humidity of the sun-heated earth, and the weakness caused by his extraordinary study of the year, produced such a severe attack of suffocation that he fell ill. Now he could no longer doubt. An interior voice gave clear and definite answers to the question that had tormented him: "God wishes you to be a seminarian. God does not wish you to be a Carthusian. He will reward your desires to abandon the world and to consecrate yourself to Him. Return to Vich." And so he did.

On recovering from his infirmity, he returned to the Seminary of Vich to resume his studies, and he built within his heart a spiritual cell, to which he retired, from time to time, to enjoy alone the regular silence of the cloister.

XIV

THE APPARITION OF THE BLESSED VIRGIN

ILLNESS—THE TEMPTATION—THE CROWN OF ROSES
THE FINAL TRIUMPH—THE STORY TOLD BY ANTHONY

The heart of Anthony was a garden where flowers of virtue grew in abundance. But among these flowers there appeared an outstanding one which surrounded and defended the others like a wall; it was the lily, a symbol of purity. 'Blessed are chaste souls, for the Lamb of God grazes among them as among lilies.'

Anthony suffered great trials in this virtue of chastity at different times of his life, but he always came out of his temptation harmless, vigorous, and pure. The demon, envious of the angelical innocence of the seminarian, presented him, by permission of God, with a last combat. Because it was the last, it was a decisive one, as well as the strangest and the most tenacious.

Anthony was in the second year of Philosophy. The Superiors of the Seminary obliged him to remain in bed because he was exhausted from the effects of a severe cold which might endanger his already delicate health. Anthony obeyed. Soon the demon let Anthony feel his presence. He caused the young man to recall the memory of the world and placed obscene images in his imagination and impure desires in his heart. This troubled him exceedingly. He feared to offend God, a God whom he loved so much! Danger was imminent. The temptation, far from relaxing, increased in intensity every moment. He struggled with all available arms that the Saints and the masters of the spiritual life advise for such combats. Sometimes he fixed his eyes on different objects; at other times he made the sign of the cross, humbly invoking the protection of Our Lord; now he took refuge, like a child, in the lap of the Blessed Virgin, his Mother, praying at the same time to his Guardian Angel and the Saints to whom he was especially de-

28

voted. But the temptation did not cease. What else could the youth do in defense of his virginal treasure?

Suddenly, a bright light illumined his room. He looked up and saw a beautiful and graceful figure; it was the Queen of the Angels, holding in her left hand garlands of roses. Taking one of them with her right hand and placing it on the forehead of a child kneeling near her, in a clear and sweet voice, Anthony heard our Blessed Lady say: "Anthony, this crown is for you, if you conquer." Who can express the torrent of joy that inundated the soul of the youth on contemplating the beauty of Our Lady and experiencing the sweetness of her words?

Later he saw a group of Saints in an attitude of prayer. These were the patrons who were praying for him in his temptation. Again there was a formidable group of dragons who crept across the room, roaring and standing erect as though they were ready to swallow him. All this lasted but an instant. The vision passed. All dangerous thoughts fled from his memory; all obscene figures, from his imagination. Peace and calm took possession of his spirit. He triumphed over the temptation; and now he felt that the crown of roses of the vision rested on his brow.

*　　*　　*

Later, in the last years of his life—1862—referring to this supernatural scene, he asserted that he was not sleeping, nor was it an illusion. In a personal manuscript he left the following annotation: "What made me believe that it was a special grace of Our Lady who freed me from the temptation was that for many years afterward I was not assailed by any similar temptation against chastity. If later on I was tempted it was in so insignificant a degree that it did not even merit the name of temptation. All praise to Mary! Victory! Victory to Mary!"

XV
AIMING AT PERFECTION
ILLUSTRATIONS OF THE FOUR LAST THINGS—THE ENGRAVINGS
IN THE ROOM—REMINDERS—VISITS TO THE HOSPITALS
DETACHMENT

The heights of perfection are ordinarily not reached by one flight of the soul. Slow, dolorous, and constant are the steps that are generally taken to ascend the heights of solid virtue, and to remain upon these heights invincible it requires constant effort. The vision of the Saints, in the splendor of their glory, is always admirable, but a study of the ingenious means to arrive at a final triumph is far more profitable to the spirit. What they did, can we not also do? Perhaps God is calling us to ascend whither they have ascended.

The process of sanctification which we are contemplating in our young seminarian allows a margin to these considerations, for Anthony put into the practice of fidelity to little things, the exquisite art of spiritual perfection.

*   *   *

In one of his retreats he learned that the frequent remembrance of the four last things of man would serve his soul to make progress in virtue; hence, he made pen-drawings of the symbolic images of the four eternal truths, writing beneath each figure short verses and allusions. He always had these pictures in sight on his study-table. He noticed that the material vision of devout images and religious pictures produced a salutary effect on his spirit. In order to awaken these sentiments, he placed a great variety of religious pictures of Our Lady and the Saints on the wall, thus converting his room into a chapel decorated with artistic objects tending to instill piety.

During the day he wished to remember the resolutions of his meditation, the lights from Heaven, and the inspirations he had received from the Holy Ghost. For this purpose he used little cards on which, in the form of ejaculations or of resolutions, he briefly expressed the ideas or the sentiments that had filled his heart and placed them, as book-marks, in his various text-books, so that they might serve as continual reminders.

Feeling the flame of apostolic zeal burning in his heart, he wished to induce some of his associates and friends, who, by their conduct, proved that they were not wholly given over to the service of God, to lead a life of greater fervor and sacrifice. With this in mind, he wrote some maxims and sayings of the Saints and ascetics on slips of paper and left them, as though through carelessness or forgetfulness, in the library, among the books most consulted by his companions.

* * *

In Anthony's youthful heart there already glowed embers of the great blaze of charity which was to consume it in later life. On school holidays and in vacation he visited the sick in hospitals, consoling them, animating them to suffer their illness with patience, performing for them, with great abnegation, humble offices, such as arranging their rooms, sweeping, trimming their nails, washing their feet, alleviating their thirst— acts by which he mortified his senses. By such edifying example he attracted many sick to God, among them a poor soldier who, while assisting at a bull fight in the Main Plaza at Vich, had the misfortune of falling and fracturing his leg. He was taken to the hospital where Anthony visited him frequently. Through Anthony's advice the soldier was converted to God, made his general confession, and lived, thenceforth, as a practical and fervent Christian.

Anthony gave private lessons in Latin and in French to students who solicited this charity, but refused remuneration of any kind for his services.

He gave another proof of his detachment on a certain occasion. Once, while passing through the street, he found a gold coin of great value. A woman who saw him pick it up cried: "Sir, I wish to have a part of it." Anthony immediately gave her the coin, saying: "Here is all of it; but I am giving it to you with the obligation of seeking the owner and returning it to him, should he be found."

The history of the youthful seminarian seems to be woven with deeds of this kind. They are the little colored stones, rich and varied, which form the mosaic of his sanctity. They are the little efforts which served Anthony to exploit the hidden treasure of virtue.

XVI

SACERDOTAL ORDINATION
The Bishop's Presentiment—Forty Days' Retreat
Enlightenment from Heaven—Temptations to
Discouragement—The Victory

"Don Fortunato: I wish to ordain Anthony at once, for
there is something extraordinary in him." These were the prophetic words of His Excellency, the Bishop of Vich, Don Pablo
de Jesus Corcuera, addressed one day to his steward and
chaplain.

What did this venerable prelate see in our seminarian to set
aside, contrary to custom, the proceedings which are generally
observed by all candidates to the priesthood? Assuredly he saw
in Anthony that exterior modesty, so natural and attractive,
which infused veneration and concentration. He saw the har-
monious blending of all his virtues, principally his prayer and
mortification, which made of him a perfect model in public
and private life. He saw his extraordinary application to
study and the great benefit he derived from the teachings of
his professors, prefects and superiors. He saw the fame for
sanctity which he enjoyed among his fellow-students and the
people, who, through a supernatural presentiment saluted him
as the man of God, who was to carry the torch of the Gospel
triumphantly through the Catalonian principality. He saw the
wisdom, the ingenuity, the zeal, and the ability that the young
seminarian had shown in the organic conception and the literary
composition of his first work "Cartas de los Angeles," which he
published whilst pursuing his Theology course. It is an original
and very profitable work. The prelate saw all these qualities
in Anthony, for they were visible to those who came in close
contact with him.

Inspired by God, the bishop removed the shadow of the
future with light from Heaven which presaged the sublime and
providential mission which the youth was to fulfill in the

Church and for his Country. For that reason His Excellency believed that he would oppose the designs of God if he delayed the sacerdotal ordination of Anthony. This revelation was enclosed in the words of the illustrious Prelate of Vich: "Don Fortunato, I will ordain Anthony at once, for there is something extraordinary in him."

* * *

The venerable bishop arranged for a ten days' retreat for ordinands before taking minor orders; twenty days for subdiaconate; thirty days for diaconate, and forty days for ordination to the priesthood. Thus he succeeded in having virtuous and exemplary clergy in his diocese.

Anthony made these preparatory spiritual exercises with great devotion and earnestness. At the close of the retreat, during the Ember Days of Advent of 1833, he received minor orders; sub-diaconate on the Ember Days before Trinity Sunday; diaconate on the Ember Days before Christmas. He was ordained on June 13, 1835, the feast of his glorious patron, St. Anthony.

A divine light came to Anthony when, in the act of receiving the diaconate, the following words, taken from the letter to St. Paul to the Ephesians were read from the *Roman Pontifical:* "Our battle is not against men of flesh but against evil spirits in high places." By this celestial light he recognized the enemies referred to in the words of the Apostle, and suddenly he recalled the vision of the Blessed Virgin and of the demons which he had had when he was following his second course in Philosophy.

The enemy, envious of the sanctity of the ordinand and fearful of the battles which he would have to fight if Anthony became a priest, assailed him with all kinds of temptations, principally against faith and his vocation, during the entire forty days of retreat which he made in preparation for the priesthood. He suffered dryness of spirit and weakness of nature; but his valor triumphed. After the shadows came the light, and from the depths of his sadness joy sprang forth. He himself affirmed that these Spiritual Exercises were the most profitable he had ever made in his life.

His desires were fulfilled. He was now a priest. Soon he would ascend to the altar. He had received the unction of regal dignity. He was a new descendant of the dynasty of Christ. Angels looked upon him with envy, and souls with hope. Like the pearly dewdrop that gleams on the leaves of the violet, there sparkled, glistening and trembling on the windows of his soul, a tear of love.

XVII

HIS FIRST MINISTRY

HIS FIRST MASS—THE FIRST SERMON
ECCLESIASTICAL ADMINISTRATOR OF
SALLENT—SUBLIME CHARITY

It was the morning of June 21, 1835. The bells of Sallent were ringing joyously, announcing the solemnity of the day. Young and old, men and women, thronged the church. The parish, the proud mother of such a son, displayed its best and most splendid adornments. The altar, with its lights, resembled flames of gold, and the flowers upon its steps formed a veritable garden. A profound silence of expectation reigned over the congregation, when a young priest appeared in the chancel, vested in priestly robes. It was Mosen Claret, who was about to celebrate his first Mass. Mothers, on seeing him, thought of their sons and wept. All, on contemplating him, remembered his holy example and loved him. When the moment came to kiss his hand, his countrymen congratulated him with affectionate veneration, and from their heart came the prayer: "May God preserve him for his people."

*   *   *

A little later, on July 25, 1835, he passed an examination with extraordinary brilliancy, whereupon he was granted the faculty of hearing confessions and of preaching. Eight days later, on the occasion of the Portiuncula Indulgence, he seated himself in the confessional for the first time. So great was the number of penitents that came to him that he remained for six consecutive hours, without interruption, at this first act of his sacred ministry.

The people still remembered the serenity, the grace and the aptitude with which, as a child, Mosen Claret gave catechetical instructions in the church, and now that he could ascend the pulpit, they wished to hear his voice as a preacher.

One day the parish priest and some of the officers of the Confraternity approached Mosen Claret to invite him, in his own name and that of the people, to preach the sermon on the principal feast of the parish. Father Claret modestly excused himself, and only upon repeated insistence of the parish priest and the officers, did he humbly accept.

When the hour for High Mass came, the people were all assembled in the church, eager to listen to the words of the young priest, who already shone with a double aureola, that of science and sanctity. His clear and sonorous voice, his graceful gestures, the fervent clauses of his discourse, the divine unction which penetrated, like holy oil, the arguments of the whole sermon, all captivated the audience to such an extent that the authorities of the town, interpreters of the general sentiment, thought of presenting a petition to the bishop asking that Mosen Claret be given a permanent position in the town.

The Capitular Vicar of the Diocese, D. Luciano Casadevall, knowing the moral prestige Mosen Claret enjoyed among his own, upon the death of the parish priest, named him ecclesiastical administrator of Sallent, when he was only twenty-nine years of age and in the second year of his priesthood.

"That cannot be," exclaimed Father Claret, when he heard of his nomination. He went to Vich immediately and presented himself to the Capitular Vicar and said:

"Pardon me, Your Excellency, I am not capable of holding this charge. Do you not see how small I am? How will my parishoners respect me?" Father Casadevall smiled and replied in these words: "Abandon that thought. Man measured by size, is neither large nor small. The greatness of man," he said, touching his forehead, "is measured here."

Father Claret obeyed, returned to the town, and amid the acclamations of the public, took possession of the parish of Sallent as administrator. All was zeal, edification, and charity in the public and private life of the new priest.

One day he returned home late owing to the many occupations of his ministry. The members of his household had already dined. He seated himself at the table alone; but, on beginning to eat, a poor man called at the door. Anthony silently served his meal to the poor beggar, while he himself did not taste a mouthful all that day. He thought this act of charity would remain known to God alone, but the grateful man made this deed known throughout the town. This act, together with other deeds of piety and self-sacrifice, surrounded the young curate with an atmosphere of supernatural greatness, which is the privilege of virtue and was the secret of the glorious success of his apostolate.

XVIII

PROJECTS AND IDEALS

A MISSIONARY VOCATION—A PASSAGE FROM ISAIAS
ATTRACTION TO FOREIGN MISSIONS
THE PEOPLE'S REGRET

A strange rumor circulated rapidly through the town of Sallent. Sadness invaded all hearts. The shadow of approaching orphanage threatened them. A torturing question was visible upon the countenances of the people. Could it be true? The friends of Father Claret gave the assurance. The parishioners looked upon the face of their venerated Father and thought his expression was sad and weary. They studied his slightest acts and decisions, and they judged everything as an indication of a speedy leave-taking. What had passed through the soul of Father Claret that caused him to wish to abandon the town? Where was he going? The people did not know.

*　　*　　*

In the rectory, in an humble interior room, the young priest, the administrator, Father Anthony Claret, walked up and down. On the table of his study lay an open book. It was the Bible. Two marked pages pointed to Chapter 41 of the Book of Isaias, and Chapter 3 of Ezechiel. He energetically pronounced different versicles of Scripture. While meditating on them he shed an abundance of tears.

"I have taken thee from the ends of the earth," he said, "and from the remote parts thereof have called thee, and said to thee: Thou art my servant, I have chosen thee, and have not cast thee away. (Isaias, Chap. XLI, v. 9).

"I will lay waste the mountains and hills, and will make all the grass to wither; and I will turn rivers into islands, and dry up the standing pools." (Isaias, Chapter XLI, v. 15).

"The spirit of the Lord is upon me, because the Lord hath anointed me: he hath sent me to preach to the meek, to heal the contrite heart. (Isaias, Chapter LXI, v. 1).

"Son of man, I have made thee a watchman to the house of Israel, and thou shalt hear the word out of my mouth, and shall tell it them from me." (Ezechiel, Chapter III, v. 17).

The fire of this biblical eloquence had penetrated his spirit, enkindling in him a burning zeal for the apostolate. The town of Sallent in Catalonia, Spain, was too small for his zeal. He wished to embrace the world. It was his desire to go to infidel countries and to enlist in the army of Foreign Missionaries. Suddenly a clear and tenacious inspiration inundated his soul with consolation. He fell upon his knees and exclaimed: "O, my God, I alone am nothing. What can *one* do in the vast undertaking of the salvation of the world? I will join many; I will found a Congregation of Apostles." He was silent. He arose with the spirit of a hero. Soon, however, discouragement came upon him. "Who am I," he said, "to perform or carry out so great a project?" He then remembered his confidante and adviser, Father Bach, who lived at Collsacrabra at the time. He confided his inspiration to him. Father Bach approved of the project at first, but advised him to postpone its realization to some future time. Claret obeyed, but said within himself: "I will be a foreign missionary some time. I long to shed my blood for Christ."

Shortly afterwards, he wrote to a friend of his: "The Charity of Christ presseth me. I cannot resist the interior impulses that call me to save souls. And now that I cannot undertake what I had planned, I shall take the road to Rome so that God may dispose of me through the medium of those who directly govern the Propagation of the Faith."

Blessed Anthony Claret communicated his decision to the Bishop of the Diocese, who used every possible means to detain him. On seeing, however, that all his entreaties were futile, he gave him the episcopal benediction and took leave of him with words of paternal affection.

His relatives and parishoners wept at his approaching departure and begged him not to abandon them, but he replied with noble firmness: "God is calling me! I must obey God rather than men." He left the village like a pilgrim following an ideal and left behind him the void of a vast solitude.

XIX
TO ROME

"Who is the young priest who so resolutely walks on the
way to France?"

"It is the administrator of Sallent, Mosen Anthony Claret."

"Who are his travelling companions?"

"No one; he is going alone."

"What are his means of transportation?"

"He does not wish any—he is travelling on foot."

"Where is his baggage?"

"He has none, save a shirt, a pair of socks, some handker-
chiefs, a razor, his breviary, and the Bible."

"What are his provisions for the journey?"

"A little bread and cheese."

"Has he any money in case of necessity?"

"None. Not even a cent."

"What is the end of his journey?"

"Rome."

"What is the object of this strange pilgrimage?"

"To give his name to the Propagation of Faith; to go to
infidel countries to preach the Gospel and to shed his blood for
Christ."

Sublime aspiration! Thus the Apostles left Jerusalem to
conquer the world.

*　　*　　*

He is now near Tosas, very near France. On arriving at a
place which the natives call *Pont del Picasso*, a man with a
ferocious aspect cried in a menacing tone, "Halt!" and pointed
a gun at Anthony. The ruffian took him brusquely by the arm
and carried him to the chief of the gang.

"Do you carry a passport?"

"Yes, sir; here it is."

"Why did you not go by way of Puigcerda?"

"It does not make any difference to me which way I go; for he who has the necessary documents may pass whichever way he wishes."

"I am going to present you to the Governor of Puigcerda."

"I am not afraid of the Governor, but *you* ought to be afraid of him for having detained a man who has the necessary passport."

They were all silent. They saw the priest did not carry money, hence they let him pass the frontier.

"Who were they?"

"They called themselves defenders of the Queen, but they were thieves, highwaymen whose livelihood consisted in robbery and plunder."

Blessed Claret, referring to the marvellous way in which he freed himself of these evil-doers, writes: "God and our Holy Mother delivered me from these thieves, for it was Saturday."

'For it was Saturday.' What a simple but significant expression!

* * *

Arriving at Marseilles he did not know the city, nor did he have a single acquaintance in it. Unexpectedly a mysterious, cultured, and amiable youth appeared before him. He called for Father Claret at his room and conducted him to the church. He bore the semblance of an angel rather than a man, and he seemed to have been sent by God to guide the young traveller. Father Claret later declared that he never saw the young man eat, for he always disappeared at meal time. Later his guide returned to him. When the day and the hour of his departure came, the youth presented himself in Anthony's room and accompanied him to the port. He took leave of him, and as he entered the boat the youth was no longer to be seen. It was assuredly the Archangel, Saint Raphael, whom blessed Anthony invoked at the beginning of his itinerary.

It was a rainy day in the month of October when the steamer "Tancred" set sail. The first night on board was a trying one owing to a storm which raged so furiously that the water entered the ship and the waves covered the deck. Blessed Anthony wrapped his Bible and his breviary in his clothing, and pressing them close to his heart, he covered them with his cassock and his hat. When the waves rose higher and higher, he bent forward to protect his books. They, however, remained unharmed and dry. His only loss was his meager baggage and the morsels of food which were saturated with the salt of the sea. To him, the food thus saturated still remained savory.

*   *   *

The exemplary life Anthony led during the trip won the admiration of all travellers. One of them, an English gentleman, who was accompanied by his servants and surrounded by every possible luxury, wished to enter into conversation with him. Captivated by his virtue, he drew him aside and presented him with a tray containing a quantity of gold coins, asking Father Claret to accept them to relieve his dire poverty. Father Claret received the money gratefully, but shortly afterwards distributed it among the religious who travelled with him. This act of self-abnegation, far from offending, edified the English gentleman, who was a Catholic. On parting, he presented his card to Father Claret and offered him his palace in Rome.

The trip had lasted five days when the rays of the lighthouse indicated the approach of land. It was night. The lights of the city of Civita-Vecchia, were reflected on the water like myriads of stars.

XX

CLARET AND XIFRE
St. Basil's Convent—A Providential Meeting
The Founder and the General—A Delay
The Designs of God

It was ten o'clock in the morning. The placid light of the autumn sun spread its golden rays over the cupolas of the Eternal City. The Tiber was turbulent. The church bells called to prayer and the silhouette of the Vatican was outlined on the horizon.

An adventurous young priest had arrived in Rome after having made the greater part of the trip from Civita-Vecchia on foot. Who can express in words what Anthony felt at sight of the Holy City, of that city which is at the same time a throne and an altar, a museum and a reliquary, and which stands like an island of eternity in the ocean of time.

*   *   *

The Providence of God ever watchful over Anthony directed him to the Convent of St. Basil, through the mediation of Reverend Father Cosmas, Superior of the Carmelite Fathers. Father Cosmas conducted him to St. Basil's to receive hospitality, but God had arranged a providential meeting there. Several young men who had gone to Rome to complete their studies for the holy Priesthood were sheltered at St. Basil's Convent. At times there was a lack of harmony among them, but, quoting the words of one of them, "Anthony Claret is an angel of peace for, since his arrival, we live like brothers."

Anthony became attached to a particular ordinand who in his manner of speech showed exceptional strength of character. This young man, in turn, was charmed at the even temper and the high ideals that the new guest at St. Basil's possessed. They understood and loved each other, but neither one nor the other could conjecture the mysteries of their meeting. Who was this young man of clear intelligence, of indomitable will, of robust faith, of a big and tender heart, tenacious in action, calm and intrepid, who could at the same time be an invincible general leading an army as a demagogue because of his fascinating eloquence; who seemed alternately a lash and a bridle, a spur and a brake? This young man was Jose Xifré.

God joined these two young men—Claret and Xifre—in a spiritual union during the course of their lives. Although they soon separated to follow different roads, they were again united to further God's designs. Claret became the Founder and Xifre the General of a new Religious Institute in the Church, dedicated to the Heart of Mary, which was to struggle for the advancement of Catholicism.

*   *   *

Neither Claret nor Xifre knew how they would, in turn, collaborate mutually under one providential plan. Anthony, mindful of the object which had brought him to Rome, went to visit the newly consecrated Bishop of Libano, His Excellency, Bishop Vilardell, for whom he bore a letter of recommendation. The Bishop, however, had left Rome for his new See. Anthony then asked to see His Eminence, the Cardinal Prefect of the Propagation of the Faith. But it being the month of October, vacation time for the members of the Sacred Congregation, all business was suspended. Anthony could, therefore, not see His Eminence, nor had he hopes of an interview before the beginning of the month of November. This provided a disappointment for Anthony, for he was anxious to begin his work of evangelizing without delay. While he was awaiting an interview with His Eminence, the Cardinal Prefect of the Propagation of the Faith, he decided to follow the Spiritual Exercises under the direction of a Jesuit priest. Nothing could have been more timely. Who can comprehend the philosophy and the theology of events?

XXI

NOVITIATE IN THE SOCIETY OF JESUS

The Retreat—Reverend Father Roothan—The Mystery of Illness—Novitiate Teachings

"Father, I am a Spanish priest. I have been assistant curate at Sallent for two years, and administrator for two years. I have felt the call to the Foreign Missions for some time and I wish to consecrate my life to the evangelization of infidels and to shed my blood for Christ. I have come to Rome to offer my services to the Propagation of the Faith, with the request that I be sent to savage lands where Jesus is not known." Thus spoke Anthony Claret at his first interview with the Father Director of the Spiritual Exercises, who replied:

"Very well, the Society of Jesus has the same mission, but we always go by twos and in groups. Would you not be afraid to go alone, exposed to hardships and dangers in those unknown and barbarous countries? Since God is calling you to the Foreign Missions, enter the Society where you can best fulfill your desires." The young priest was silent for a moment and then replied: "Who am I that I should be considered eligible to admission into the Society of Jesus?" The director admired the humility of Father Claret and encouraged him, saying: "Do not fear. Address a letter without delay to the Very Reverend Father General asking admission."

The earnestness portrayed in Anthony's letter caused the Reverend Father Roothan, Superior General of the Society, to send for him in order to make his acquaintance. He approved of Father Claret's vocation and told him to present himself to the Father Provincial who resided at St. Andres of Monte Cavallo. Soon afterwards, on November 2, 1839, he was vested with the habit of the Society of Jesus in the celebrated Novitiate which was sanctified by the examples of St. Aloysius Gonzaga, of St. Stanislaus Kostka, and of St. John Berchmans and many other illustrious men.

"All was done so rapidly that overnight I found myself a Jesuit," Father Claret wrote later and added: "When I see myself vested in the holy habit of the Society I can scarcely believe what I see. It seems a dream, an enchantment."

* * *

Three months were spent amid the spiritual delights found in the practise of virtue, studying the Constitutions and following the Rules; in fine, in imbibing the spirit of the Society of Jesus. Sound in body and in a joyful spirit, he began, on the second of February, the "Spiritual Exercises" which were to last thirty days. But here another trial sent by God awaited him.

Anthony felt a sudden, sharp and mysterious pain in his leg. He was carried to the infirmary, but in spite of medical care the pain returned after momentary alleviation. After careful examination the physicians feared that Anthony would be crippled for life. The Father Rector visited him frequently and one day, seeing the progress of the disease said to him: "This infirmity is not natural. You were so contented, so happy, and in such perfect health, and now when the "Spiritual Exercises" have scarcely begun, this strange illness appears. It makes me believe that God has other plans for you. Let us consult Father General, who is so kind and has a knowledge of the things of God." Both went to Father General's room. Addressing the novice, the Father General assured him that it was the will of God that he return to Spain as quickly as possible, counselling him, at the same time, not to fear, but to take courage.

The novice did not understand this supernatural mystery, and the prophetic truth contained in the words of that man of God. He, however, obeyed and returned to Spain.

* * *

Later, Father Claret received a letter from Reverend Father Roothan in which he said: "God brought you into the Society, not for the reason that you remain there, but that you might learn to gain souls for heaven."

These words Father Claret expressed in his Autobiography as follows:

"God granted me a great favor by directing me to Rome and by bringing me, although for only a short time, into the company of such virtuous Fathers and Brothers. God grant that I might profit by it!

"If it has not been to my personal advantage, it has served well for the benefit of my neighbor. There I learned to make the Spiritual Exercises of St. Ignatius, the method of preaching, catechizing, and confessing with profit. I also learned other things which, in time, have served me well.

"God be praised for having been so kind and merciful to me. Make me love Thee, serve Thee with fervor, and let me cause Thee to be loved and served by all creatures. O all ye creatures, love and serve God. Try to find out by experience how sweet it is to love and serve God! O my God; my only Good!"

XXII

REGENT OF VILADRAU

Appointments—Dancers Dispersed—The "Fire at Noguer"—The Miracle of Benedictions

"Go to Manresa, a fortified city defended by the party of the Queen, Maria Cristina, and there you will be able to fulfill the ministrations of your apostolate freely without incurring the suspicion of the Governor of Madrid." Several Fathers of the Society of Jesus offered Claret this advice. Others, among them the Very Rev. Firmin Alcaraz, Vicar General of the Hieronymites, and later Bishop, told him to go Berga, a town ruled by the Carlists, where the religious enjoyed full liberty in the exercise of their ministry. Anthony was grateful for these counsels, but thought it prudent not to follow them, but rather to place himself unconditionally at the disposition of his Bishop. Father Claret was accordingly sent to the town of Viladrau as parish priest.

Viladrau is situated on the slope of the majestic Montseny Mountains, a center of flourishing Christianity and of natural beauty.

The new curate took up his assigned duties with brilliant hopes and earnest zeal. His parishioners received him with the warmest welcome and veneration.

* * *

The fame of his sanctity soon spread through the town. His words were religiously listened to, and his counsels followed. Through this esteem he could exercise his zeal in a way that might be considered indiscreet in others.

A popular festival was organized on a certain day in Viladrau. A public dance formed a part of the program. The servant of God heard of it, and when the music began and all was in readiness, Father Claret appeared among the dancers with crucifix in hand and spoke in a pathetic tone of sin and eternal punishment. The merry-makers grew serious, and soon dispersed.

The villagers applauded the act, and several of the young people were moved to compunction and approached the Sacrament of Penance the following day.

Several prodigious happenings, attributed to the supernatural power of the young priest, were told and retold. The people were confirmed in their belief by referring to a new public event.

Noguer, property of D. Jaime Bofill, became a prey to flames. Father Claret, on being informed of the fire, hastened to the place. Men and women made every effort to extinguish the flames, but all in vain. Father Claret made the sign of the cross over the burning building and the flames ceded to the blessing, the devouring fire obeyed a strange power and ceased suddenly.

"A miracle! A miracle!" came the cry from all the bystanders. "The fire was quenched when Mosen Anthony Claret had blessed it."

Claret fled from the acclamations of the public, but this prodigy augmented the moral prestige of his apostolate and contributed to the welfare of souls.

Anthony rose in the admiration of the people to even greater heights than when he cured their ills.

* * *

A young boy, named Francisco Pladevall, suffered a long time from intense pains caused by nervous disorders. All medical aid seemed practically useless. The child appeared to be incurable. One day, the child's parents carried him to Mosen Anthony Claret, requesting him to cure their child. Claret declared that he was not a physician nor had be the gift of miracles. The parents, however, pleaded, insisted, wept. Claret then ordered that softened clay be applied to the sufferer. In the meantime the priest prayed. The cure was instantaneous, and the malady did not return.

A young man, twenty-five years of age, lay dangerously ill. He was unconscious and apparently at the point of death. Anthony Claret applied a simple remedy and offered prayers for his recovery. In a few days the young man, well and happy, was able to return to his work in the fields.

Another young man, about eighteen years of age, who was so crippled as to be unable to move, recovered perfect health through the application of a simple home-remedy and the blessing of Father Claret. In a few days the crippled boy was able to go to church, where he assisted at the Holy Sacrifice of the Mass celebrated by Father Claret, in thanksgiving for this favor. All were in admiration at this remarkable cure.

The news of these cures spread through the district, and soon the house of the Curé resembled a hospital, for crowds of sick people gathered there. Anthony, however, wished to cure their souls rather than their bodies. He adopted the method of imparting a general benediction to those who were physically ill, but he devoted himself principally to cure the infirmities of the soul.

Rejoice, ye souls, held captive by sin! Leap with joy, ye hearts, poor victims of the world, for now your liberator engages in battle with you. His weapons are such as the demon fears and the world needs.

XXIII

THE TECHNIQUE OF THE MISSIONS

EXTRAORDINARY GRACE—DURATION OF HIS MISSIONS
PLAN OF THE MATERIAL—STYLE OF HIS PREACHING
PARABLES AND COMPARISONS—THE BEST EULOGY

There are, in the therapeutics of the body, radical remedies that alleviate infirmities. There is also an efficient remedy in spiritual therapeutics to cure the grave malady of the people, namely, religious indifference. Parish Missions provide the cure.

What are Parish Missions? Missions are a solemn and public call which God addresses to the people so that they may not be left in the hands of weak nature. Missions are an organized, conscious, rapid, and clamorous assault made by the soldiers of Christ on the city of the soul that lies sleeping, happy, and confident in the power of the enemy. Missions are the austere and grave proclamation of the four last ends of man and of the cardinal dogmas that the world has abandoned as a heavy weight upon it. For that reason, one of the greatest graces that God can give a parish is the grace of a holy Mission.

*   *   *

Father Claret understood the exceptional importance of this apostolic ministry first by calculation, later by experience, and always by inspiration from heaven. Consequently, he devoted all the energies of his life to Missions.

His Missions, which lasted nine, fifteen, twenty and even thirty consecutive days, did not tire his audience; in fact, eagerness and enthusiasm rose among the people. The subjects upon which he generally developed his sermons were on the importance of salvation, the gravity of mortal sin, the necessity of confession, bad confessions, death, the death of the just and the sinner, judgment, hell, eternity, heaven, and perseverance.

At Missions of longer duration he, moreover, treated of other subjects such as the prodigal son, the mercy of God, final impenitence, the last judgment, the conversion of St. Augustine, scandal, the conversion of Magdalene, proximate occasions of sin, the holy Rosary, the Passion of Our Lord, and the Sorrows of Our Lady.

His style of preaching was based on the readings and imitation of St. John Chrysostom, St. Alphonsus Liguori, Fray Luis de Granada, *Sinisculchi,* and, above all, of Blessed John of Avila, whom he chose as a model. Serious study was always brought into the preparation of his sermons, and prayer gave them unction. Study and prayer united gave his oratory the persuasive power which convinced the learned as well as the ignorant.

*   *   *

Anthony Claret wished to have his Missions well organized. He had previous communication, by means of letters, with the respective parish priests, and arranged the slightest details to a finish.

When preparing for a Mission in some indifferent or rebellious place, Father Claret asked the prayers of the most saintly persons he knew, and wrote especially to communities of Religious recommending to their prayers the success of that apostolic enterprise.

His voice was grave, sonorous, and flexible; his gestures were moderate and calm; his discourses were written in sentences neither too extensive nor too brief. Interpolated exclamations and interrogations gave his sermons vibrancy and dramatic art.

"Arguments in the pulpit," Father Claret used to say, "are out of place; the world is lost, not by a lack of arguments, but by a lack of truths." He often exclaimed: "Poor preachers, how useless would your labors be if you were not assisted by the grace of God, and if the soul were not naturally Christian. He walks in evil ways who deals with and disputes with the devil; for the most stupid devil is more alert than the wisest philosopher."

Experience in preaching taught him to descend in word and concept so as to make himself understood by the most ignorant. He frequently repeated the maxims of St. Augustine:

"I would prefer to have grammarians criticize me rather than not be understood by the uncultured." It was his custom to apply, in his sermons, similes, comparisons, practical applications, examples, and parables. There were some who criticized that simplicity and that abundance of comparisons and parables. D. Enrique Ojero de la Cruz, however, defended him valiantly when he wrote: "His language was allegorical; he made himself clearly understood by all, save by his enemies who tried to reduce Father Anthony to the level of an ordinary man. I myself challenged some of these latter at different times, saying to them: 'If the parable is something so ordinary, invent one.' And when I saw those who believed themselves wise and gifted in the spoken word, so confused, I corrected their facility in passing judgment by placing before them the example of our Divine Master, who always spoke in parables."

Great conversions and resounding triumphs were the result of Father Claret's sermons which were delivered with noble, simple, strong, and convincing eloquence. An influential and perverse leader in a town, on seeing the success of a Mission said:

"If this preacher does not leave, all the theatres, cafes, and recreational centers will be deserted."

Can a greater eulogy be paid an apostolic missioner in fewer words?

XXIV
THE FIRST MISSIONS
Silhouette of the Missionary—The Center of His Vocation—Reply and Counter-Reply
The Patroness of the Missions

"What is the meaning of this gathering in Viladrau today?" asked a traveller, looking at the town from the slopes of the majestic Montseny. There was a reason. All the people of the surrounding districts gathered at Viladrau in the afternoons. The casinos and the taverns were closed. Songs and prayers resounded in the air. The church was the center of attraction. What was happening in Viladrau?

A priest, a missionary, an apostle, is speaking from the pulpit. His face seems transfigured. His voice is raised in imprecation; it trembles and resounds like an echo of eternity. His hearers are moved to repentance, and they break out in tears and sobs.

Early in the morning, before the dawn of day gilds the mountain top, the people again hasten to the parish church. They crowd around the confessional, where during long, long hours the missionary hears confessions. It is the seed that has quickly brought the harvest! Here the father gathers in his arms the prodigal son who is returning home.

What has happened in Viladrau? It is seen that families at variance with each other are reconciled; centers of dissipation have disappeared; public morals have become better; indifferent men and distracted women have given up their scandalous habits and hear Mass, assist at sermons, and receive the Sacraments.

The holy Mission given by Father Claret is the load-stone that attracts all the people; it is the secret of this spiritual transformation.

"Blessed be God! Thanks be rendered to Almighty God," exclaimed Father Claret on seeing the fruit of the Mission, the first that he gave according to his organic plan and liturgical outline. "To be a missionary shall be the great work of my life."

* * *

Father Claret immediately began another Mission in the Parish of Espinelvas, and later one in the Parish of Seva, which were followed by two Missions at Iqualda and Santa Coloma de Queralt, respectively.

His vocation was now clearly defined. His call was to a missionary life. All he needed was to obtain, from his Superiors, a release from parochial duties so that he could devote himself freely to the preparation of his sermons. The bishop acceded to his request. Father Claret then began a series of missions which proved to be spiritual prodigies and which deeply affected the principal towns of Catalonia and Canarias.

A deep theologian of the bishopric, Anthony Claret's teacher in the Seminary, on hearing his first sermon said: "Mosen Anthony Claret has been my pupil, but now I am willing to take him as my teacher."

Father Claret preached at a seven-day devotion in honor of Our Lady of Sorrows in a very indifferent town. His audience listened in profound silence. Soon, a coarse, nervous voice broke the stillness with the cry: "No, no, that is not true." The missionary serenely repeated the truth and explained it with a comparison. After having listened and understood, the same voice was heard again: "Yes, you are right, that is true."

This discourteous man remained tranquil and satisfied amid the ire of the public. Moved by the manner in which Father Claret proved the truth, he made his confession to the missionary that very day. It was the turning point of his life.

* * *

The first thing Father Claret did on beginning a Mission was to put it under the protection of the Blessed Virgin. "Mary is the Mother of Mercy," he said, "and mercy is principally shown to sinners."

Travelling one day in company with Father Antonio Potellas, Father Claret began speaking of devotion to the Blessed Virgin. Father Potellas, noting the enthusiasm that animated Father Claret when mentioning Our Lady, interrupted him saying: "It seems to me, Anthony, that you are very devout to the Blessed Virgin."

"Why not," he replied, "when she grants me all I ask of her?"

His companion marvelled at this affirmation and asked him in wonder:

"What's that? Explain to me your method of addressing Our Lady."

"Listen," Anthony replied, "I ask for whatever I wish with fervor and confidence, and if I see that Our Lady does not listen to me I draw near her image. I pull her mantle and say to her: 'If you do not obtain this favor, I will pull harder; I will tear the mantle,' and then she listens."

These words of ingenuity and of deep theological sense point to one of the most salient characteristics in the spirit of Father Claret, and the secret of his great success in the apostleship, devotion to the Blessed Virgin.

FLASHES OF ZEAL

Traits of an Apostle—Stop, Sinners! Stand Back!
The Voice of Obedience—The Preamble of
the Mission—An Invocation to
The Blessed Virgin

What words could express the ardor of the apostolic zeal that burned, at that time, in the heart of Father Claret?

The best and warmest words are those he himself employs in his Autobiography. "Would I not be," he writes, "the greatest criminal in the world if God, my Father, did not hinder the outrages of men?

"Ah, my Father! I will defend Thee, even though it may cost me my life. Glowing with love for Thee, I shall say to sinners:

"Enough of offense! Stop, sinners! Stop! Do not lash my Father. You have heaped sufficient lashes upon Him; you have opened too many wounds. If you do not wish to desist, then beat me, for I well deserve it; but do not lash or maltreat my God, my love, any longer. Ah, my love! Ah, my love!"

In another part he continues:

"If a mother, through the natural love she bears her child, runs, cries, and snatches it from the brink of the precipice, this, and more, is what divine grace does for me and in me.

"Charity urges me on, it impels me; it causes me to walk, to run from one town to another, it obliges me to cry out:

'My son, sinner, look here, you are about to fall into the infernal regions.'

"Ah, how many times I asked Almighty God for that for which St. Catherine of Sienna pleaded; namely, that God would grant me the favor to place myself at the gates of hell and detain those who are about to enter there, and to say to everyone of them: 'Where are you going, unhappy one? Stand back! Go, make a good confession and save your soul, but do not come here to be lost for all eternity'."

*   *   *

These flames of the fire of charity and zeal, nevertheless, were checked by obedience to his bishop.

Father Claret was Parochial Regent in Viladrau for a period of eight months. He then moved his residence officially to Vich, where he lived subject to the orders of his bishop, who assigned places where he was to preach.

"Often," wrote Blessed Anthony, "prelates of other dioceses invite me to give Missions in their dioceses. Whenever my bishop consented, I went, for I had taken the resolution never to preach in any parish or diocese without the express order of my ordinary.

"The necessity of being sent and of having the bishop himself designate the place, is what God made clear to me from the very beginning. And so it is that, although the places to which I was sent were bad and demoralizing, great good was always the outcome of my Missions, because God sent me and disposed and prepared the hearts of the people.

"Let missionaries be warned not to go to any town, how good so-ever the people may be, unless they are sent by obedience; but with the sanction of obedience, let them go to any place, no matter how bad the people may be. Even though difficulties may arise or persecutions be raised against them, let them not fear, for God has sent them through obedience. He will take care of all."

*   *   *

Mistrustful of his own strength and prompted by his deep humility, he placed his entire confidence in the Blessed Virgin. On the first day of the Mission he directed the following prayer to Our Lady:

"O Virgin Mother of God, Mother and Advocate of poor unhappy sinners. Thou well knowest that I am your son and minister, formed by thee in the forge of thy mercy and love. I am like an arrow placed in your powerful hand. O, my Mother, hurl me with all the strength of thy arm against the impious, cruel and sacrilegious Achab wedded to vile Jezabel, I wish to say: 'Cast me against Satan, prince of this world, who has made alliance with the flesh.'

"Let victory be thine, O Mother. Thou wilt conquer. Yes, thou hast the power to overcome all heresies, errors, and vice. And I, confident in your powerful protection, will engage in the battle, not only against flesh and blood, but against the princes of darkness, as the Apostle says, grasping the shield of the Holy Rosary and armed with the double-edged sword of the divine word.

"Thou art the Queen of Angels. Command them, my Mother, to come to my aid. Thou knowest my weakness and the strength of my enemies.

"Thou art the Queen of the Saints. Command them to intercede for me and tell them that the victory and the triumph will redound to the greater glory of God and the salvation of souls.

"Repress, O Lady, the pride of Lucifer and his followers who have the audacity to usurp souls redeemed by the Blood of Jesus, the Son of your virginal womb."

All these expressions, and a thousand others that animate and give warmth to the writings of Blessed Anthony, are flashes of his interior fire, but these flames of zeal developed and expanded by a rule not to be deviated from, namely, obedience.

XXVI
APOSTLESHIP OF CONVERSATION
AT THE FIRESIDE—CONVERSION OF A SAMARITAN—THE MULETEER'S BLASPHEMIES—THE SCENE OF CONFESSION

There is an apostolate of powerful efficacy for the conquest of souls, intimate and hidden, strong and vanquishing, whose glory is not often inscribed in the archives and annals of human vanity. It is the apostolate of familiar conversation.

As Father Claret knew, by his own experience and that of others, the spiritual influence of a good or a bad conversation, he, therefore, endeavored, on principles of art and virtue, to make his conversations attractive, instructive, and exemplary.

* * *

During the course of a Mission, a certain person of quality in the town offered Father Claret hospitality in his home. As it was winter, they seated themselves at the fireside when the repast was over, and there engaged in a familiar conversation.

Father Claret spoke of God and spiritual things with ingenious simplicity, apparently without any intention of conquest, because this person enjoyed a good moral reputation in the town. They then took leave of each other. A short time after, however, a penitent approached Father Claret's confessional. It was the friend who, moved by the conversation of the evening, wished to make a general confession, as he himself declared afterwards to a companion, stating at the same time that he had, for a long time, been making sacrilegious confessions.

* * *

God granted our Father the favor of supernatural enlightenment by means of which states of consciences were revealed to him, and thus many souls were converted and consoled in their tribulations.

One day, while passing near Manresa, he met a woman of ill repute. God suddenly manifested to him all the woman's

sins. What was he to do? Despise her? Flee from her presence?
No. He drew near and spoke to her politely. At first the conversation touched on different topics; then on things of God;
and later, on the sins of her life. The woman was surprised,
for she could not imagine how an unknown priest could know
her hidden sins; he could even point out when and where they
had been committed. Like another Samaritan this woman awoke
from her lethargy and wept bitterly over her sinful life. She
made her confession to Father Claret, and in future led a
fervent and exemplary life.

*   *   *

The following incident happened in the suburbs of Ribas,
not far from Ripoll.

The holy missionary travelled on foot to a place where he
was to begin a series of sermons that very day. Panting and
covered with perspiration, he seated himself on a mound, and
opening his breviary, he began to pray. A coarse muleteer
happened to pass that way, and on seeing the priest, cried out:
"Listen, Father; close that book and come hear my mule's
confession."

"Unfortunate one," replied the priest, "it is you that need
to go to confession; for it is now seven years since your last
confession."

The poor muleteer was amazed at hearing an unknown
priest make such a disclosure. The eyes of his soul were
opened, and seeing the sad state of his conscience, he soon
made his confession with extraordinary signs of repentance.

*   *   *

Something similar occurred on another occasion. It was on
the plains of Barcelona. Father Claret, after finishing a Mission, was returning with his habitual modesty from the field
of his operations. He walked along the road reciting the rosary.
A cart-driver observed him from a distance; then drawing near
to him with a sarcastic smile, said:

"Good morning, Father. Are you very busy? If you have not much to do, I can give you occupation. My mules have not made their confession yet. Will you hear them now, Father?" An infernal smile was reflected in his eyes, on his lips, and in his face when he uttered these insolent words.

Father Claret, repressing an impulse of saintly indignation and looking upon him fixedly, with sweet sadness, said to him:

"Unhappy, unfortunate one! Do you know what you have said? Do you know that you have pronounced a sacrilege? Ignoramus! Do you not know that mules are incapable of confessing? You are the one who should make your confession, because you need it badly. Well, tell me, when did you make your last confession?"

"I do not remember, Father, for I do not keep an account of such things; we have to attend to many other things."

"Well, I will tell you. Fifteen years ago. It is fifteen years since you last confessed your sins?"

"That is true, but who told you so, Father?"

"And, moreover, you are guilty of many and grave sins. You have done this, that, and that."

Father Claret continued, mentioning the principal sins that weighed upon the conscience of that insolent man. The poor cart-driver was terrified.

"Who told you so," he repeated, "because it is true, it is true."

"I do not know you," Father Claret replied, "but I can see the state of your conscience. You are bad, very bad. May God have mercy on you."

As though wounded by a stroke of lightning, the poor cart-driver was overcome. He tied his mules to a tree and knelt down to go to confession. A little later, a road-side traveller saw a strange scene. A priest was seated on a stone and near him knelt a cart-driver confessing his sins.

XXVII
THE BOOK OF NATURE
The Poem of the World—Sources of Inspiration

The creation opens like an immense Bible on the background of space, and the stars write the words of God in letters of gold. The assiduous reader of this book is man, supreme monarch, who extends his sceptre over the circumference of the world seated on his earthly throne.

Father Claret was a great lover of nature; in the contemplaton of its marvels and its beauty he found sublime comparisons which he used to advantage in his sermons. From nature he also learned the secrets of love that led to his ecstasies and raptures. Why should it not be so, for creation is a stanza written by God, an international museum of artistic works, which no one has ever been able to imitate perfectly. Every feeling heart and every great soul cannot help but love nature because nature is the synthesis of all arts. The architecture, sculpture, painting, music and poetry of nature have God as their author, the Genius of eternity, the inexhaustible Artist Who has engraven on matter all the plastic forms of thought.

*   *   *

"How great must Thou be, my God, since Thou hast created such wonderful things," Father Claret repeated frequently. He often took natural scenes as subjects for his familiar talks, ingeniously interpreting their symbolism of things. In his autobiography he quotes the following simple words:

"If death was spoken of or bells were ringing, the opportunity was offered me to speak of the frailty and inconstancy of our being, of the certainty of death and of rendering an account to God. When it thundered and lightened, I thought of judgment, and I spoke of Judgment Day. When standing near a fire, I spoke of the eternal fire. On seeing flowers, I said to my companions that, as these plants produced such beautiful and sweet smelling flowers, so should we produce flowers of virtue. At the sight of fruit-bearing trees, I pointed to the good works we are to perform, for if we are not productive of good works, we would be like the two fig trees mentioned in the Gospel. The flowing current of the river directed our thoughts to the stream of life that flows into eternity. The song of the birds and the sound of music recalled the eternal and ever-new canticle of Heaven. Thus I dealt with all the other phenomena of nature. These familiar conversations I observed were productive of much good."

XXVIII
REMEMBRANCE OF THE MISSION
The Psychology of the People—Miguel Iter—The Child's Picture—The Conversion of the Child's Father

Father Claret was one of the men who best knew the psychology of the people; a realist and not a schemer of sterile projects. He adopted such resources of spiritual combat that most impressed the people and attracted souls to God.

He remembered that when a child, it was the contemplation of such holy pictures as graphically reproduced the four last things, the mysteries of Our Lord and of the Blessed Virgin that stirred his conscience. He observed, too, the prodigies that were worked in souls and the devotion inspired in hearts by the reading of pamphlets that briefly told a story, or related the power of the rosary, or of medals, scapulars and other sacramentals. He, himself, used all these things in his Missions, and it was his wish that other missionaries do the same, convinced of the fruit that the people would derive therefrom.

* * *

Miguel Iter was a young diligent religious. Knowing the itinerary of Father Claret's journeys he followed him on his apostolic mission. He loaded a little beast of burden with booklets, pictures, rosaries, and medals, and displayed his religious merchandise at the doors of the churches in which Father Claret was to give a Mission.

He did not seek material advantage in his sales; his purpose was the good of souls, for thus he had been taught by Father Claret. Both, animated by the same zeal, distributed liberally these various articles of piety which led the way quietly to many conversions in families.

One afternoon, when Father Claret had concluded a Mission, he was, as usual, modestly walking along the street, when a little child approached, who, kissing his hand, said:

"Father, give me a picture. God will repay you."

An angel seemed to speak through that voice. Father Claret drew a picture from his pocket. One side showed a damned soul, and on the other side were reflections on hell.

On the following day as he was making his thanksgiving after Mass, in the vestibule of the Church in which he was preaching, an unknown man approached him secretly. The husky man, heavily bearded, covered his face with his cloak so as to hide in shame, and on drawing near to the priest said:

"Father, I wish to go to confession, but in a place where no one will see me."

"Come to the sacristy at once, and I will hear your confession," said Father Claret.

Both went to the sacristy. The penitent knelt at the feet of Father Claret and wept bitterly, exclaiming:

"Father, O Father, I am a great sinner! Will God pardon me?"

The abundance of tears he shed and the unusual signs of contrition caused Father Claret to ask the motive that prompted him to make his confession.

"Ah, Father, yesterday when you passed my house, one of my children kissed your hand and asked for a picture. He amused himself a while with it; then he left it on the table; he then went out to play with other children. I, through curiosity and pastime, looked at the picture and read the corresponding leaflet. Oh, Father, what an impression it made on me! Every word was an arrow that wounded my heart. I determined to change my life. God has made use of you to convert me. I wish to make my confession to you. I am a great sinner. Will there be pardon for me?"

Father Claret consoled and encouraged him; he heard his confession and absolved him from his sins. This man, who had been indifferent and unbelieving before, and who had been the chief of a perverse and corrupt crowd, was now a source of edification by his Christian and exemplary life. Such was the fruit of a picture and a leaflet.

XXIX

REWARD OF HEROISM

The Missionary's Map—Between Banolas and Figueras
Desert of Snow—The Angel of Orista

Why is that poor, humble priest stopping on the wayside and examining a map, backed with canvas, which he always carries with him? He is calculating the distance that remains to be traversed before he reaches the town where he is to open a Mission that very night. He has walked five leagues; five leagues more separate him from the town. The wind blew; rain fell upon him; the sun scorched him; he lacked food; his feet were swollen. What difference did it make? That Missionary carried within himself a heart burning with apostolic zeal, and this heart is the motor that energizes weak human nature.

*　　*　　*

God rewarded these heroic acts. One day he went from Banolas to Figueras. He had finished one Mission and wished to begin another without loss of time. But how was he to get to Figueras since a terrific storm had just arisen? How could he leave Banolas while terrifying thunder rolled, and, amid dense and sombre clouds, serpentine lightning flashed! God wills it! So, forward!

He arrived at the banks of the river which he had to cross in order to reach Figueras. On account of the heavy rain the river had risen, and it was dangerous to cross it.

A rocky cliff stood out in the middle of the stream, the ends of two beams from opposite banks of the river were supported by the cliff, their other ends were resting on the banks. Father Claret crossed the first beam safely, but a man who walked ahead broke the second beam and the waves carried him away. It seemed impossible to open the Mission at Figueras that day! He looked about, but saw no one to help him. He would have to return to Banolas.

"O, my God! Come to my assistance. The souls who are awaiting me at the holy Mission are pleading." Thus exclaimed the Missionary with all the fervor of his heart. Suddenly an unknown, modest, and courteous youth appeared on the cliff on which Father Claret stood. He took the missionary on his shoulders, quickly waded the turbulent stream and carried him safely to the opposite bank of the river. Father Claret wished to offer a reward for this heroic act, but the young man smiled and mysteriously disappeared. It was an angel from heaven.

*   *   *

Another similar event happened one day while Father Claret went from Vich to Orista. A servant named Ramon Prat accompanied the missionary on this trip. It was he who later gave a detailed story of the happening.

It was a stormy afternoon. Rain fell heavily from a dark sky. The wind howled furiously. At a distance, a fireless sun showed rents of gold among the clouds. For several days snow had spread its mantle over the fields and roads so that the direction of the paths was obliterated.

When they found themselves still at a distance from the city, Father Claret, having compassion on his companion said, "Ramon, return, for it is late."

Ramon knew that Father Claret did not know the road and that he could easily lose his way in that desert of snow; therefore, he did not wish to leave the missionary alone.

"Ramon, return, for it is late," Father Claret repeated. Ramon looked about and not seeing any footprints, not even the lightest, in the snow, replied: "No, Father, I cannot leave you. You will lose your way. The town is far distant, and there is not a trace of anyone who may direct you."

Father Claret was silent, but Ramon suddenly saw an unknown young man, neatly and elegantly dressed, wearing a barretina on his head. He was also going to Orista.

"Ramon, return, my son, for it is already late. See, I do not need your service. This young man will accompany me."

Ramon was convinced and took leave of the two, but as he proceeded along the way over which the youth was supposed to have come, he noticed that there were no foot-prints in the snow.

"What is this?" Ramon asked himself. "Whence has this young man come?" Instead of returning to Vich immediately, Ramon stopped on the road and watched the two travellers on their way. When Father Claret came in sight of the village and there was no longer any danger of being lost, the young man disappeared. Upon his arrival in Vich, Ramon publicly announced this happening, and all praised God.

Later, in the course of a familiar conversation with Father Claret, it became known that this young man was an angel.

XXX

THE BLESSINGS OF FRIENDSHIP

Tenderheartedness—Don Fortunato Bres—Flights of
an Angel—Spiritual Conversation—The
Miraculous Sewing

Love buds forth from the heart as the first-born of all sentiments, and one of the most intimate and most human manifestations of love is friendship.

Our Lord, the Saints, the wise, artists, and all classes of men have had friendships. A good friend can be a source of consolation, the guiding star, the sudden impulse of heroism, the origin of virtue, the cause of scientific progress, merely by his conversation and sacrifices. Therefore, it is an error to condemn all friendship.

Father Claret possessed a fine sense of spirituality. In every epoch of his life he cultivated friendships, and in regard to them he tried to abide by prudence in his selection and by the virtue of constancy; in the matter of selection he chose those whose friendship would be both good and useful, and in regard to constancy he chose those whose friendship could be distinguished by sacrifice, the character of its legitimacy.

*   *   *

God blessed the holy union of these spiritual friendships. The following case bears proof:

Don Fortunato Bres, protector of Anthony Claret while a seminarian, to whom he owed the opportunity of pursuing his studies towards his ecclesiastical career, and in whose house at Vich he lived for several years as a member of the family, rather than as a guest, while on his way to the cathedral to celebrate Holy Mass had the misfortune to slip and fall on the ice. This resulted in a broken leg. Don Fortunato requested his friends to communicate his misfortune to Father Claret at once. "Let Father Claret come to me! Let him come immediately, for I wish to speak to him!" was the saintly old priest's request.

Father Claret was preaching in Olost, four leagues from Vich. A young man hurried to him with the message. All at once a knock was heard on the door. On opening it, Father Anthony Claret was there. It had been snowing, but Anthony's clothing was not even moist. His path led through muddy places, but his feet were dry. What had happened? Father Claret was asked, and the latter replied with genuine simplicity:

"An irresistible impulse brought me here. An interior voice said to me: 'Go to see Don Fortunato.' So here I am without knowing why I have come."

"Have you celebrated Mass?" Father Claret was asked.

"Yes, and, moreover, I heard confessions and took my breakfast in the rectory."

"At what time did you leave Olost to arrive here so soon; it is only a quarter past seven?"

"I heard confessions until seven and then started out on the road. I cannot explain how I arrived here."

All were astonished at the fact that a journey of four leagues, over mountain paths covered with snow, could have been made in ten minutes. At the first opportunity the people asked the Pastor of Olost how this prodigious event came to pass. The parish priest's sister replied: "I saw him in the confessional until seven. He came out suddenly saying that he was going to Vich; I ordered a servant to saddle the horse. He followed Father Claret with all possible speed, but could not overtake him, nor could he even catch a glimpse of him. Strange to say, no foot prints were left upon the falling snow."

"A miracle!" all exclaimed. "The angels carried him to see and console his friend."

Father Don Juan Coma, a native of Manleu, parish priest of Figueras, a priest distinguished for his virtue and science, was also a good friend of Father Claret.

One day, after preaching, he had to leave Figueras so as to arrive at Gerona that same afternoon. That distance was about six leagues. Father Claret invited his friend to accompany him a short way. He accepted. As they went along, they engaged in spiritual conversation, and in a short time, without knowing how, they found themselves at the Orriols Inn, three leagues from Figueras.

"How is this, Father Anthony?" Father Coma asked.

Father Claret replied smilingly, "I do not know. Accompany me a little farther. It is so sweet to speak of the things of God." They continued their journey. So engrossed were they in their conversation on spiritual things that Father Coma became entangled in briars and tore his cloak.

"All will be well," exclaimed Father Claret, and resumed the pious conversation.

In a few moments they both, greatly surprised, arrived in the city of Gerona. As soon as they had reached the rectory, Father Coma wished to mend the rent in his cloak, but, quite astonished, he saw that it was untorn. He could neither detect the rent nor the mending.

Father Coma mentioned the incident to his friends, and they all exclaimed: "The doing of Father Anthony Claret! God works his miracles to honor his servant. Happy those who can claim friendship with so holy a missionary."

XXXI

PERSECUTION AND DEFENSE

Conspiracy of the Passions—The Circular of an Archbishop—The Defense of the Missionary—Valor
of Father Claret—Hospital or Scaffold

All the Saints have received in a greater or less degree an inheritance from God, the inheritance of persecution. Father Claret had a triple persecution to combat in the work of his Missions, viz: the persecution of envy, of scandal, and of tyranny. He triumphed over all his enemies, brandishing only one weapon, that of innocence.

Envy tried to lessen his success, attributing it to the forces of circumstances, and to the ignorance of the people, and not to the merit of his sermons, nor to the divine, supernatural intervention of Heaven.

Scandal wished to discredit his apostolate, because the response to every Mission was the certain closing, for lack of attendance, of every center of dissipation and orgy.

Tyranny, finally, tried to muzzle his word, and to exile him, because the political leaders of the town, with the pre-occupations of their gubernatorial zeal, feared that at one word of his the Catholic population would arise against the liberal government.

* * *

Tarragona was the province in which Father Claret preached most. While many there took advantage of his Missions, others, although few, hated him even to the point of wishing to assassinate him.

The persecution of wicked men rose to such an extreme that the Archbishop of the Diocese felt himself obligated to come to the defense of the priest. In a circular letter addressed to all the parishes of the diocese, His Excellency defended Father Anthony Claret publicly. Among other things this memorable document reads as follows:

"For the purpose that the evil may not spread, and that prejudice may be removed from those who have harbored it, I charge you to effectively retract such accusations, and affirm with all certainty that Don Anthony Claret never has taken the least part in any political faction, that he began his missionary career with the permission of competent authority, with universal applause, gathering copious fruits of conversion and virtue without ever incurring the least censure on the part of his civil and ecclesiastical authorities.

"His private life is blameless; his habits are edifying; his works conform to the language of a minister of the Gospel; his abnegation and disinterestedness are complete; he never receives stipends for the sermons he preaches, not even for the Holy Sacrifice of the Mass, which he celebrates daily. If for some special reason or other, he finds it necessary to receive some alms for other services, he immediately invests the money in some laudable object.

"As regards the booklets and other religious articles which he disposes of for the purpose of his Missions, he never seeks temporal gain, for in nowise does he bother about money matters.

"His penitential, mortified, laborious life is that of a true apostolic missionary. He always travels on foot, without provision for food or clothing. The people of Catalonia and other provinces know and publish his saintliness. I can vouch for it without fear of being contradicted by those who might wish to pretend otherwise, or to try to deceive others."

*   *   *

Father Claret well knew the persecution that had been raised against him by his joint enemies; and his spiritual state, in the midst of all these storms, is reflected in these words:

"In the midst of the alternatives of tribulations and consolations I passed through agreeable and bitter moments. Sometimes I was very weary of living and then my only thought and my only conversation were of Heaven, and this consoled and animated me in the extreme. Generally, I did not refuse to suffer; on the contrary, I wished to suffer and to die for Jesus Christ. I did not wish to place myself voluntarily in danger, but it pleased me to have my Superiors send me to dangerous places, so that I might have the good fortune to die for Our Lord at the hands of assassins."

Father Claret was generally greatly beloved in the province of Tarragona, but there were also perverse men who made attempts against his life. Knowing this, Father Claret said one day to the Archbishop: "Your Excellency, I am not terrified, nor would I stand back for that reason. Your Excellency may send me to whatever diocese you may wish, I will go gladly. Even if I knew that a double file of assassins was awaiting me, I would go forward. My desire is to die in the cause of preaching the religion of Jesus Christ. My aspiration has always been to die in a hospital as a pauper, or on a scaffold as a martyr. I would wish to seal with my blood the virtues and truths that I have preached and taught." Neither the words of the priest nor the Archbishop's circular need a commentary. They are clear, sincere, and definite!

XXXII

THE DEMON'S IRE

Wound in His Side—Cured by Our Lady—The Fall of
a Stone—Fire! Fire!—It is the Demon

Father Claret saw a squadron of demons at the left side of
his bed, when, while he was a seminarian, he had a grievous
temptation, which was driven away by the apparition of the
Blessed Virgin. This infernal army fought him particularly
at the time of the Missions, when he snatched so many souls
from them and won these souls for God as so many spoils
of the battle.

The holy missionary was in Vich at the time of the following occurrence:

One morning the persons in the house in which he lived
noted, with surprise, that he did not come to breakfast at the
usual time. They feared he was indisposed. They knocked at
his door, entered the room, and asked if he were ill.

"I have a severe pain in my side," he replied. Alarmed at
this, because Father Claret was not accustomed to complain of
slight pains, they called the doctor and the surgeon. They
came, and on examining the afflicted part found a frightful
wound in his side, as if his flesh had been torn by the claws
of a wild beast; it was such that several ribs were exposed.
No one knew the cause of this, because Father Claret never
mentioned it, but it was believed to be the effect of the demon
who wished to torment the flesh of the innocent missionary.

The doctors came to see him twice. Noticing that gangrene
was about to set in, they agreed to perform a surgical operation, and set the following morning for its performance. They
came and knocked at the patient's door; there was no response.
They asked for him anxiously, and while they were speaking
the amazed patient presented himself before them smilingly

"Do not be frightened," he said, "but help me give thanks
to God, for last night the Blessed Virgin cured me."

The astonished doctors asked to see the place of the wound. To their surprise they noticed that not even a scar was to be seen; it was covered with white firm skin.

"A miracle!" exclaimed all the bystanders.

"It is not natural," replied the doctors.

At the request of Don Fortunato Bres, in whose house Father Claret was residing at the time, an official entry was made of the happening.

*   *   *

The persecutions of the devil were more frequent at the time of his Missions. While Father Claret was preaching in Sarreal, a province of Tarragona, crowds were so impressed that they took the church as though by assault; they filled it to its utmost capacity and people even crowded the portico, for it was impossible to gain admittance into the church. One day when the missionary was most fervent and pathetic in his sermon, an enormous stone fell from the arch of the tower upon the congregation.

"That is nothing," cried Father Claret from the pulpit. "Let no one move! It is the demon who wishes to impede the fruit of the Mission. But God does not permit him to do you any harm."

So it was. Not a fragment of the stone touched any one. This miracle augmented the fervor and enthusiasm of the audience and so the devil was defeated.

*   *   *

One day, Father Claret was preaching to a large gathering. It was in the middle of the Mission. The people were showing signs of greater and greater compunction. It was night and nearly all the inhabitants were gathered in the church. When the missionary had taken the Crucifix into his hands to end his sermon with a final stirring appeal, an unknown man burst into the church and disturbed the audience, crying: "Fire! Fire! The house is burning. Help!"

Father Claret, interrupting the sermon, said in a loud voice: "It is the demon. The house is not on fire. Let the sacristan go and see. If there is a fire we shall all go to extinguish it, but while we are waiting to be advised, let us all be silent and tranquil." The sacristan returned; he said there was not even the slightest sign of a fire. The public wished to beat the man who had alarmed the people, but he had mysteriously disappeared.

"Did I not tell you so?" exclaimed Father Claret. "It is Satan, the enemy of souls, who fears that you will profit by this holy Mission."

Profiting by this happening, he preached a new sermon on the importance of salvation. Tears and sighs of the people mingled with the words of the missionary. The downfall of the demon could not have been greater nor more humiliating.

XXXIII
THE NEW PERSECUTIONS
The Blessing of a Cloud—The Lash of the Sermon
Protection of Heaven

"The Conquest of Souls," was the motto which the heroic
missionary wrote on the program of his apostolate, and in
order to develop it, he reproduced in his life, the sufferings
and persecutions that the great Apostle of the Gentiles suffered
in his time. And how could it be otherwise, if hearts that he
won for Christ were spoils snatched violently from the claws
of the enemy? For this reason the demon greatly hated the
missionary, Father Claret. It was through his combat with
the demon that he obtained the triumph of his conversions.
In order to prevent them, the prince of darkness used every
possible means.

* * *

One day, Father Claret was preaching in the open air.
Thousands congregated to hear the sermons of the famed missionary. It was a solemn religious function. When the apostolic
word resounded with the greatest eloquence and unction, the
sky became covered with clouds; thunder rolled; lightning
flashed, and the whirlwind burst into a hurricane. The assembly
became frightened and restless and began to flee, but Father
Claret calmed them, shouting: "Let no one move. It is the evil
spirit which comes in the midst of this storm. He will soon flee
conquered."

And so it happened. The missionary blessed the clouds and
the storm disappeared.

* * *

At another time, Father Claret was preaching a Mission
in a church. The attendance was so large that he was obliged
to improvise a pulpit on the plaza. Under the sway of his
supernatural eloquence, the people broke out into tears and
sobs, asking God's pardon for their sins. Soon a sound was
heard like the blow of a lash. It came from the pulpit. The

countenance of Father Claret indicated pain, he staggered; and when it seemed that he was about to fall, the alarmed people rushed forward to grasp him, but he said in a serene voice: "Leave me; do not be alarmed. It is the demon who has given me blows so that I may cease preaching to you."

Father Claret remained silent some moments while the people, amid tears, raised their hands in prayer and exclaimed: "Pardon, O my God! Pardon, and have mercy!"

*   *   *

The Mission in Igualda was having splendid results. Many and great converts were seen even in public. Others were on the point of being converted. In order to move those who still remained undecided, Father Claret prepared, by prayer and study, a special sermon, a sermon on Mary Magdalene. All wept on hearing it. His word was a luminous and palpitating concentration of the tenderness, repentance, and love which the sublime penitent felt in the hour of her conversion. At the moment when the audience was most attentive, many among them weeping, a terrible noise disturbed the people. The frightened multitude cried out in consternation. Then Father Claret extended his arms over the people saying: "Be calm, brethren; do not be alarmed. These are demons who fear that you will profit by the Mission. Scorn them and they will soon flee."

The people became tranquil on hearing these words of the holy missionary. The demon fled.

Later, Father Claret, on referring to this epoch of the Missions, in which he had been, by supernatural help, so manifestly freed from danger and persecutions, wrote the following simple words in his autobiography:

"The persecution which hell raised against me was great, but the protection from heaven was even greater. I saw visibly how the Blessed Virgin, the angels, and the saints conducted me through unknown paths; they delivered me from thieves and assassins, and they carried me safely to port, without my knowing how."

XXXIV
THE CATECHISM OF THE MISSIONS
Vocation of the Catechist—His Catechism Books
Methods of Catechetical Instruction
Documents of This Mastery

One of the most ingenious and sublime scenes in the life of Our Lord is that in which the Divine Master is seen surrounded by children, teaching them, simply and patiently, His celestial doctrine. He was the first catechist in the world. Father Claret had that immortal picture engraved on his mind and in his heart. On beginning a Mission his first care was to gather the children and to teach them the catechism.

"The first thing that I do," he wrote in his autobiography, "is to instruct the children in Christian Doctrine, either because of the liking I have always had for this kind of teaching, or because I knew it to be most necessary, for the Catechism is the foundation of the edifice of religious and moral instruction; and, then again, it pleases the children and leaves the deepest impression; it preserves them from error, vice, and ignorance; it forms them to virtue more easily, since they are more docile than adults. With children, one has only to do the work of planting, but with adults one has to uproot and then plant."

"There is, besides, another advantage. Through children, grown people and their parents are easily conquered. Giving children prizes in the form of pictures or leaflets for attendance and for application, causes the parents and adults to read them through curiosity. Often they are converted, as I well know by experience."

*   *   *

The profound conviction which Father Claret had of the exceptional importance of catechetical instruction led him to compose and edit four treatises on Christian doctrine. The first, a very short one, was for the use of children up to the age of seven; the second was for the less gifted; the third was for the more intelligent and wide-awake children; this was more extensive; and the fourth "The Catechism Explained" was intended for adults. It was an admirable work in depth and form, in method and adaption. Even to-day, after the appearance of so many similar books, it is considered, in material, one of the most classic and precise.

Father Claret not only wrote the catechism but he also taught it, and the manner in which he exercised this difficult mastery is found, described in detail, in his book "The Instructed Collegian," from which his biographers have taken it, saying that, in the beginning of the Missions, he called the children to the church, placed them in a semi-circle so that he could see all at a glance. If the number was too large he distributed the children into groups, asking the assistance of other catechists. If the number of catechists proved insufficient, he called upon one or two of the most instructed and reliable of his pupils and had them teach the youngest and most backward of the group.

He began his teaching of the catechism with the sign of the cross, followed by the recitation of three Hail Mary's to the Blessed Virgin, and an Our Father in honor of the Guardian Angels. His method was to begin by asking a child whom he thought would know how to answer. If he found that there was no one capable of answering he would teach one the answer, word for word. He asked the same question alternately and individually; then the children all answered in concert. When all knew how to answer the first question he taught the next. Then he reviewed the first question before proceeding to the third. Thus he continued as long as time permitted. On the following day he repeated the questions and answers of the previous day. When they knew their catechism well, he asked the same questions using different words, in order to find out if they had grasped the thought.

He used to say that the principal defect of the catechist in teaching catechism is that he talks too much. He himself never corrected a child who did not answer correctly, but had another child do it. Thus he held the attention of the children, particularly when he obliged them to recite in unison.

At the close of the allotted period he gathered the groups and made a few minutes' talk suited to their age, talent, and occupation, in clear and simple terms. He placed before them some example with a short, final reflection to encourage them to be good Christians. In conclusion, they recited three Hail Mary's, and Father Claret distributed holy pictures and instructive leaflets before they left the church.

After due preparation, he admitted the children to general Communion. In the afternoon of Communion days, a procession, in which the children took part, marched through the principal streets of the city. The songs of the children and their little banners gave a touch of color and holy joy to the picture of the Mission, which is ordinarily austere.

Father Claret, remembering the great spiritual good he had obtained in childhood from the study of the catechism, always taught it not only when he was a seminarian, a priest, and missionary, but also when overwhelmed by the complex occupations as Archbishop of Cuba and Confessor of the Queen. He wished to simplify and to make the teaching of the catechism uniform in all the dioceses of Spain by using one official text-book, hoping thus, with the identity of questions and answers, to facilitate the teaching and learning of religion.

XXXV

THE TRIUMPH OF HIS ENEMIES
THE TRIUMPH OF THE SECTS—ATTITUDE OF THE MISSIONARY
THE VISION OF SINS—SURROUNDED BY BRILLIANCY

Good news had just circulated through Vich. It was that the great missionary, Father Anthony Claret, would preach the Lenten sermons that year—1841, in the cathedral. Vich was the official See to which Father Claret retired after his apostolic journeys. There the fame of his preaching and miracles resounded unceasingly. For this reason everyone awaited the Lenten season with holy impatience, and families from neighboring towns even rented houses in the city of Vich to move there during Lent, so as to be able to attend all the sermons of the missionary.

But the demon, who had been powerless so many times in his attempts to interrupt the preaching of Father Claret, triumphed this time by means of earthly agents. The political head of the Province of Barcelona directed a secret communication to the mayor of Vich, in which he textually said: "Try, by all means, to prevent Anthony Claret from preaching the Lenten sermons in the Cathedral." No one knew the impious and unjust motives of such a suspension. Only sectarian hate could inspire such an order.

The mayor of Vich was perplexed and hesitated for some time before alluding to the prohibition to preach, fearing an explosion of popular ire; but, in order not to become unworthy of the consideration of his political chief, he called Anthony Claret into his presence. The latter appeared immediately in the mayor's office. He entered the room in a grave and tranquil manner, and listening to the order by which he was forbidden to preach, responded:

"The Gospel says that if they persecute you in one city, flee to another. But I will put myself at the disposition of my ecclesiastical superior."

Later, in a moment of intimacy with a friend of his, he expressed his desire to shed his blood for Jesus Christ, adding these words:

"Although I should know beforehand that on ascending the pulpit, they were awaiting me with a dagger in hand to assassinate me, I would not have turned back. My Superior is the one I must obey."

*　　*　　*

The ecclesiastical governor, fearing greater evil, counselled him to suspend his sermons, at least for a time. Obediently Father Claret retired to the picturesque town of Pruit, which lies at the foot of the Collsacabra Mountains. His occupations in the silence of this solitude were study, prayer, and penance. Eye-witnesses affirm that his mental prayer ordinarily lasted seven hours. He fasted daily during entire weeks and months, and would have lived on bread and water, if his spiritual director had not forbidden this austerity.

Clamorous cries ascended to Heaven; these were cries of souls, yearning to hear the words of the apostolic missionary which would guide them to conversion. This his Superiors believed, and at the end of May, 1842, they sent him to govern the parish of St. John of Olo temporarily. The first thing he did in the towns of that district was to captivate the sympathy of local authorities. With their acquiescence and the permission of his Superiors, he began his missionary work anew, but only in bordering parishes.

*　　*　　*

One day while he was preaching at San Juan of Olo, he paused an instant while preaching. Inspired by the Divine Spirit, Who gave him an insight into the consciences of his hearers, he said in a solemn voice: "Brethren, I could point my finger at those who among you are in mortal sin." These words filled his hearers with salutary fear, and the following morning they thronged around the confessional to purify their consciences by sacramental absolution. Referring to this epoch, a venerable parish priest, whom he dealt with intimately said: "In our days, on our Catalonian soil, there has never been a more exemplary priest, neither of better fame nor of greater zeal than the servant of God, Don Anthony Mary Claret."

God manifested this holiness by extraordinary signs. Among these was the resplendent light that surrounded him while he celebrated Holy Mass. This declaration was made by Father Paul Coma of the Oratory of St. Philip Neri, in the informative process. The following are his words:

"When I was fifteen years of age I entered the parish church of St. Eugenia of Berga, diocese of Vich. At the "Rosary" altar I noticed an unusual splendor surrounding the then unknown celebrant. I drew near and then recognized Father Claret, whose face was transformed. This strange brightness spread its rays as far as the sacristy. I do not remember whether there was, besides myself, any other person in the church. This happened while the servant of God was giving Missions in Catalonia."

A political happening at that time brought days of hope and joy to the Church of Spain. It was the fall of the minister, Olozaga, progressionist and radical. Gonzalez Bravo, who succeeded him was conservative. By means of the relative liberty which he conceded to the Church and her ministers, Father Claret recommenced the task of his missions.

XXXVI

RODA AND BARCELONA
Impressions of a Hearer—Santa Maria del Mar
Prophecy of the Temple—Cure of a Cancer

It was soon known in the different towns of the Catalonian province that Mosen Anthony Claret had resumed his missionary labors in the parishes. The first town to solicit his service was Roda.

His Excellency, Bishop Don Francisco de Asis Aguilar, of Segorbe, wrote his impression of this Mission, for he had been an ocular witness during his seminary days:

"One Monday morning, in the month of December, 1843, a seminarian told us that on the previous day he had heard, in the church of Roda, an orator who spoke for one continuous hour, without coughing or hesitating while his eyes were constantly turned towards Heaven. He related this with such enthusiasm that we became anxious to hear him also. We satisfied our desire the following Sunday."

"The roads that lead to Roda were thronged with people who were, like ourselves, to hear the missionary. The surrounding towns and houses were left almost deserted."

"The rather spacious church was filled to overflowing; the audience spread over the nearby plaza up to the adobe-partition that served as a wall over the precipice at whose base the river Ter flows."

After reciting the rosary, Father Claret began his sermon in a clear, vibrant voice so that all could hear him perfectly, those who were within as well as those outside the church. Not a murmur or movement on the part of the audience, and not a coughing spell on the part of the missionary interrupted the flow of words and of doctrine that came from his lips.

Some said, "How can he talk so long a time without tiring?"

Others asked, "Whence does he draw all this doctrine?"

"What exact, simple, and opportune comparisons!" others said.

"What well-brought-out examples! What a wealth of sacred texts and how well applied!" exclaimed others.

"He is a saint!" many added, and some even told various miraculous happenings which had come to pass.

From that time on his fame was propagated in all directions and to great distances.

* * *

The renown as apostolic orator, which Father Claret acquired from day to day, resounded through the royal city.

In the month of May they invited him to preach in the magnificent church of Santa Maria del Mar (Our Lady of the Sea) in Barcelona. The May sermons had previously been delivered by the most celebrated orators of the Catalonian principality. Father Claret accepted the invitation, and so great was the enthusiasm awakened in the public that a venerable priest said:

"I cannot remember, in more than forty-eight years, that an orator attracted so large a crowd."

Another priest added: "He will reap more fruit than all the other priests in Barcelona together."

Rich and poor, learned and ignorant, teachers and pupils, priests and seculars, gathered around his pulpit, forming an immense spiritual family. The crowds were moved to say, as they left the church:

"This man is a saint. He is a man of God. He is not like the rest of the priests. He is an Apostle."

It seems that God was pleased to confirm the opinion of the people by prodigious deeds.

One night, during one of the sermons which he was preaching during the month of May in the church of Santa Maria del Mar, he stopped suddenly, struck a blow on the pulpit, contrary to his ordinary custom, and said in a solemn voice, "Spiritus Domini super me."

He was silent for a moment, and he again struck the pulpit and repeated: "Spiritus Domini super me." And so for a third time. The hearers fixed their gaze on the speaker and remained in suspense.

Then he exclaimed, "What I am saying is as true as the fact that within a short time a dreadful storm, which will cause great damage, will come upon Barcelona."

And so it happened. The sky rapidly became cloudy, a torrential rain fell, and the fury of the tempest was so violent that, inundating streets and plazas, it destroyed several warehouses on the beach of Borne.

* * *

The following incident took place also during the same month of May. Men and women took their places in the church, two and three hours in advance of the hour for services. One among the early arrivals was Doña Francisca Soler, widow of More, who had suffered from a cancer of the eyes for sixteen years, and which, according to the opinion of physicians, would cause her death in a short time. God inspired her with the thought: "Father Claret must cure me! He is a saint! He must cure me."

The celebrated missionary descended from the pulpit. The sick woman approached him, begging him to cure her. The expectation of the people was great. What would happen? Will God perform a miracle in the presence of everyone through the intercession of His servant?

Father Claret put his hands upon the eyes of the afflicted woman and said a short prayer. The cancer soon dried, leaving the woman completely cured.

So abundant and select was the doctrinal material which Father Claret developed in his May sermons, preached in Santa Maria del Mar, that some visited him only through curiosity to see the holy missionary's library. Curiosity was soon transformed into edification and astonishment, for they found that the breviary and the crucifix formed Father Claret's library.

XXXVII

OLOT AND VALLS

Inez Ferrarons—Fifteen Hours in the Confessional
The Mission of the Twenty-five Confessors
The Punishment of the Orange

The greatest blessing that could fall upon a parish was to hear the sermons of Father Claret. So said the parishoners and the judicious people of the town. For this reason, requests to have the zealous missionary preach in their respective localities came from all parts. The fact that he was unable to respond to all the petitions, which, to him, represented the conversion of so many souls, tormented his heart.

The one who, with greatest persistence, came to beg Father Claret to give a Mission in his parish, was the parish priest of Olot, a town in the diocese of Gerona.

Father Claret finally consented. It was soon made known that the people owed this Mission to the prayers of a holy soul, a virtuous invalid, Inez Ferrarons, who during twenty years suffered horrible pains with heroic resignation and who died in the odor of sanctity.

*   *   *

It was in the year of 1844. The mission began in the middle of August and lasted until the middle of September. Every night the church was overcrowded with people, and such was their eagerness to go to confession that not content with assailing the confessional from six o'clock in the morning until half-past nine at night, when Father Claret retired to his room, they even sought him there. They begged him, for the love of God, to hear their confessions. This he never refused to do.

The copious fruit of this mission may be gathered from the following declaration made by Abate Vila, arch-priest of the parish of San Mateo in Perpignan, who, as a sub-deacon, assisted at the Mission.

"I declare," he says, "that the crowd was so large that twenty-five confessors were needed to hear the people's confessions, and they scarcely sufficed. On the day of the General Communion three priests distributed Holy Communion during the whole morning. Uninterruptedly for three hours the servant of God spoke on the manner of preparing for Holy Communion. In the afternoon the rosary was chanted. The voices of those present responded with such fervor that they sounded like a crash of prolonged thunder."

People three leagues distant from the village came to the Mission, forming numerous troops and leaving their respective towns depopulated. In one of the chapels of Olot persons were continuously occupied in making the Way of the Cross.

*   *   *

The triumph of grace in the Mission of the year 1846, given in the town of Valls, was also far-reaching. The Mission lasted a month, and the people asked that it be even prolonged, such was the enthusiasm of their religious fervor. Their eagerness to make their confession to Father Claret was such that they spent almost all night in the church so as to be first in line on the following day; that is, at half-past four in the morning.

God sanctioned the word of his messenger by a marvelous event. He was preaching one night with extraordinary fervor. Carried away by zeal and the copiousness of apostolic doctrine he prolonged his sermon longer than usual. Three young men sat beneath the pulpit, chattering and grumbling to the disedification of all about them.

"How long he preaches," one said.

"And what terrible things he preaches," exclaimed another.

"It is past the hour! It is time to go home!" added the third.

Then one of them, the most daring and vile, said to his companions, "Just watch how soon he will be silent!"

Saying this he drew an orange from his pocket and threw it at the missionary. Father Claret, without the slightest change of countenance, continued his sermon. The disrespectful youth admired the serenity of the priest, but, amid the laughter of his companions, he threw another orange at him.

The sermon ended. The sacristan came to close the doors of the church. He noticed the young man seated beneath the pulpit. It was the youth who had thrown the oranges at the priest. The sacristan ordered him to leave the church, as all the other people had gone, and it was now the hour to lock the doors. The unfortunate man, however, was unable to move, incapable of arising from his seat. The sacristan grasped him by the arm, but all in vain. The youth replied weepingly:

"I cannot move! I cannot move! It is a punishment of God!"

Overwhelmed by fright, the sacristan communicated the happening to Father Claret, who said to him: "Yes, it is a punishment of God. Nevertheless go and tell the young man that tomorrow I shall await him in the confessional."

The sacristan did so, and at the same moment the youth arose. Early in the morning of the following day, the faithful saw a young man on bended knees and bathed in tears at the feet of Father Claret. It was the one who had thrown the oranges, but who now, amid sobs, confessed his sins.

XXXVIII

INTERESTING TESTIMONIES

THE EULOGY—LIFE OF PENITENCE—A SIEGE OF THE MULTI-
TUDE—THE CURE OF A CHILD—THE RELIC OF SHOES

A constant miracle seemed to be taking place in the life of
Father Claret, the miracle of health. He scarcely slept. He
fasted for entire months. He spent long hours in prayer during
the brief intermissions in his apostolic works. Duty in the confessional absorbed the hours of the morning and of the afternoon; at night he preached sermons of one, two, or three hours'
duration, to which his hearers listened with rapt attention. On
completing a Mission in one town, he immediately began
another elsewhere without allowing himself rest for body and
mind. Have we not reason to believe that some supernatural
force sustained the nature of the heroic missionary?

On February 4, 1846, immediately after the sermons of
Valls, he began a solemn Mission in the cathedral of Tarragona. The Mission was so animated and the spiritual fruits
so plentiful that the Cathedral Chapter of this metropolitan
church—a thing which had never been done in any previous
case—issued an act drawn up officially, stating and describing
these happenings, and transferred it to the capitular book "De
Rebus Gestis." It is one of the most solemn and authorized
public documents which verify the marvelous triumphs of the
preaching of Father Claret.

A little later he preached another Mission in the town of La
Selva, and referring to it, an illustrious prebendary of Tarragona wrote:

"I was very young; and I remember that I, with another
young man, more pious than I, took a two-hour trip in order
to hear him preach in the town of La Selva. It was three o'clock
in the morning when we tried to gain admittance into the
church. Many people had spent the night in the open, so as to

hear his sermons, or to have the good fortune of making their confession to him."

"His sermon on St. Mary Magdalene is ever present to my mind. I felt myself called to the religious life quite forcibly and was drawn to a missionary's life. Besides many extraordinary occurrences, relative to his many conversions, were related."

Father Claret next went to Falset, a town also in the diocese of Tarragona, where no less marvelous results of the Mission were evident. The archpriest of the villa later expressed these results very synthetically in the following words:

"Rev. Father Claret gave a Mission in this parish with such evangelical unction, zeal, erudition, and learning, that people from the neighboring districts were drawn thither. The crowd far surpassed the capacity of the church, and listeners stood on the surrounding plaza and in the streets."

The souls that he conducted on the path of penance and salvation were innumerable. To reach such happy results, he did not allow himself a moment's repose. He spent the nights in prayer. His short rest and sleep was taken on the floor, or either seated or reclining in a chair, for he did not avail himself of the bed that had been prepared for him. He fasted almost every day and ate with excessive frugality. It was observed that he never fixed his gaze upon one of the other sex. The modesty, sweetness, temperance, and other moral qualities of the chosen of the Lord imparted to him an odor of virtue and sanctity that many called him "the saint."

*　　*　　*

At this Mission an extraordinary event happened to a child, Antonio Forcadell. One day, during the mission, at night-fall, Reverend Father Claret, accompanied by other priests, walked along the street upon which the house of the Forcadell family faced. The child was eight years old at the time. Owing to an eye disease, he was unable to see the light. As soon as the child heard the name of the venerable missionary, he suddenly rushed into the street and with the simplicity and candor natural in children, he said: "Father Claret, you must cure my eyes."

"My son," the priest replied, "I am not a doctor."

"That does not matter," replied the child. "You can cure me, if you wish."

Then the servant of God, with the greatest kindness and sweetness, touched the eyes of the child, adding, "My son, wash your eyes every day with clear water." Instantly the disease disappeared, and the child saw perfectly well. Thenceforth, not the slightest impairment of vision was ever noted.

*   *   *

This Mission ended in April. A little later we find Father Claret in Lerida. In the morning, he preached at May devotions in the cathedral, and in the afternoon, at the church of the Holy Rosary. The Archbishop of Tarragona, referring to those sermons, wrote later, saying among other things the following:

"The audience was immensely large. He heard confessions in the cathedral in the morning, and in the hospital chapel in the afternoon. He converted many and great sinners. Some came from great distances to make their confession to him, and many passed the whole night in the church, so as to be able to find a place in line at his confessional."

"During the hours he remained in the house it was necessary to place a guard at the door to avoid confusion among the many people who gathered around him."

"In spite of all, the stairs on which he ascended to his rooms were filled with people; in the event that they were unable to speak to him, these good people contented themselves with kissing the crucifix which the servant of God generally wore on his breast, and which for that purpose Father Claret entrusted to one of the employees of the house."

"People who had noticed that Father Claret always wore the same clothes, wished to give him a new suit; but he would not accept it. They only succeeded, without his notice, in changing the old shoes he wore for new ones, leaving the old ones to a family which still preserves them as a treasure of great price."

We would be able to cite many and valuable testimonies of this kind, but those referred to suffice to sketch, with firm lines, the figure of our great missionary.

XXXIX

NEW FIELDS OF OPERATION
THE STRIFE OF THE PENITENTS—THE HERETIC OF ALFORJA
THE TRIUMPH OF GRACE—THE CANARY ISLANDS

A storm cloud, charged with hatred, calumnies, suspicions, envy, surrounded the apostolic man of Catalonia, and soon he was to be wounded by the lightning of persecution.

Father Claret, in the meantime, fixed his gaze on heaven and did not cease to conquer souls for God through the work of his Missions.

In a letter which he wrote to his bishop from Tarragona on February 23, 1847, he gave a vivid impression of them.

"The work is great," he said, "but the fruit, which, through the mercy of God, is gathered in all the towns where we preach, is not less."

"We hear confessions morning and evening; besides, we have other priests help us, but even then we cannot take care of all the penitents that present themselves."

"They wait from morning until night, and when they see that there is no possible chance of approaching the confessional, they begin arguing, each setting forth his own rights to confession."

"Another said, 'I am a great sinner; for the love of God, let me approach the confessional, for I need it more than anyone'."

"One said, 'It is so many years since I made my confession'."

"Another, 'I have never made a good confession; I have always failed to tell my sins through shame'."

"It moves one to compassion to hear such strife, but what grieves one more is to see daily hundreds of persons gather around the confessional, without being able to console them other than by merely hearing their confession."

"If we are in the towns, they surround us; if we go to the wilderness, they follow us. It is a pity that we do not know how to multiply the loaves and the fishes as our Divine Master did, because it is necessary that they bring food with them from their homes."

*   *   *

Thus the holy missionary expressed himself. While he was working for souls, burning with divine love, others conspired against him, burning with satanical hatred.

In reality, a rebellious apostate, a licentious man, commonly called the "heretic of Alforja" was scandalizing, for some time, the people of various towns of Tarragona. He wished, at any risk, to propagate his errors and heresies among families, but first thought it necessary to discredit the preaching of Father Claret or to banish him from Spain. He, therefore, wrote to the Military Commander General of the Province of Tarragona an anonymous letter filled with insults and calumnious accusations against Father Claret. The Commander, with incredible precipitation, ordered young men from Ruidoms to go to arrest him. The order for arrest was not executed, because the Archbishop of Tarragona very opportunely interposed his authority, presenting at the same time a heated defense of the innocence of the missionary.

But who was this heretic of Alforja, who fought Father Claret? What was his doctrine, and what became of him?

He was Don Miguel Rivas, a rich proprietor of the said village, at one time a good Christian. He even annually made the Spiritual Exercises at the celebrated Franciscan Convent of Escornalbou, where his brother-in-law, a religious, lived. His pride, his exalted imagination and his tendencies led him to very grave errors. His great economic position, his mysterious life, and his austere exterior example made many proselytes in that district. Being publicly declared an apostate, he preached day and night with the faith of an *illuminato* and the obstinacy of a heresiarch.

"My people are lost," the parish priest of Alforja said one day to Father Claret. "Come here to give a Mission. Leave other towns, where perhaps there may be sins, but where there is at least faith. Faith, the foundation of moral life, is in danger here."

Father Claret already had knowledge of the heretical propaganda, and he judged it opportune to combat it at the Mission, which the parish priest proposed.

The Mission began, but the attendance was small.

"These people are lost," said the parish priest with discouragement and pessimism.

"Do not fear," Father Claret responded. "I have met with greater problems among people, and yet grace overcame them. Let us trust in God."

The Mission continued. One night, moved by curiosity, the heretic came to listen to Father Claret. God awaited that moment to break his obstinacy. The words of the missionary penetrated the depth of his soul. They served, at the same time, as light for his intelligence and strength for his will.

"I wish to speak to that man. I wish to consult him about some doubts," said Don Miguel to a friend of his, after Father Claret's sermon. The next day the heretic called on the missionary, and a little later, weeping, he fell upon his knees in the confessional.

He publicly abjured his errors. He submitted to the penance that was imposed by the Archbishop of Tarragona. In the future, by his humility, his abnegation, and his fervor, he became the model of practical Catholics.

On taking leave, after the Mission, the parish priest, embracing him, said to Father Claret: "You have saved my parish. Blessed be the hour in which God inspired us with the idea of this holy Mission."

* * *

The devil, however, did not cease his attacks, but increased his fury at the new conquest of the missionary. Pictures and caricatures, libels and poetry were drawn and written, and exposed to the gullibility of the people, showing Father Claret with cartridge belt and blunderbuss, affirming that he was seducing the people and inciting them to revolt against the government. Father Claret bore all silently, but he felt that these calumnies would make his sermons useless.

Men wished to muzzle the apostolic word of Father Claret, but God permitted this apparent triumph of his enemies, for other souls and other countries claimed the presence of the apostle,—the Canary Islands.

Don Bonaventura Codina, a friend of Father Claret, was at the time, appointed bishop of the Great Canaries. The new prelate sounded out the missionary in regard to taking him with him to his new diocese.

"I have no pleasure nor will of my own," replied Father Claret; "I will gladly go wherever my superiors may send me, be it to the Canaries or to any other part." Whereupon His Excellency, Bishop Codina, wrote to the bishop of Vich, asking him to authorize Father Claret to give Missions in the Canary Islands for some time.

After having obtained the permission he immediately began his missionary work under the direction of the new bishop.

Fortunate Islands! Soon you will be doubly fortunate, for you will receive the visit of a saint! Simple and abandoned souls, who are hungering for the truth, rejoice because an apostle will come to you who will fill you with peace and who will open the gates of heaven to you!

Father Claret left Catalonia carrying with him his famous missionary baggage, which consisted of a small bundle containing a change of clothing, some papers and his breviary.

Madrid, Seville, Cadiz, and Tenerife were the four points at which he stopped in the company of the bishop. Father Claret took advantage of these brief stops to deliver sermons. In March, 1848, he arrived at the episcopal see of Las Palmas.

XL
THE APOSTLE OF THE CANARIES
<small>List of the Missions—Sixteen Hours in the Confessional
Pulpit on the Plaza—Communion Rail in the Court-
yard—Condescension of a Saint</small>

The Canary Islands!

The glance of Father Claret, enkindled by zeal, fixed itself upon the new panorama of souls that Providence offered him for conquest. His norm always was obedience, and he hoped that his bishop would trace for him the lines of his apostolic itinerary.

We have, fortunately, an authentic account of the series of sermons which Father Claret developed here; they are the brief and precise notes which the bishop compiled under the title of "Lista de las Misiones."

We know, through this document, that the places on the Canary Islands at which Father Claret preached missions were· the Cathedral of Las Palmas, Telde, Arguimes, Arucas, Galdar, Guia, Moya, Teror, San Lorenzo, San Bartolome de Tirajana. Tejeda, Vega de Santa Brigida y San Francisco.

*   *   *

There are details concerning the Mission at Santa Brigida, which it behooves us to note, because these particulars show the fervor of the people and the work of the missionary.

"The mission lasted twenty days," wrote Don Ignacio Mederos y Oliva, parish priest of the said town, in an official letter. "Father Claret was occupied, almost without ceasing, in preaching and in hearing confessions."

"In spite of its vast dimensions, the church was inadequate, by far, to hold the people who came from the neighboring towns; therefore, Father Claret had to preach on the plaza every day. Confessions were heard until one o'clock, and some-times until two o'clock in the morning. Then, after a rest, which ordinarily did not last longer than two hours, he returned to the confessional until the afternoon, the time for the sermon."

"During the days of the Mission he reconciled couples who had lived apart, and married many who had lived in concubinage. The reform was so general and lasting, that there was not one of those who had lived in evil ways who was not converted to God, and who did not persevere in his good resolutions."

"It was impossible to distribute Holy Communion in the church on the last day of the Mission—on the general Communion day—so large was the concourse of people. It had to be distributed on the stairs leading to the main door of the church. Some who had received entered the church for their thanksgiving; after a while they made room for others to enter.

"Such was the anxiety of the faithful to receive the Sacrament of Penance and to wash their souls in the salutary waters of this sacrament, that they crowded around the confessionals, rivalling for a chance to be the first, that sometimes, in order to maintain order, authorities had to intervene."

* * *

Father Claret travelled on foot from one town to another; only once, through humble condescension, he mounted a camel.

At the close of the Mission in Gran Canaria, the bishop sent him to the island of Lanzarote, and assigned him a religious companion. This religious, however, was very stout and walked with difficulty. They alighted at a port of the island, and as their destination was still at a distance of two leagues, the good friar asked Father Claret, "How are we going, on horseback or on foot."

"You know," Father Claret humbly replied, "I always go on foot."

"Well, I," replied the friar, "cannot make so long a stretch on foot; but I will not ride if you do not do so."

The dialogue ended, and Father Claret said: "I cannot consent that you, through respect for me, should fatigue yourself. Both of us will ride, since you so desire." A camel was brought to them, and both the missionary and the friar rode.

Beautiful virtue of condescension, daughter of charity, and therefore, proper to saints.

They alighted from the camel before arriving at the town so as to enter it on foot. Some, however, had seen them mounted. The news that this was not Father Claret, the missionary who was coming to preach to them, spread through the town.

When they arrived, a man, determined and vexed, approached Father Claret and asked him, "Are you the missionary who preached in Gran Canaria?"

"Yes, sir," Father Claret replied.

"Be it known to you," the man concluded, "that some say you are not the same, basing their assertion on the fact that the former always travelled on foot, whilst you have come riding. Many have said that they will not go to hear your sermons, because they think you are not the missionary who preached in Gran Canaria."

The Mission, in spite of this, bore abundant fruit, but Father Claret took note of this observation and of the case. He was again convinced of the fact, that examples of mortification and sacrifice are what principally move and attract people.

XLI

BOUQUET OF PRODIGIES

SUBTERRANEOUS OUTCRIES—SIN OF CURIOSITY—THE DEMON
AND THE LANTERNS—DISCERNMENT OF CONSCIENCES

Great was the natural eloquence and penetrating was the
divine unction that always accompanied the sermons of Father
Claret. His popularity, wherever he preached, was attributed
to his fame for sanctity and accompanied by prodigies and
miracles.

The Missions of the Canaries were filled with prodigies. So
great is the number of miraculous events that it would be difficult to refer to them all.

A Mission began in a town. The church was overflowing
with people. Suddenly the crowd became alarmed because
subterranean noises were heard. There were cries and howls
like an army of men in hours of combat.

Father Claret ascended the pulpit and said, sweetly and
serenely. "That is nothing. Be calm."

When the sermon began the demons were silent. The people
believed themselves singularly blessed to be able to draw near
the missionary, or to touch the hem of his cassock, or to kiss
his hand. His body and his garments seemed to exhale a perfume of purity and a fragrance from heaven which calmed
temptations and pacified spirits.

*　　*　　*

During a mission he was the guest in the home of another
very religious family. Every morning the lady noticed that
the bed had not been used.

"This missionary priest," she said to her husband one day,
"must not go to bed, because I always find the bed the same.
If he does not sleep nor rest, how can he work so much?"

Once, moved by curiosity, she wished to observe what
Father Claret did in his room during the hours of the night.

She silently drew near the door and looked at him through the key-hole. Father Claret was on his knees praying.

The following day the lady made her confession to the missionary, and before leaving the confessional the priest asked, "Have you no other sins?"

"I do not remember any," the lady replied. And then with grave accents, the holy missionary said: "Yes, there is another. Last night you observed me in my room through the keyhole; that was a sin of curiosity."

The same happened to a young man who had looked at him through a crack in the door during the late hours of the night, while Father Claret was on his knees at the foot of the crucifix.

* * *

The following happened in Arucas. The spacious parish church was too small to contain the crowd. An improvised pulpit was placed on the plaza of the village. As all the sermons were given at night, naturally the question arose: "How are we to furnish light for the large plaza?"

"Quite simply. Each family bring a house lantern."

They did so. The numerous lanterns gave the plaza a fantastic aspect at the beginning of the sermon. Suddenly an invisible and simultaneous gust of wind extinguished the lanterns. At the same time a mysterious hand snatched them violently from their owners and threw them on the ground. A cry of terror was heard.

"Ah, my lantern," cried one.

"They have broken my lantern," exclaimed another.

The crowd became excited in the midst of darkness.

Then Father Claret, in a loud voice that dominated the entire plaza called out: "Brethren, do not be frightened. The demon has extinguished the lanterns. The demon has thrown them on the ground. Be assured that not one lantern has been broken. God has not given him permission for that. Pick them up from the ground and relight them."

They did so, and all saw, with surprise, that in spite of having struck the stones, not a lantern was broken.

*   *   *

Discernment of consciences was one of the singular graces with which God favored His servant. By a single word of the penitent he knew the secrets of his soul. There were occasions on which, without ever having seen the persons, he knew the state of their consciences.

On a certain day a lady presented herself for confession to him for the first time.

Father Claret, without even having heard her confession, said to her: "Madam, God bless you and preserve you in His grace. You may receive Holy Communion, for you are not guilty of even a venial sin."

The lady was greatly surprised and received Holy Communion with all tranquillity. She told the story herself, affirming that in reality she was not conscious of having sinned. Other penitents said that if, through ignorance or forgetfulness, they had failed to confess some of their sins, Father Claret would ask them:

"Do you not remember other sins? My son, why do you not confess such or such a sin, which you have committed on such a day, with such a companion, and in such a place?" And he reminded them of the minutest circumstances of the sins not confessed.

Many persons knew that Father Claret had this particular gift of penetrating into the secrets of consciences, and for that reason they tried to place themselves under his authority and direction.

XLII

PROPHETIC ANNOUNCEMENTS

The Fruit of the Harvest—The Obedience of the Beasts—The Hailstorm—Prophecy of the Cholera

Charisms and marks of divine love! While the hand of Father Claret was performing miracles, his words, filled with supernatural light, were sending forth prophecies.

Father Claret was preaching a Mission in the parish of Moya. The heart of the missionary was moved to compassion. Some of the people had walked several leagues just to hear him. The docility of the audience was edifying. All approached the sacred tribunal.

On the last day, from the plaza pulpit, he spoke inspiringly to his audience, saying:

"I am well pleased with you, my brethren! You will be rewarded in eternity. But, in the name of God, I announce to you that this year there will be a more abundant harvest than ever. Remember what I am telling you, when the time of gathering comes."

It was sowing time when Father Claret spoke those words. The people believed and hoped. The harvest season came and the old people of the town affirmed that such an abundant crop had never been seen in that district. The prophecy was fulfilled!

*   *   *

The sacristan congratulated Father Claret as he descended from the pulpit, adding: "You must, indeed, be satisfied; for, excepting a few shepherds who are out in the fields, all the town has come to the Mission."

The following day Father Claret was in the field with the shepherds. "Why do you not come to the Mission?" he asked.

They replied: "Father, we regret it very much. We cannot, because the cattle would over-run the cornfields and the keepers would punish us."

"I tell you no. The cattle will not do any harm. Come to the Mission."

The shepherds obeyed, leaving the cattle alone in the field. The latter soon ran into the oat and wheat fields, but were unable to eat. An invisible muzzle kept them from opening their mouths.

*   *   *

Father Claret tried to organize the Missions so that they were held at a time most favorable for the people, but at times his excessive work and the commands of his superiors arranged the date. This happened in a certain town. He was obliged to give a Mission during harvest time. The wheat was ripe, and the people were anxiously and hopefully urged to work in the field.

Father Claret visited the homes of the principal workmen and told them:

"Do not fear to come to the Mission; God will bless you."

"But, Father," they replied, "that is impossible. The entire harvest may be lost in a single day. We are Catholics and appreciate what pertains to the church, but we cannot lose so many days."

"God is the master of the fields, of the wheat, of the rain, and of hailstorms," was Father Claret's reply.

"In God's name I say to you, that if you come to the Mission, your wheat fields will be more productive, and all danger of rain and hail-storms will be averted. If, however, you do not come, your harvest will be destroyed." Father Claret said no more and began his Mission. Some heeded the call; others did not.

In two days all the people saw the fields of those who did not attend the Mission in ruins and their crops lost. A heavy hail-storm unexpectedly fell upon the wheat fields. On the other hand, the fields of those who made the Mission were preserved. The stalks heavily laden with the golden grain remained erect and not a grain was touched by the hail in spite of the ruined adjacent fields.

The news of this happening spread rapidly through the district, and it served as a salutary warning.

Once the bishop ordered Father Claret to go to a rebellious and obstinate town. The word "Mission" was enough to frighten the people. Their forgetfulness of eternity was complete. Religious ignorance reigned in their intelligence, and corruption in their hearts.

They were, nevertheless, attracted by the fame of the apostle, and consequently, they went to hear him through curiosity.

The voice of Father Claret became superhumanly powerful. Fixing his gaze on an indefinite horizon, he pronounced these words:

"I announce to you, in the name of God, that within a short time a great mortality will come upon you. Parents will be bereft of their children, and children of their parents. Confess your sins and do penance, for God's hour is near at hand."

Many, hearing these words, repented of their sins, and, filled with fear, made their confession. Others, not wishing to believe the missionary, continued in their levity and dissolute life.

The prophetic announcement made by Father Claret was fulfilled in 1851. Cholera morbus was the lash of God. Thousands became victims in the Canary Islands. Recalling the words of the missionary, all said:

"It is a punishment of God! Ah, if we had but heeded the call to the Mission given by holy Father Claret."

XLIII

MIRACULOUS CURES

A Miracle Through Contact—Saved from Fire
Cure of an Epileptic

The name of Father Claret attained great publicity in the Canaries while the self-renouncing missionary worked there. All had at least something to be grateful for, and many, also, for health of body and family happiness.

His zeal as apostle prompted him first to heal the soul, but his fatherly heart beat with pity and tenderness at the sight of bodily infirmities. For that reason, he often asked God to cure many sufferers, and many times the Lord listened to him in a miraculous way in order to satisfy the desires of good Father Claret.

A lady who had been suffering with a very painful eye trouble for a long time came to him. No one knew the cause of the trouble, but the disease was growing. She had consulted the most famous specialists, but their medicines and treatments, far from curing her disease, only caused it to grow worse. The poor woman became impoverished; yet her eyesight failed her. She would soon be blind, according to the opinion of the doctors. She then remembered the miraculous cures which were attributed to the servant of God, Father Claret.

Full of faith, she said to herself, "If I could but meet the man of God, he would certainly cure me."

She went to the church and there patiently awaited Father Claret's entrance. As soon as she was carried to him, she took the priest's hand to kiss it, but instead of carrying it to her lips, she placed it on her eyes. The touch of that blessed hand upon the eyes of the lady wrought a sudden and permanent cure.

"I am cured," the lady cried. "I now see perfectly well. Blessed be the saintly Father Claret."

On a certain occasion our father was preaching in the

church of St. Brigid. Every hearer, on leaving the temple, was a living inducement for others to attend his sermons.

A poor woman on hearing such eulogies, wept with regret, because, on account of her family duties, she was unable to attend the Mission. She, however, made an effort. She left her little son sleeping in the cradle near the hearth in which she had kindled a fire to keep him warm, while she went to the church, one night, at the hour for the sermon.

Father Claret had been preaching for three-quarters of an hour, but it seemed only an instant to the woman. She was so interested and moved by the sermon that the thought of home left her mind. Soon the missionary became silent. He looked at the woman, and inspired by a supernatural light, he said to her: "Lady, go home immediately. The cradle has caught fire; if you do not go quickly, your son will die in the flames."

She left hurriedly and found that, on her child's awakening, a part of the covering had fallen from the cradle into the fire-place and had already begun to burn. The poor mother cried with fear. On remembering that she owed the life of her son to Father Claret, she did not cease blessing God and His servant.

*   *   *

In the city of Telde lived an epileptic young girl of tender years, who had suffered nervous attacks during which she completely lost the use of her senses. Six and even eight men were required to hold her during her convulsions. The slightest ill-humor sufficed to cause an immediate attack.

Father Claret happened to be preaching a Mission in that city. The young girl wished to assist at the evening service, which was the most solemn act of the Mission. After the sermon, Father Claret went to the sacristy, and on seeing so many persons about, asked the cause.

"My sister has taken a nervous spell," answered a man, "and in that case she needs all our help."

Father Claret, without saying a word, entered the church, saturated her handkerchief in holy water and returning to the sacristy, said to those who held the young girl, "Let her free; let her free."

"Father," they all cried, "we cannot do that. She will throw herself upon the ground and injure herself."

"Let her free, I say," repeated the missionary. "Do not fear; no harm will ensue."

They unfastened her, and the young girl remained quiet. Father Claret then placed the handkerchief, moistened with holy water, on her face and the maiden seated herself tranquilly on the floor upon which she had been lying.

"Take the cloth from her eyes," Father Claret said. All wondered at seeing those eyes, usually distended and glassy after her attacks, now shining with their natural brightness.

Father Claret retired, and the young girl walked home accompanied by her brother. She spent the night in peaceful sleep; she arose early the next day went to church, and with other persons accompanied the servant of God, on foot and without tiring, to the neighboring town of Valsequillo, a distance of about a league.

The girl afterwards went to work, suffered and lived many years, but her nervous attacks did not return. Her cure was complete.

XLIV

IN THE PATH OF AN EVANGELIST
INVITATION OF A POOR MAN—HORROR OF MONEY—THE ANGEL OF BESOS—THE HIGHWAYMEN ASSAULTED

Blessed be the steps of the evangelists of peace and good will! May the angels guard their ways! From the apostolic word will bud forth, like blood-tinted roses, sacrifices and conversions. Thus did Blessed Father Claret cross the path of life.

And what were the lines of his moral portrait? They were calmly traced by the Bishop of Cadiz: "I remember," he wrote, "with profound edification, that very modest countenance, so sweetly grave; his glance always reserved; his words well thought out and kept within limits, spoken with ineffable suavity and penetrating unction, all indicating his almost continuous union with God. I remember that rigid mortification, even to the point of eating, even at the table of kings, only vegetables; nor did he sleep in a bed, but on the floor or in a chair, and that, at most, for three or four hours.

And what was the plan of his apostolic journeys? The Apostles dispersed to all the zones on the map of the world to conquer souls. But they traveled like the poor, because they had received the mandate from Our Lord who said:

'Do not possess gold, nor silver, nor money in your purses, nor scrip for your journey, nor two coats, nor shoes, nor staff, for the workman is worthy of his meat.' (Matt. IX, 9, 10).

So also Father Claret; he traced the long routes of his apostolate on the map of Catalonia, the Canaries, Cuba, Spain, Italy and France. He was always accompanied by "evangelical poverty," as a fellow traveller.

Let us hear his own words. They constitute a poem of simplicity and realism which St. Francis of Assissi, the Poverello, might have signed. His autobiography relates the following:

"Travelling one day from Igualada to Barcelona, I approached the town at mid-day. On passing an inn, a poor beggar, taking compassion on me obliged me to enter with him. He asked for a plate of beans which cost four 'cuartos,' or twelve cents, and paid for it from his own pocket. After this meal I felt stronger. That same afternoon I arrived at the town which was at a distance of about five leagues."

In another part we read:

"It was at the end of June, and the weather was very hot. I was going from Vich to Capdevanol to give the Spiritual Exercises to priests who had gathered at that parish. On passing in front of an inn, the landlady, seeing me all bathed in perspiration, greatly fatigued, and tormented with hunger and thirst, invited me to dine."

"I thanked her, but she insisted; I told her that I did not carry money."

"That does not matter," she replied. "Come in and eat and drink, for it gives us pleasure to offer you hospitality."

"I then gratefully accepted the invitation."

* * *

But why is this cult of poverty so extreme and so fervent? Father Claret himself replied:

"I knew it was the will of God that I should not have money nor accept anything, except the necessary food, only at the moment in which I should take nourishment, but not receive provisions necessary to take me from one point to another. Noticing that such abnegation edified everyone and made a deep impression, I did all in my power to continue the practice."

Whence such an attraction to what the world hates and repulses? Let us listen to the secret of his ascetic philosophy.

"One thing I have observed," wrote Blessed Claret, "and that is, when one is poor, and wishes to be so through good will, and not through force, he experiences pleasure in the virtue of poverty. God sends relief in one of two ways. He will either move the heart of the rich to give what is necessary or cause one to live without the need of nourishment. I experienced the ways of His Providence in both manners."

This habit of holy poverty created a horror of money in his heart which the world does not understand.

The case is proved in an ingenious phrase referred to by Blessed Anthony Claret:

"Putting my hand into my pocket one day, I became frightened because I thought I had a coin in it. I took it out to throw it away or to give it to a beggar, but on looking at it, I found it was a medal."

"If at times," he said, "money was offered me for sermons, I refused it saying that I did not need it, for on my trips I neither need horses nor coaches; I always go on foot, even though the roads may be long and rough. Neither do I lack money for clothes or shoes, because God preserves them for me for a long time."

*   *   *

And how did God respond to these sacrifices of the apostle? He blessed him, consoled him, and in some cases, commanded an angel to guide him on his way. Thus it happened at one time. On a rainy day the Besos River had risen; nevertheless, Father Claret had to wade it because he had a Mission scheduled in a town on the other side of the river.

What was to be done in this critical moment? Was he to postpone the Mission? And who knows if there was in that town one single soul awaiting the missionary's word to be converted.

No, he would not turn back. He resolved to cross the river. Seated on the bank, he took off his shoes.

Soon a child appeared to him, and looking smilingly at him, said: "Father, do not take off your shoes, for I will take you across."

"What! You will take me across? You are too small; you could not sustain the weight of my body for one moment, much less could you take me across the river! But tell me from what town are you?"

The child looked at him sweetly but did not reply.

"Go, my son; go home, for it is going to rain, and you will get wet."

The child then said firmly and resolutely, "Let me help you, Father. You will see that I can sustain you and bring you to the other side without becoming wet."

And so it was. The child transported Father Claret to the opposite bank. Father Claret was astonished. He opened his breviary to give the child a picture as a remembrance, but in the act of giving it to him, the child disappeared. It was an angel.

*   *   *

Let us close this collection of episodes with a scene that has been produced many times by writers' pen and artists' brush. It is an immortal page written in the life of Blessed Claret, portraying serenity, valor, sacrifice, and faith.

Near Olot was a town whose parish priest was a friend of Father Claret. Preparations were being made for a great celebration of the patronal feast of the parish. The principal number on the program, without doubt, was the sermon which the celebrated missionary was to preach at High Mass. The servant of God started on his way to his destination alone and on foot. Suddenly, at one of the cross roads, he was assaulted by three fierce looking men who shouted:

"Halt, Father! Your purse or your life!"

"My life perhaps I can give, but I do not carry a purse," Father Claret responded serenely.

"Then prepare to die," said one of them. "Companions, away with him! If not, he will denounce us before the authorities."

There was no change in the countenance of Father Claret at this threat; he addressed them quite tranquilly:

"I am not afraid to die. I only ask one thing of you. I am going to preach a sermon on the occasion of a great feast in the village. All has been organized. They are awaiting me at the fixed hour. Now give me my liberty. After having preached my sermon, I will return here prepared to die."

"All right," said one of them. "Let us set him free; he will return."

"And what if he does not return? And if they take us to prison? It is best to kill him!"

"Do not fear," Father Claret answered. "I give you my priestly word that when the sermon is over I shall not stop even to eat; I will return here, ready to die. Let me go to preach the sermon first."

These words, such moral fortitude, disarmed the assassins; and all three said, "Then go in peace, but return soon, for we shall await you here."

Father Claret, expressing his thanks, left them. He preached the sermon, made his confession, and prepared for death. Within an hour he returned to the appointed place. The highwaymen were hidden. On seeing Father Claret approach, a sentiment of veneration and surprise turned their criminal hearts.

"He is a saint! He is a hero! He deserves to be pardoned for his courage!" said the three men. But dissimulating their resolution, they came into the road and shouted, "Halt! Father! Do you come prepared to die?"

"Yes, my friends, but I first want to thank you for the favor you granted me."

"What are we going to do?" the three asked themselves.

"Pardon him; let him go in peace! He is brave! And besides, he is a saint. I want to make my confession to him right now. Father, will you hear our confession? We are thieves and assassins, but we wish to change our criminal lives. You have converted us through your greatness of soul. Please hear our confessions immediately."

Father Claret sat down beneath a tree, and the three men made their confessions. What a supremely simple, deep, dramatic moral picture! Let us repeat in conclusion the words with which this chapter opened:

Blessed be the steps of the evangelists of peace and good will! May the angels guard their ways! From the apostolic word will bud forth, like blood-tinted roses, sacrifices and conversions.

XLV

AUREOLAS OF HIS APOSTOLATE
THE INCURABLE—BORAGE WATER—GO IN PEACE—ANA
VIGNER—THE CHILD OF TEYA

Jesus passed through the world doing good; good to souls by converting them, to bodies by curing them. The catalog of his cures, like a spiritual symbol and like a material reality, was that which Our Lord taught the emissaries of St. John, the Baptist, when he gave them this mission:

"Say to John, the blind see, the lame walk, the lepers are cured, the dead arise, and the poor are evangelized."

In imitation of Our Lord, Father Claret passed through the world doing good; good to souls by preaching Missions and the spiritual exercises; and good to bodies by curing them with that prodigious virtue which God granted His servant as a grace of his apostolate.

The sick awaited the missionary along the streets through which he passed; full of faith, they flocked to the church in which he was preaching; they crowded about the rectory where he was lodging during the Missions, begging a blessing, a word, a look, an advice, a hope of health. They believed that the least manifestation of that saint would be the beginning of their cure.

"For that reason," using the expression of an eye witness, "wherever Father Claret went, an improvised hospital was set up."

We have gathered here a few facts in the original simple version of the people. Critical history has curtailed some of the prodigies.

*　　*　　*

The following happened in Lerida. Father Claret was preaching a Mission. The fame of his eloquence was great, but greater still was his moral prestige, gained by his virtue and the prodigious deeds which the public attributed to him.

On a certain day, when he was passing through the street, a little old woman, weeping, came to him. A child of about eleven was at her side. Father Claret, as was his custom, gave a picture to the child and a leaflet to the woman. The old lady then said to the servant of God:

"Father, have compassion on me. I am a poor grandmother, and this is my only grandchild. But as you see, Father, he is sick; he has a double hunchback, and the doctors cannot cure him. Have compassion on me, Father, and cure my grandson."

"Poor child!" exclaimed Father Claret, petting the little one paternally. "How long has he been so?"

"Since his earliest years."

"And what do the doctors say?"

"That he is incurable."

"What can I do, if the doctors cannot do anything?"

The poor woman began to weep.

Father Claret then touched the chest of the child, and its back, and said:

"God will cure you, my son! Be a good Christian."

All Lerida knew in a few days that the child was cured and that his supernatural physician had been Father Claret. Not a trace of the deformity remained in the body of the child. He grew robust and was always the consolation of his grandmother.

*   *   *

There was an expression which became celebrated in Vich. It was this: "Borage water, worth nothing."

Doña Antonia Vila de Calderon was seriously ill. The principal doctors of Vich visited her and all declared her incurable.

The priest was called, and he hastened to administer the Last Sacraments so as to prepare her for her journey to eternity upon which she was about to enter. The patient herself believed that death was approaching. After giving maternal counsels to her children, she thought only of God and heavenly things.

Father Claret was at Vich at the time. At the request of the sick lady he came to see her.

"I will go immediately," Father Claret said, "although it is not necessary that I go."

No one then understood the meaning of those words. On entering the house, he beheld a picture of the saddest and most profound desolation. There were tears and moans.

"Be calm, very calm!" Father Claret said to them smilingly. "There is no reason for such weeping! Where is the sick lady?"

Father Claret was shown to her room. In a few moments he was with the patient, bringing her consolation. On leaving the house, he assured the family that she would be cured. The bystanders breathed freely. This was the first alleviation they had felt in their anguish.

"She will be cured. To obtain her cure, give her this drink."

This was only a disguise under which the miracle was hidden.

The doctor came and after examining the drink exclaimed scornfully: "This is borage water! Worth nothing! Let her drink all she wishes. It will not harm her."

Upon saying this, the doctor left the house not to return again.

A few days later, a lady, well known in the city, was on her way to the church to make her confession and to receive Holy Communion in thanksgiving. It was Doña Antonia Vila de Calderon. Father Claret had cured her. The people on seeing her alluded ironically to the phrase the doctor had used, "Borage water! Worth nothing!"

*   *   *

Father Claret, in the opinion of the people, seemed to be a specialist for all infirmities, and, therefore, they came to him in crowds to consult him in their afflictions.

"But I am not a physician," said Father Claret to his un-expected clients.

But they, having at times come from long distances, responded: "Cure me, Father."

A man and a child were traveling to Figueras early one morning. Who were they? Pedro Llobet and his son.

Whence did they come? From Trias very near the village of Navata.

What was the object of their journey? The cure of their child.

Who was the doctor? Father Claret, who was then preaching a Mission in Figueras. The child had been suffering for five years from a kind of leprosy which covered his whole body, causing him such horrible pains that the poor creature frequently gave out heartrending cries and fled in despair. He could not bear any close-fitting clothing. The only garment which covered his pitiable body was a pair of wide pantaloons of coarse cloth, which could be thrown over his head and fastened up to the waist.

One day, when he was tired of consulting doctors in vain, the father of the child heard that the saintly missionary was at Figueras and that he had cured many in a marvelous way. He took the child there as a last resource.

Father Claret was in the church, making his thanksgiving after Mass. Pedro Llobet waited and then took his child to the rectory. Drawing near he said:

"Father, have compassion on me. I have brought my son to you to be cured. Look at his poor little body."

Father Claret raised the garment that covered the little boy, and on seeing it exclaimed: "Poor little thing! How he must be suffering."

"He has suffered very much. Only God and we are witness to his sufferings."

Turning to the child, Father Claret said amiably: "Be a

good Christian. You will be cured, God willing. I will recommend you to God. Go in peace."

The father hoped that Father Claret would, like other doctors, prescribe for his child. On noting that he neither said nor did anything for him, the father took for granted that the priest was busy and that they had come inopportunely Therefore he retired respectfully saying:

"Father, I see that you are at your prayers now. If you wish we will return tonight for the prescription."

"No, you will not have to wait. Obey your doctors."

"But, Father, we have gone to many doctors, and by doing so, I have spent all my earnings."

"Do not fear; go in peace. I will recommend you to God."

The father and son left Figueras sorrowfully. When they were midway, however, the child suddenly cried out with joy:

"Father, I am cured. Nothing pains me now!" And he began to leap for joy.

The father could not believe his eyes. Was it perhaps an illusion on the part of his son? The child then tore off the coarse cloth that was fastened at the waist, and showed his father his back and his chest, all free from the disease and covered with new, soft skin.

A little later all the town of Tria, on seeing the child, were convinced of the miracle. The two fortunate travelers remembered the words of Father Claret:

"I will recommend you to God."

*   *   *

Father Claret used two means in the cure of illnesses, the one spiritual, the other corporal. Both served to protect his humility from the applause of the people.

He first commanded them to say some prayers and then prescribed some inoffensive medicine and inculcated obedience to their doctors. Thus he intended to hide the gift of miracles. Let us read the account of Marie Ana Vigner.

"I was a young girl of about fifteen years of age when I

suffered from stomach trouble of such a nature that I became completely prostrated. The doctor had little hope of saving me, and my depression was such that my fainting spells were frequent. This sad state was the effect of four years of suffering from my infirmity. All remedies seemed to be exhausted, and the doctor declared death inevitable. A pious woman then advised my mother to take me to Father Anthony Claret, who was then at Vich, for he had cured many miraculously. Provided with cordials and medicines, my mother determined to take me to the priest. Since Vich was about two leagues distant from my home, mother rather dragged than accompanied me. It was necessary to revive me several times on account of my fainting spells. Walking at a regular pace, we spent more than triple the time necessary to make the trip. On arriving at Vich my mother presented me to the servant of God. I told him of my ailments and he replied:

" 'I am not a doctor.'

"Then charging me to have a particular devotion to the Blessed Virgin he said:

" 'Be a good Christian. You will be cured.'

"We left. On passing the door of his room, he prescribed a potion of an herb for dropsy. In the same instant I felt that I was cured. I regained my strength and returned home as if I had never been ill. On seeing this change, my mother was astonished. So was the doctor who had visited me and all who knew of my illness. My health continued so perfect that I even forgot to take the medicine the servant of God had prescribed for me."

*   *   *

Father Claret cast a double glance at the sick. With one glance he looked upon their sufferings of body and with another, profound and efficacious, he saw their souls, which perhaps were also sick. It often happened that a double cure was wrought. The cure of the soul by conversion, and the cure of the body by restoration to health.

In the town of Teya, in the Bishopric and Province of Barcelona, there lived a boy, about fifteen years of age, called Juan Girbau. One evening at seven o'clock, while the Blessed Sacrament was carried as Viaticum to a sick person through the plaza, this boy took an epileptic fit, the first he had ever had. After this, these spells continued to come upon him frequently. Another affliction, a great repugnance to acts of religion and pious practices followed. He was unable to assist at Mass and at sermons. Nor could he bear to have anyone pray at his bedside. He fled from the images of Jesus and Mary and was repelled by the crucifix, wherever it was, even though it was in pockets or around the neck.

The boy was seemingly good, but an interior strength, against his will, impelled him to every irreligious act. His deeply grieved, but good Christian mother and father, wished him to see Father Claret. In company with four neighbors of Teya, they brought him to Barcelona where the servant of God was at that time.

"I do not wish to see the priest," cried the boy. "Take me away from here."

All believed that he was having an attack. Finally, he was brought into Father Claret's room. Contrary to all expectations, he was as calm and meek as a lamb. Father Claret, putting his hand on the sufferer's head said affectionately:

"Listen, my son; you will recite daily the holy rosary; three Hail Marys to the Mother of God; and one Our Father to your Guardian Angel, and another for my intention. To-morrow you will go and make your confession. If the confessor were to ask you if you were sick, you will answer: 'No,' and if he should wish to know who cured you, you will say: 'God, our Lord'."

Addressing those who accompanied him, he added: "If, within some days there should be a recurrence of the malady, do not heed it, for it will be of little or no importance."

When they left the presence of Father Claret, the boy was

able to pray. The following day he went to confession and to
Holy Communion. Afterwards, he attended all the religious
exercises of the parish. He was cured of his infirmity.

The people of Teya, on seeing the boy who had been an
epileptic and a blasphemer the day before, now in good health
and piously inclined, said with enthusiasm and gratitude:

"A miracle of Father Claret."

They were right. God gave the first Apostles of Christianity,
as a guarantee of their ministry, the grace to cure, a grace by
which they healed the sick with a blessing, with a word, and
even by mere contact with their shadow. So, too, Father Claret
spread his wonderful cures along the way. They were the
aureola of his apostolate.

XLVI
THE SEER'S GLEAMS OF LIGHT

Dr. Masmitja—Cure of an Orator—Miracle on Good
Friday—The Book of Consolation—The Horror
of a Reprobate—The Death of a Priest

"Draw near to God, and you will be enlightened," says
the Psalmist. Father Claret lived in God, and God lived in
him. By this means he bore in his spirit the light of eternity.
At its reflection, time and space are folded in its shadow. The
glance of the seer contemplated, as clear as days, the panoramas of the future!

These horizons of his vision, clear and smiling, as in innocence and happiness, gladdened the spirit of Father Claret. But
when they were sad and gloomy, as the conscience of the
sinner or the mourning of an unfortunate one, then his great
and sensitive heart suffered profoundly because the suffering
of his fellowmen found an echo in his heart. For this reason
the life of the saintly missionary was so human and attractive.

Let us consider some signs of his clear-sightedness.

One of the great friends whom Father Claret had among
the clergymen of Catalonia, was Dr. D. Joaquin Masmitja,
arch-priest of the Cathedral of Gerona. They had known each
other for a long time; and the more they associated, the more
intimate and spiritual their affection became. Father Claret was
the confidant of his friend in matters of conscience, and only
in him did Don Joaquin find consolation and calm in his
troubled spirit.

For some time a secret anguish tormented the latter's soul.
Father Claret continued his Mission. As soon as Dr. Masmitja
saw him within his sight, hope of recovering his tranquillity
of conscience came to him. The two met on the road.

"Where are you going, Father Claret?" asked Dr. Masmitja.

"To look for you, Don Joaquin. And, moreover, to console you, because I know that you are in spiritual tribulation. See, the remedy against your anguish is this. . . . Practice it, and you will be cured."

Dr. Masmitja was astonished at the fact that Father Claret had ascertained his most intimate spiritual secrets. But he was also consoled by the fact that the advice of his friend sufficed to relieve his soul from tribulation.

*   *   *

Father Claret had the greatest respect and admiration for all his companions in the apostolate, when there shone in them true zeal for the conversion of souls. He keenly felt their illness and their death, because they were honored members in the army of the Church. From his hands came prodigies in the form of cures of priests, religious, and seminarians.

Father Pedro Nolasco Tenas was an illustrious and pious religious of the Order of Mercy. He lived habitually in the Convent of Barcelona, and was engaged in preaching. Father Claret fostered a singular affection for him, because he noted that the latter's sermons brought great good to souls.

For some time Father Tenas' health was very delicate, but, notwithstanding all, he did not wish to slacken his labors.

One day he was unable to move in his bed, because a coughing spell caused a hemorrhage.

"I consider his condition grave," said Dr. Saques, "and I dare say that he has only a few days to live."

Father Claret knew of the illness of his friend and immediately went to visit and console him.

"That is nothing!" said Father Claret smilingly.

"Brace up and have confidence in God."

They conversed briefly on matters pertaining to the ministry. Shortly before taking leave, Father Claret put his hand upon the sick man's head. After saying a short prayer, he said, in a happy jovial way:

"Father Pedro, take courage. You will even help me explain the catechism and preach sermons."

"May God hear you," the sick priest replied, stretching out his hand to him.

*   *   *

The following day joy reigned in the Community of Mercy, for Father Tenas had been cured. The previous day had found him in a dying condition and now he was following the Rule perfectly. In order to prove to all the power of his lungs, he began to preach immediately. For many years he continued one of the most eloquent and pious preachers in the city. Father Claret took him as a companion on some of his most important missions. Father Tenas then remembered that prophecy which Father Claret had made while he was ill:

"You will even help me to explain the catechism and preach sermons."

Father Claret paid his friends the courtesy of friendship with the most delicate affection of his heart. In moments of danger, or in real pain, he often did what only saints could do—he performed a miracle.

Pedro Homs was a seminarian in the course of philosophy. His desire inclined towards the sanctuary. All his efforts were so concentrated on saving souls by means of the sacerdotal ministry. On a certain day he had a fall. As a result of the fall, his eyes became inflamed; his eyelids closed. The doctors believed that he would lose his eyesight. Sadness and discouragement fell like a shadow on the spirits of the young seminarian. He felt that he could not now be a priest. His father was a great friend of Father Claret. Distrusting doctors, he placed all his confidence in the prayers of the servant of God.

"He will be cured," said Father Claret. This was the hope of the afflicted family.

It was Good Friday of the year 1847.

While visiting the repositories during Holy Week, it happened that the two friends met in a church. On leaving the church the servant of God repeated the same words to the afflicted Father:

"He will be cured."

In the afternoon the Holy Missionary preached the sermon on the Seven Last Words in the Church of Our Lady of Mercy. On coming to a passage on the "lance that pierced Our Savior's side," he paused a moment, and changing his tone of voice, said:

"At this moment there is one who has recovered his sight in virtue of the blood of Christ."

The audience, in surprise, asked themselves: "Who can it be?"

A man came running to the church; he was beaming with joy. He was the father of the seminarian. He waited in the sacristy until the servant of God descended from the pulpit and then addressed him saying:

"My son is cured! My son can now open and close his eyes; he can see perfectly."

Father Claret was not amazed at the news, and he modestly retired, shunning all conversation on the matter.

Later the young man was asked the hour in which he had been cured. It was in the same hour in which Father Claret pronounced those mysterious words:

"At this moment there is one who has recovered his sight in virtue of the Blood of Christ."

*   *   *

Children were particularly dear to the heart of Father Claret. When children approached him with a two-fold beauty —the beauty of innocence and the beauty of sorrow—he overflowed with tenderness and offered them the treasures of his counsels—counsels that would bring them happiness.

The servant of God was giving a Mission in Pobla de Lillet. One day, while passing along the street, a girl of thirteen called Candida Villalta, approached him saying:

"A picture, Father! Please give me a picture, and God will repay you!" The child continued her pleading with candid insistence.

"My daughter, I will not give you a picture, but I will give you what you need more," said Father Claret.

In the act of giving her a copy of "Camino Recto" ("The Right Road") he said:

"Take this book, for you will, in time suffer much, and it will serve as a consolation."

The child received the book with a double sentiment, one of joy, because it was a gift from Father Claret, and one of sadness, because of a mournful augury of her future.

Candida at the time enjoyed perfect health. She had good parents and her family enjoyed a splendid economic position. Nevertheless, Father Claret's prophecy was fulfilled with absolute exactitude.

While still young, she suffered grave tribulations of body and spirit; in her family and in her affairs; dislocation of bones; difficult operations; painful sickness; danger of death; reception of Holy Viaticum five times in as many grave illnesses. All this caused the life of Candida to be a prolonged martyrdom until her death, which occurred at an advanced age.

She confided to her confessor, Father Coma, of the Oratory of St. Philip Neri, the following:

"Father Claret prophesied all these things when I was but a child. At the time he gave me a book which would prove a consolation. Here it is always at my side. It has given me patience and resignation in the midst of sufferings."

*   *   *

This was, indeed, a prediction of sorrow, sweet and resigned, but the following was a prediction of horror, profound and tragic.

Father Claret was preaching in La Selva del Campo, in the Province and Diocese of Tarragona. One night, on leaving the pulpit, the sacristan came up to him and said:

"Father, an urgent sick call has come. A lady, seriously ill, wishes to make her confession."

Father Claret did not know her family, much less the mentioned lady. He was silent a moment and reflected. Then, raising his eyes to heaven, he exclaimed:

"Tell the family not to expect me. Ah, it is useless to go, because this woman is lost before God."

Horror took possession of all who heard those words.

The family later called the parish priest who went to the house without hesitation. He entered the room of the sick person. Upon seeing the priest, it seemed as though she became possessed by the demon and began to hurl insults, imprecations, and blasphemies upon him. The priest spent all the resources of his zeal in order to bring this stubborn heart upon the right path. But all was useless. The woman continued blaspheming. On leaving the room, the priest repeated the prophetic words of Father Claret:

"She is lost before God."

The sick woman continued perverse and obstinate a few days longer and then died suddenly. She was lost before God.

*   *   *

A note of fright also emanates from this event. It was in 1849. The Bishop of Vich had organized the Spiritual Exercises for the clergy and had chosen Father Claret as Retreat Master. All the priests of the diocese wished to attend the retreat, attracted, principally, by the fame for sanctity of the missionary. But this could not be; those who were obliged to remain said to those who went:

"You are fortunate to be able to listen to a saint. Bring us notes of what he says."

A number of priests headed by the virtuous bishop gathered in the Seminary. Father Claret gave the first meditation with unction and simplicity, but before he began the conference they noticed a strange paleness in his countenance.

"What can be the matter with Father Claret?" the priests asked themselves. "Is he perhaps ill?"

Father Claret began speaking slowly and after a few brief words he said:

"You will notice, venerable brethren, that I am affected. My voice trembles and I am growing faint without being able to help it. God has just revealed to me that there is one of you who has begun the Spiritual Exercises and who will not be able to conclude them. He cannot even surmise his approaching death."

These words surprised his hearers and each one began to fear. On the following day a young, robust priest took sick mysteriously. The physician's services were useless. The priest died. Many years later, one of the retreatants told the story and added:

"I am still moved and terrified on remembering those solemn words, pronounced by Father Claret."

XLVII

THE VOICE FROM THE CLOISTER

Miss Maspons—The Son of Jose Rouira—The Possessed Vision of Consciences

Blessed Father Claret spent long hours of the day and night conversing with God in prayer. In these hours he received from heaven deep secrets regarding states of conscience and the particular vocation which each one is to follow in order to do the will of God.

And what did he do with those secrets? They were the messages that God gave to him to communicate afterwards to souls. And he, prudently and opportunely, with liberty and strength, gave integrally to his hearers the content of the revelation, and his enlightening words were darts that pierced hearts and made souls submissive.

During Lent of 1845 the following incident took place at Mataro. Miss Maspons belonged to a very distinguished family of Mataro. Because she was young and rich, intelligent and beautiful, good and charitable, she was universally loved. A young man of good habits, holding a brilliant position, sought her hand in marriage. The matter was treated to the satisfaction of both parties and the date for the approaching marriage was set.

Father Claret did not know Miss Maspons. One day a friend of hers, Teresa Figueras, told him of the approaching wedding, when Father Claret interrupted her saying:

"No, that young lady will not marry. Such is not the will of God. God wishes her to become a nun, a Capuchin religious."

Teresa was astonished at these words, but since the wedding was to take place very soon, she did not believe them.

One night Miss Maspons went to hear a sermon preached by Father Claret at Mataro during the Lenten Season of 1845. God caused the words of Father Claret to prove mysterious darts that wounded the heart of that elegant young lady. Deep confusion overpowered her. She prayed and wept. After the sermon she went home without joining in the conversation, as was her custom, with her friends.

"What has happened to Paquita Maspons?" they asked one another. "She is probably ill."

In the meantime a heart-rending scene was taking place in the Maspons family.

"What has happened to you, my daughter, for you are weeping and are so disturbed. Have you had a fright?"

"No; nothing has happened. I have heard Father Claret's sermon, and God has opened my eyes to see and depreciate the things of the world. Tell my friend to forget me; if he should think of me, let it be only to recommend me to God. I wish to be a religious, a Capuchin nun."

"Ah, not that. Everything except that. We will do all in our power to prevent it."

"There is no authority against the authority of God. I feel that God is calling me. I shall be unhappy outside the cloister. You are good Christians and love me; I beg you to let me follow God's call."

The battle within the Maspons family lasted three months, but, finally the constancy of the daughter conquered. She entered the Capuchin Convent of Mataro. The parents resigned themselves to the vocation of their daughter, but the loved one did not conform himself to the resolution of his beloved. He pleaded, insisted, threatened, wept, but all in vain. Finally, he guessed the origin of the determination. On knowing that it had been a sermon of Father Claret, he heaped all sorts of calumnies against the servant of God; these were published by the revolutionary press of Spain and America.

Father Claret, in the midst of the unjust complaint which, for the reason mentioned, had been made against him, said with serenity:

"This comes from God. I have nothing to do with the resolve of Miss Maspons, for I do not even know her."

It is recorded in the annals of the convent that Sister Maria Francisca Maspons lived and died as a holy religious.

*   *   *

The prestige and authority of Blessed Father Claret in regard to souls was very great. He was appreciated not only by penitents, but also by spiritual directors, who came to him in hours of uncertainty concerning grave matters. This occurred in the case of Candida Rovira.

There lived in the town of Estany, province of Barcelona, diocese of Vich, a couple named Jose Rovira and Rosa Malats. They were blessed with two daughters; the younger always delicate and sickly, died very young. The parents then concentrated all their hopes and affection on Candida, now their only daughter. Candida was attracted by the vanities of the world for some time, but one day she felt the impulse of a religious vocation.

"The world is not for me. Its diversions tire me. I feel sad in the midst of noisy joy. I wish to be a religious. But how can I make my resolve known to my parents?" Thus said Candida to herself in pensive hours, and she let the days pass in silence and retirement. But one day she made a sudden start. She presented herself to her parents calmly, yet resolutely, and said to them:

"I have been thinking of it for some time. It is not the impression of a moment. I wish to be a religious. I know what grief this will cause you, but it is the will of God."

"Have you thought it over well, my daughter? Do you know in what a situation you leave us? We do not wish to oppose the call of God, but what if you deceive yourself? We will consult a wise counsellor in the matter and we will do what he shall tell us."

On the following day, the father and daughter went to Father Canals, Prior of the Carmelites of Vich, who after examining the vocation of the girl, seeing that the parents were poor and somewhat advanced in years and needed the help of their daughter, did not believe it prudent to approve of Candida's resolve, but neither did he dare to disapprove it. He said thus to them:

"I find this case a difficult one, but Father Claret is here. You know he is a man of science, virtue, and experience. Present yourself to him, explain matters, and then do as he shall tell you."

They went to the servant of God. Father Claret received and listened to the father first and then interviewed the daughter. He reflected for some moments; he said a short prayer and then called both together. He spoke thus to them most resolutely:

"It is the will of God that Candida becomes a religious. Do not fear to give your consent, because within a year God will grant you the blessing of becoming the father of a son who will be your consolation in your old age."

On hearing these words the man smiled skeptically, because he and his wife were advanced in years. On taking leave of Father Claret he said to him:

"If, within a year, we have a son, we shall give our daughter permission to go to the convent."

Jose Rovira, as soon as he came home, told his wife the result of the interview and soon the whole town of Estany knew of it. One year later, not more nor less, there was great rejoicing in the Rovira family, for a male heir, robust and beautiful, had just been born. All remembered the day of Father Claret's prophecy and exclaimed:

"The boy is born miraculously."

Candida reminded her father of the fulfillment of the promise to permit her to enter the Convent. To the satisfaction of all, Candida took the habit of the Third Order of the Carmelites of Charity, for her vocation was now recognized as the express will of God.

The heaven-sent son advanced in years. Through his labors

and his honorable conduct he became the consolation of his parents and the staff of their old age.

* * *

Father Claret looked upon convents as residences of God and as the paradise of souls. And for that reason, when the world, the demon, and the flesh wished to disturb those asylums of sanctity, he was always there to re-establish, with his words, the empire of peace.

An incident, told by the parish priest, D. Mariano Sanias, as heard from the lips of the servant of God himself, took place in a convent of Barcelona. It is recorded, moreover, in the handwriting of Blessed Claret among his personal manuscripts. While Father Claret was giving a Mission in Barcelona, a confessor of nuns presented himself and said to him:

"Father, in the convent under my charge there is a religious upon whom the community looks as useless. She never receives Holy Communion and she often omits the community exercises. I, as her confessor, have never understood her spirit, nor have I been able to make her reveal herself after having had her under my direction so many years. Would you kindly come to the convent and hear her confession to see if you can understand her."

Father Claret acceded to the request, went to the convent, and heard her confession. On taking leave of the Father confessor, Father Claret said to him:

"I have commanded the religious to receive Holy Communion with the community. Let us see what will happen."

That same day, Father Claret went to Barcelona to preach a Novena. Upon his return he immediately went to the convent. He was told that the religious was unable to receive Holy Communion because when she went to the railing with the others, the demon caught her by the waist and threw her against the religious at the railing, causing them to fall upon the platform. She herself was so bruised that she could not move. As a result, she was carried to her bed and was unable to leave it for a week.

Father Claret heard the story and said to the community:

"Tomorrow morning I will give her Holy Communion myself. The poor thing! She is so good and angelic! It is for this reason that the demons are tormenting her so!"

Father Claret celebrated Holy Mass and distributed Holy Communion to the community. He failed to see the tormented religious, but found that she was in a corner of the choir. He called her loudly and commanded her through obedience to communicate. The religious came down, trembling. At the moment in which she received the Sacred Host, she remained entirely tranquil. After that she was able to communicate every day with the community.

* * *

The news of this and other happenings soon spread. The fame of Father Claret's sanctity, the number of his conversions, proved throughout all Spain his genuine spirituality. For this reason the religious communities begged with insistence that Father Claret conduct their retreats. They knew that the fervor of his word would increase love of regular observance in the religious.

The Order of the Discalced Carmelites of St. Theresa was one that profited most by the advices of Father Claret. All of the religious of the various houses were anxious to hear him. When they were granted this honor, they mentioned this favor to the other communities and looked upon it as a favor from heaven.

In Vich, when Father Claret was giving the Spiritual Exercises to the Discalced Carmelites of St. Theresa, a deep and serene joy inundated the souls of the religious. What was the reason? The Mother Prioress, Sister Maria Esperanza of the Conception gave the explanation:

"Father Claret has heard our confession. He told us in one of his conferences not to be uneasy about these confessions, because at that very moment he was reading our consciences. All of us have experienced that he was telling the truth; he knew the faults of each one better than the interested person."

The Mother Prioress, wishing the same happiness to the religious of other convents, wrote to the Superior of the Third Order of the Carmelites and told her to engage Father Claret for their retreat. She told her what had occurred in her convent.

She received this reply:

"Many thanks be given to God. We have made the retreat under Father Claret. The community is consoled and edified. He told us on the eve of the retreat that we were not to be distressed nor to have the least anxiety of mind, because he could see perfectly the state of our consciences. Thus have we experienced it. May God be praised!"

The people acclaimed Father Claret with vociferous exultation. But another voice, grateful, but restrained, also blessed his name. It was the voice of the cloister.

XLVIII

ARCHBISHOP OF CUBA
Reward of Humility—Mandate of Obedience
The Third Class Coach—The Grand
Cross—The Three Visits

God exalts the humble!

The Church placed the pompous robes of the episcopate over the missionary's cassock, and in order that the Missionary Archbishop might have greater prominence, he was assigned the most suitable of Spanish colonies—the island of Cuba.

The Island of Cuba, discovered by Columbus in 1492, is on truth one of the most beautiful that gives life, as a charming oasis, to the desert of the seas. The moral beauty of its inhabitants, on the other hand, must have been inferior to the charms of the land, when in June, 1834, General Tacon, in an official report affirmed that "an increasing number of assassins and thieves circulated through the streets of the capital, killing, wounding, and robbing not only during the hours of the night, but also in broad day and even in the public and most frequented streets. The vagrants are innumerable, and astounding is the number of those who earn their living by all kinds of deceit."

The capital city had been for a long time deprived of its legitimate shepherd, on account of political disturbances. In order to form an idea of how demoralizing the Island was before Father Claret was appointed Archbishop of Santiago, suffice it to say that, in the Archdiocese of Santiago, of the 41,167 baptisms that were administered from 1842-1846, more than one-half, or in exact numbers, 22,517 were of illegitimate birth. Could a better field of operations for the apostolic zeal of the new Missionary Archbishop have been found?

The See of Santiago of Cuba was made vacant by the promotion of its Archbishop, Rev. Fray Cirulio de la Alameda, to the Metropolitan See of Burgos, April 20, 1849. Since the political and moral conditions of the Island were in such a critical condition, the election of a new bishop was a most delicate and transcendental matter.

"Who do you think," asked the Señor Nuncio, addressing the virtuous priest, Don Jose Ramirez y Cotes, "would be the Archbishop that Cuba needs? I have been thinking over the matter for some time, and I am still perplexed."

"Señor Nuncio," replied Don Jose, "Cuba needs missionaries! What it needs is a missionary bishop."

"That is true, Father, but where can one be found? Where is the person that would be a missionary bishop in Cuba?"

"He is in Catalonia. Father Claret, the missionary who went to the Canaries, is the best choice. There is no better."

A superior light illumined the mind of Señor Nuncio, and he exclaimed:

"That is true!"

*   *   *

How was the news of Father Claret's nomination to the Archbishopric of Santiago de Cuba made known to him? Who was the first to communicate it to him? Was it the Papal Nuncio? Was it the Queen? Was it the Minister of the Interior? Surely, no one would guess that; it was the demon.

Father Claret was in Barcelona, guest of the chaplain of Religious Magdalens. His open breviary, from which he was praying, was on the table. Soon a slip of paper fell mysteriously on his book. It was of brown color about four inches long, and on it were written these words:

"Now you will be content, for they have named you Archbishop of Cuba. There you will work for your own, but I also will work for my own."

The paper bore a strange signature. Three scratches made by a finger nail.

On another day the demon repeated the notice in a monologue of rancor.

A religious was greatly tormented by the demons. One night they thrust her out of her bed violently; they fastened her to a column of the cloister, beat her vigorously, and tore her habit off.

Father Claret had a high opinion of the virtue of this religious. He animated and comforted her in her tribulations.

Another night while the demons were passing the door of the religious, they were heard to say:

"Now they wish to make him Archbishop of Cuba! We shall see!"

This occured several months before the appointment. The religious communicated it to Father Claret, but the humble missionary exclaimed:

"Do not heed the father of lies!"

Again the demon spoke with rabid disdain, pointing to the boat and the cabin which the future Archbishop was to use on his trip.

A soul greatly favored by Almighty God, yet tormented by the demon, had been for a long time under the spiritual direction of Father Claret. This person asked the prayers of a religious community in favor of Archbishop Claret.

"Pray much for him," she said, "because the demon hates him since he draws so many souls from his satanical power."

Later on it became known, by an authentic document, that one night a religious was violently torn from her bed by evil spirits, who carried her on board a merchant vessel, "Teresa Cubana," and said to her:

"This cabin is for the thief who is going to Cuba. We have not been able to prevent it, but know that we are going to wage war against him and not let him do anything."

*　　*　　*

The enemies challenged the skill of the Papal Nuncio in appointing the holy Missionary Archbishop of Cuba. Father Claret, however, was far from suspecting the appointment.

How he opposed with humble firmness the acceptance of this dignity!

Father Claret was giving the Spiritual Exercises to the clergy of Vich. One day, the 11th of August, after one of the acts of the retreat, word was left in the sacristy that the bishop had summoned him. He went to the palace immediately and the bishop gave him the royal order received by the Minister of the Interior, D. Lorenzo Arrazola, in which his appointment as Archbishop of Cuba was announced.

The servant of God, on hearing the decree, was struck dumb with surprise; but shortly after, addressing the bishop, he said:

"This cannot be! I cannot accept! I would ask Your Excellency to kindly reply that I have not the knowledge nor the virtue necessary to discharge that office."

Having said this and believing firmly that he would not be molested with the same subject again, he began anew his beloved missionary work, giving, during his free hours, conferences on Moral Theology, Sacred Oratory, Asceticism and Mysticism to his fellow missionaries.

Father Claret's objections did not convince the Papal Nuncio nor the Minister of the Interior. Thus, in spite of Father Claret's opposition, they wrote to the Bishop of Vich, asking His Excellency to impose upon him the acceptance by virtue of Holy Obedience.

This was a new surprise for Father Claret; yet he still had recourse to his humility. He asked the bishop to permit him to make a retreat, in order to think it over well and to consult several prudent persons. The bishop acceded benignly.

Father Claret consulted four venerable priests who had known him well—Don Jaime Solar, Don Jaime Passarell, Padre Pedro Boch, and Padre Esteban Sala. All four told him:

"It is the will of God that you accept the charge!"

Father Claret then obeyed resignedly, and to his bishop, who was making his pastoral visits at the time, he wrote:

"Your Excellency knows that I have always allowed myself to be led by the hand of obedience. In view of the much appreciated letter of Your Excellency, together with that of the Papal Nuncio and of the Minister of the Interior, I humbly accept the Archbishopric of Santiago de Cuba. 'Behold the servant of the Lord: be it done unto me according to thy word.' "

*   *   *

What modifications were introduced into his spirit and into his customs by this exalted appointment? None. He retained the same humility, unchanged simplicity, and identical zeal for the conversion of souls.

This suggested a story which had been witnessed and lived through, and was told by His Excellency, the Bishop of Segorbe, D. Francisco de Asis Aguilar. Dr. Aguilar was a pupil of Fr. Claret and accompanied him from Barcelona to Gerona. His testimony is as follows:

"At dawn of a morning in April, 1850, a priest and a student left Barcelona, taking the road that led to the railroad station of Mataro. The priest, dressed in a well-worn and almost tattered cassock adorned with patches, but neat and clean, the best his impoverished condition allowed, carried nothing else than a walking cane.

"The student carried on his arm a long cloak of about the same age, more or less, as the cassock of the priest. The cloak was tied with a band, and contained a shirt, socks, and some books, which made it clear that this bundle held the belongings of the priest on the road.

"On nearing the station, the young man asked his respectable companion in what class he would travel, for he wished to buy his ticket.

"I do not know; they have given me six 'reales'," replied the priest.

"The student received the six 'reales' from the travelling priest and went to buy a third class ticket. Undoubtedly the priest was poor, and the student was not rich!

"This priest was Don Anthony Claret, Archbishop-Elect of Cuba; venerated even more than respected in all the towns of Catalonia and the Canaries; famous in all Spain; renowned and loved in distant parts. The student was the writer of these lines. From all the things that he related, quite simply, he had done the day before leaving Barcelona, I inferred that he was still working at twelve o'clock at night and that at two or three o'clock in the morning he was at work again."

Father Claret was to preach a Mission at Gerona. The church being too small to contain the immense crowd that came to hear the sermons, the balcony of the priest's house was converted into a pulpit.

At the time of the sermon, the plaza, the adjacent streets, the windows and the balconies of the houses, all were filled with people who listened with amazement and compunction to the fervent preacher.

Who would have recognized the celebrated missionary and the Archbishop-Elect in the guise of the poor chaplain who traveled third class on the train, with money that had been given him as alms? Thus he went along until he was consecrated Archbishop.

It was stated that in the Mission given in Gerona in addition to the great number of sermons, preached to thousands upon thousands in the open air, because the cathedral could not contain the crowds, he gave retreats to the Cathedral Chapter and the clergy of the city, to parish priests of the diocese, to seminarians, to religious in their convents and to the sick in hospitals.

"Where did he get the time?" "When did he study? How could his health resist all that work?"

With these questions His Excellency, the Bishop of Segorbe, closed his references as eye-witness of the life of Blessed Anthony Claret.

Father Claret was preconized by Pope Pius IX, May 18, 1850, and a little later the Pontifical Bulls were sent. His consecration took place in the Cathedral of Vich, October 6, 1850; on October thirteenth of the same month the new Archbishop received the Pallium at the hands of the Papal Nuncio, Monsignor Brunelli, in Madrid. Later on, October 18, the Minister of the Interior, Sr. Arrazola, proposed his name for the reception of the Grand Cross of Isabel the Catholic, and on the twenty-second the royal order made the nomination.

"I do not merit the Grand Cross! I cannot accept it," said Father Claret to those who communicated the proposition. "Jesus bore the wooden cross, and I wear a cross of glory? I cannot accept it!"

But being obliged to do so, he accepted it. He, however, placed so little importance on that honorable insignia that, leaving it behind him, he left the court, and thus he neither wore the cross nor fulfilled the obligations of the title. On the twenty-fifth of the same month, he was advised that he had to pay 300 reales to be a Knight in reality, but since he did not have that amount of money, a charitable friend paid for it for him. Having left Madrid, a royal order authorized him to bestow the cross upon himself. Thus he became a Knight of the Order. This was done on November fourth.

*　　*　　*

The appointment of Father Claret as Archbishop of Santiago caused joy and sorrow among his friends; joy at the hierarchical exaltation of the humble missionary, and sadness at the necessary approaching separation.

The one who most deeply experienced these contrary sentiments was, assuredly, his faithful friend, Don Fortunato Bres. One day, in order to mitigate somewhat the sorrow of Father Claret's approaching absence, he said to him:

"Archbishop, before Your Excellency leaves for Cuba, I ask that you leave us a remembrance for all time. Know that I merit it, for I have always been your protector."

"Ask whatever you wish," the new Archbishop replied. "But let me first make the request that you will always treat me familiarly by addressing me as 'you' and not 'Your Excellency.' "

"I agree. The remembrance that I ask is your picture."

"That, by no means. I cannot consent to have my picture painted. Ask me anything else; but that, no."

"I know that this mortifies you, but do it for me and for my family. Look, you will leave me, and probably we shall never see each other again in this world. If something can mitigate my sorrow it is to see your picture."

Such was the respect and the courtesy which Father Claret showed his intimate friend and benefactor, Don Fortunato, that to please him he had his portrait made. One of the most skillful artists was called to paint the picture. On seeing the Archbishop always so occupied, he exclaimed:

"A difficult task! Who will keep His Excellency quiet long enough to delineate his features?"

In spite of all, the picture came out well in oil painting. It shows him modest, graceful, and natural, and it is even today, one of the most exact and devout pictures of the servant of God.

As soon as he had received the episcopal consecration he wished to unite, as much as possible, the height of the new dignity with the simplicity of the missionary. For that reason he imposed upon himself the most rigorous poverty in the robes and jewels that were proper to his new dignity.

A wealthy man of Barcelona came to one of the missionaries of Vich one day and said:

"Do you wish me to present to the new Archbishop the robes of his dignity? It would give me the greatest pleasure, and my family would be greatly honored in doing so?"

"Very well; there are no objections. Only I warn you of one thing. They must not be luxurious, but modest and ordinary. If they are the contrary, the Archbishop will not receive them."

"They will be made of the same cloth that is used in making the robes of the other bishops."

"No, very much more modest. Do me the favor to heed my wish, and you will do right."

So he did. The Archbishop then accepted the robes with deepest gratitude. He ordered a tin-plated pectoral cross, but soon, for reasons based on prudence, he was obliged to use the cross that was offered him.

*   *   *

Father Claret, who, at the time of his episcopal consecration, added the name of Mary to his own, gave a delicate example of his devotion to the Blessed Virgin.

"I must leave Madrid in a hurry, because before departing for Cuba I have to make three important visits," the Archbishop said one day to a friend of his who was urging him to prolong his stay at court.

What visits could those be that were so imperious and urgent?

They were three. The first was to the Shrine of "La Virgen del Pilar," Patroness of Spain, which he had visited in the month of February of the same year, and which he had desired to visit again to place his pastoral ring on the column upon which Our Lady stands. He later wrote to the chaplain asking that a "Salve" be recited, after the rosary, for his intentions.

The second was to Our Lady of Montserrat, Patroness of Catalonia. He arrived at Montserrat on the second of November. A solemn religious function was organized in commemoration of the day.

A large crowd of people from the neighboring towns gathered in the church. Ascending the pulpit, the archbishop gave a very fervent sermon on devotion to the Blessed Virgin, causing the faithful to shed an abundance of tears, particularly when he bade a tender farewell to the sweet "Morenita" of Montserrat.

As a souvenir of this visit a magnificent picture that represented Archbishop Claret was left in the Monastery Church. It was painted on the arch of the case that encloses the sacred image, in the gallery of illustrious visitors.

The third visit was to the Virgin of Fusimanya, Patroness of Sallent. The Sallentinos prepared a splendid reception for him. Music and poetry, enthusiastic acclamations and tears of affection were offered on his arrival in his native town.

When it was known that, on the following day, he was going across the craggy mountains, in pious pilgrimage, to take leave of Our Lady of Fusimanya, a great place for pilgrimages, all the town awaited him, anxious to hear his words for the last time. The Archbishop spoke to his countrymen on the love for the celestial Patroness, Our Lady of Fusimanya, which they should cultivate.

Father Claret was satisfied now. He had consecrated his three loves at the feet of the three images; namely, his love for Spain, before Our Lady of Pilar; his love for Catalonia before the Virgin of Montserrat, and his love for his village before Our Lady of Fusimanya.

The three visits! Preamble of a happy omen for his episcopate.

XLIX
REMEMBRANCE AND LEAVETAKING
The Criminals of Villafranca—Farewell—Story of the Trip—Mission on Sea—Presentiments
The Prelate of Cuba

Two angels, the Angel of Spain and the Angel of Cuba, ascended to the presence of God. The prayer of the Angel of Cuba was this: "Lord, listen to the clamors of thousands of abandoned souls. They are without a father and without a shepherd! Send them your apostle, and they will be saved!" The prayer of the angel of Spain was this: "Lord, he has been a missionary in Catalonia, but not of all Spain. The clamor of thousands of souls who wish to hear his voice arises to Thee, asking that the word of Thy apostle may resound throughout all Spain."

God said to the two angels: "From 1850-1857 he shall be Archbishop of Santiago and missionary of Cuba; from 1857-1868 he shall be Archbishop of Trajanopolis and missionary of Spain."

The angels were silent. On descending to earth, they saw the great apostle taking leave of Catalonia, recording as a remembrance, four conversions of glorious renown.

*   *   *

A short time before Archbishop Claret left for the episcopal see, a very extraordinary event occured, which put the apostolic zeal of the Blessed in bold relief. It was the conversion of four criminals in Villafranca of Panades.

The criminals had been put into prison on Saturday afternoon and were to be executed on Monday morning. All four had sworn that they would not receive the last Sacraments. All efforts of the priests were useless. The culprits were obstinate. Monday morning came. It was known that Archbishop Claret would pass through Villafranca at that time. This coincidence seemed to have been sent by God.

All the priests went to beg the servant of God to stay over in Villafranca that morning, so as to try to convert the four impenitent criminals. Father Claret consented.

"Your Excellency must be fatigued from the trip. Come to my house first for breakfast," the venerable parish priest of Villafranca said to him.

"No, no," replied Father Claret, "let us first go to recommend this business to God."

"All the priests have gone, in turn, to visit the criminals; but all our efforts have been fruitless. The criminals have declared that they would not confess."

"Ah, that is serious, very serious! When will they be executed?"

"This very morning."

"Let us, then, go quickly to the church. God will remedy the matter."

Father Claret knelt before the Blessed Sacrament and prayed for a few moments. On leaving the church, he said to the priests who accompanied him:

"Let us go to the prison! They will confess. They are but boys."

Three of the criminals were mere youths, and the fourth one was about forty years of age.

The holy missionary arrived at the prison. By the warmth of his exhortations, the three young prisoners were conquered and confessed. But before giving them Holy Communion the missionary asked them if they pardoned everyone, and one of the group said aloud:

"I pardon all, except my mother."

An exclamation of surprise came from the bystanders.

"No, I do not; I cannot pardon my mother, because she has been the cause that I am brought to the gallows today. If she had corrected and punished me in time, I would not be here today. Therefore, I do not pardon her."

On hearing these words pronounced before the Blessed Sacrament, Archbishop Claret, filled with emotion, fell at the feet of the condemned man, beseeching him:

"For God's sake, my son! Look; you are going to appear before the tribunal of the Eternal Judge this very day! Pardon your mother from your heart."

"No, no, I do not pardon her. She has been the cause of my misfortunes."

"My son, you will be damned if you will not pardon your mother. I beg of you to pardon her in God's name and in my own."

"I need not pardon you, for you have not offended me, but I do not pardon her."

The people were in consternation. Some prayed; others wept; and all had their eyes fixed on the Archbishop and on the culprit.

Then Father Claret said to the chaplain: "Do not give him the Sacred Host."

In a little while the four criminals, clothed in the mantle of infamy and mounted on mules, were on the way to the scaffold; behind them came Father Claret saying the rosary for the two obstinate criminals. The moment of execution came. Then one of the impenitent men cried:

"I pardon my mother from all my heart. Pray for me."

Then the older man who had not wished to go to confession, extended his arms, asking to make his confession. Seated on the bench with head covered, he confessed. Father Claret ascended the scaffold and standing beside the four bodies preached an emotional sermon to the immense crowd that had gathered at Villafranca.

"Blessed be the hour that brought Father Claret here!" exclaimed the people. "God brought him."

Later God revealed to Father Claret that the four criminals had been saved, and in a public conference he emphatically pronounced these words:

"The criminals of Villafranca were saved."

*　　*　　*

The multitude that witnessed this consoling scene, with tears and sadness repeated: "Why will you not continue as our missionary?"

"I have other sheep that are not of this flock; and it is necessary that I go to bring them into the sheepfold."

Like the good shepherd, he went to look for them.

It was at ten o'clock in the morning on a sunny day, the twenty-eighth of December, 1850. A large crowd filled the wharf of Barcelona and all the avenue of La Riba. At a distance stood the castle of Montjuich, as vigilant as a sentinel. Across the plains, the great city was given over to the fever of work. In front of it, and to the sides, was the sea, lost in the haziness of the horizon, with its light undulation of ripples, which reflects the blue sky on the mirror of its waters.

Soon a clamor was heard. The multitude knelt. Near the balcony of the sailing vessel a priest appeared. He raised his hand and traced a cross on the air, the cross of benediction and of parting.

The new "Theresa Cubana" went furrowing slowly and majestically through the waves, leaving behind it a swiftly disappearing wake.

Now two great oceans opened before his eyes: above, the ocean of the sky, crossed by stars, and beneath him an ocean of water, crossed by boats. Times of fair weather and hours of storm, such are the alternatives of the sea. Well, what difference does it make! Never did that boat cross the sea in greater security. It was carrying on board the "Envoy of God" and God defends His anointed from the fury of the storms.

*　　*　　*

The passengers made a good choice in naming Padre Paladio Currius as historian of the trip. His elegant and facile pen wrote rapidly the different happenings on board. These notes are today, after the Autobiography of Blessed Anthony

Claret, one of the best sources of historical documentation. Father Currius writes as follows:

"This is the state in which we found ourselves. The sky brilliant with light; the sea, in repose; the boat, motionless. It seemed as though the Lord had paralyzed the elements so as the better to hear the prayers of the friendly crew. There was a mingling of priests and seculars, of pure virgins and sinful men, the cultured resident of the city and the rustic mariner, all of us forming a little town floating on the waves of the ocean. The same petitions make us equal at this moment, in the eyes of our Maker.

"But soon the hour of trial came. We were very near the Strait of Gibraltar when a terrible storm arose, putting the boat in danger of shipwreck. The waves penetrated the steerage cabin. The boat was in such a critical condition that the captain set out the boom-sail at the stern so as to balance the boat. But as this did not abate the danger we returned to Malaga, the nearest port, the following day."

*　　*　　*

But all the happenings in history, among men as in things, have a profound theology, whose secrets are guarded by Divine Providence. The mystery of the tempest and return to safe port was soon discovered. We know it today by words in the Autobiography of Blessed Claret:

"I believe that our coming to the city of Malaga was a singular disposition of God for its welfare; an assertion which I could not help but make in a sermon, is that the Lord had brought me here as He brought the prophet Habacuc to Daniel in the lions' den. It was exactly four days since a Mission was begun by four Capuchins. So my arrival was quite opportune.

"I was well received by the Bishop. The authorities came to see me, and the bishop and canons requested me to preach. The people assembled, in order and devotion, in the great cathedral. I also preached in various other places. During the four days that we were there I believe that I preached fifteen times. The people of Malaga seemed pleased with me, and I liked them. What a great harvest was thus presented to me!"

As the sea was calm, the "Theresa Cabana" resumed her journey. Currius, whom the archbishop appreciated highly, expressed his impression thus:

"How magnificent is the ocean! The wind, agitating its surface, carries the waves from one side to the other, forming moving mountains which now rise, now sink, changing mountains into valleys. The boat clawed the waters, which, ceding to violence, leaped, rose, and then vanished in silver foam; the waves dashed against the sides of the ship, forming thousands of capricious playthings. They seem to feel, to know, and to bid us welcome, calling out, dancing, and playing, in order to please and entertain us.

"Some cross each other and bar the path of those that follow; others join each other and leap, at the same time moving their heads, that seemed to be adorned with pure white plumage; others bend their necks to let us pass over them and then rock us like children in a cradle. Some, with a sinister air, threaten to attack the ship and to sink it; but on approaching, they open wide and let us pass free, although the sea's breast heaves, sighs, and even groans. Along the horizon which is as green as the meadows, one sees, here and there, waves converted into foam, that look like flocks of sheep that graze at leisure in an endless field."

* * *

Very soon, on passing the Gulf of Damas, an idea suddenly came into the mind of Father Claret. What idea? To give a Mission to the crew of the "Theresa Cubana," which he did. His voice which had been heard in the great cathedrals, resounded in the immense cathedral of the sea, from the pulpit of the boat. I do not know, but I believe that before that grand spectacle the fish must have come afloat and the angels must have come down to listen to the words of the new Saint Anthony. What was the spiritual fruit of that Mission?

Father Currius wrote in his notes of the trip:

"There was not a passenger, nor a sailor, from the captain to the last cabin-boy, who did not go to confession and receive Holy Communion."

Father Lobo, in a letter adds:

"All the priests lent their services to hear confessions, but in vain, for almost all went to confession to Father Claret."

On the fifteenth of February the voyagers sighted the Cape of "Mayri" of the Island of Cuba. With a heart full of joy the servant of God entoned the "Te Deum," and then they sang the "Salve" in thanksgiving to Mary, "Star of the Sea." It was the Saturday before Septuagesima Sunday, when the "Alleluias" are suspended until Easter Sunday; Father Claret closing his breviary and looking toward the Island of Cuba, where he was to suffer so much, said with a deep sigh: "The last 'Alleluia'!"

He landed upon an abandoned but fertile soil that, beneath the feet of the saint, trembled with emotion, and budded forth and gave to the Church a glorious crown composed of the fruits of conversion and saintliness.

February 17 was the day of his solemn entry into the city of Santiago; on the 18th he took possession of his archiepiscopal see. Two weeks later he made a pilgrimage to the Shrine of Our Lady of Cobre, Patroness of Cuba, where he consecrated the archdiocese to Our Lady so that she might ever be, in the words of Father Claret, "the sweet Prelatess of the Island."

A short time later, he, in union with his domestics and missionaries, made the Spiritual Exercises as a preamble of retirement and prayer to commence the work of evangelization of the towns and cities of Cuba.

The Apostles did the same to conquer the world; they went into solitude. All this Father Claret did under the presidency of the Blessed Virgin, who is the "Evangelist of the World."

L
PASTORAL MINISTRY
Grain Fields—Few and Good Seminarians—Betterment of the Clergy—Visits—The Faith of the People Five Thousand Horsemen

Sublime scene! One morning in February, 1851, Archbishop Claret was in his palace. He called a meeting of his missionaries. Showing them the map of Cuba, he repeated the words that Jesus Christ addressed to his Apostles:

"Raise your eyes and see the regions. The fields are white, and it is time for the harvest." He then divided the reapers into all the zones of the wheatfields to gather the harvest. The owner of the field, the Archbishop-missionary, marched at the head of the reapers.

Who could condense, in the composite vision of a picture, the wonders of charity and of zeal, of sacrifice and abnegation. of struggle and triumph, of miracles and prophecy, which form the history of the saintly Archbishop during his six years' administration in the Island of Cuba?

On this canvas of reminiscences we give a few touches of historical truth and emotional suggestion. These sketches of bold central lines will project the image of this hero of militant Catholicism on the mind of all.

*   *   *

What shall we say first, of his seminary, of his cathedral, and of his churches?

The seminary building was in ruins; the rooms without furniture; the classrooms without tables or desks. For the past thirty years not a seminarian had studied there; and the few that were ordained had not followed an ecclesiastical course. Thus it was that ignorance of the sacred sciences and relaxation of morals was general among the clergy.

Father Claret made radical changes. He reconstructed and improved the building, spending 12,000 dollars of his own rentals on it; he formed a staff of professors; named a rector and prefects; organized a plan of studies and ordered careful vigilance regarding the conduct of the seminarians.

"Few and good seminarians; not many ill-formed!" That was his motto. He explained:

"I know by experience that the greatest punishment that can befall a people is a bad priest! It is best to leave a town without a priest than send one unworthy. If God does not send me men who are truly called, God Himself will have to take care of the people and souls by means of the angels. A call is God's gift. I must not bring the unworthy into the sheepfold to destroy it, instead of tending it.

The earthquake of Santiago had cracked and demolished a part of the cathedral. He invested 24,000 *duros* from his own pocket and from donations of his friends in repairing it.

For the rebuilding of the houses which had been destroyed and the churches which had been demolished, he obtained from the Governor of Madrid five million *pesetas*. Countless were his works and sacrifices for the economic, scientific, and moral betterment of his clergy.

The Archdiocese was unorganized in regard to parishes, nor was there any designation of fees. A Diocesan Council meeting was held to study and establish a vast system of spiritual upbuilding for the good of souls. The poor and neglected clergy were without endowment. He obtained for canons and curates, parish priests and co-adjutors, a subsidy analogous to that which the clergy of Spain received.

The priests were without liturgical or moral instruction. He, therefore, organized Ecclesiastical Conferences for them, with plans of the matter to be discussed and dates of the meetings, pointing out, as places for assembly, the principal parishes of the diocese.

The clergy were dispersed through cities, towns, and ranches, without a place for spiritual retirement to repair their moral strength. He arranged for priests to meet annually at

Santiago for a retreat; he himself paying the expenses of the trip and their stay.

In order that none of the ecclesiastics, whether diocesan or outside the diocese, should be lodged in hotels or public boarding houses when passing through Santiago, he made the archiepiscopal palace a free hotel for all priests. There was one who abused the goodness of the archbishop, a canon of the Island of Santo Domingo, Don Gaspar Hernandez, who lived three years with the domestics of the Archbishop without any expense for board or maintenance whatsoever.

The palace was an asylum and a hospital, church, and school. There the poor, the sick, the children, and the aged flocked. In order that he might exercise material as well as spiritual charity toward them, he gathered them and gave audience every Monday of the year. He appeared kind and affable in the midst of that assembly of poor beggars. After giving each one of them a *peseta* in alms every time, he taught them the catechism and prepared them for confession during Lent.

A true picture of supernatural grandeur and at the same time a school of moral philosophy!

The poor are for the Christians sacred persons, because in them is seen Our Lord disguised, passing through the world, knocking at our doors for charity.

*   *   *

Who can now recount all the heroism of his pastoral visits, journeys, in which the sweat of his brow was mingled with tears of consolation? Let us read what Blessed Claret wrote in his notes on these pastoral visits:

"A bishop should visit his diocese every year, or at least every two years. He must not remain stationary in his palace! If the sun were always to shine upon the same spot on the earth what little profit that would be; but revolving continuously from one point to another, it illuminates it, warms it, and makes it fruitful. So should the bishop illumine, warm, and make the diocese productive."

This is the theory which was stamped in his writings. What was his practice? Let us briefly consider his deeds. They are the best touches of the brush in the picture of the Missionary Archbishop.

During the first two years of his stay on the island of Cuba he visited the entire diocese four times, covering an extension of 45,000 square miles.

There was not a town nor a ranch which he did not visit, often having to cross high bleak plateaus or wide stretches of land, always on horseback or on foot, through more or less unknown paths. His journeys were not less than twenty leagues at a time, and there were occasions in which he went without tasting food in twenty-four hours, beneath the burning sun of the tropical zone. Sometimes he gathered the people from two or three rural districts to give them a joint Mission. At times a tobacco factory, which was nothing more than a shed, served as a church. He then erected an altar and a pulpit. The confessionals were merely chairs, but for the confessionals for women a railing which they carried with them was attached.

The fruit of the missionary labors of the Archbishop was copious. During the first three years alone of his apostolate in Cuba, 12,000 marriages of persons who had lived in concubinage, were blessed. 40,000 children were legitimatized, to whom their parents, in the future, gave an education. Nearly 300 couples, who had been scandalously separated, were reunited. Some 80,000 persons, who before had not approached the Sacraments received during the general Communions at the Mission. 30,000 was the number converted by the labor of the apostolic missionary. During his first visit he distributed 38,217 books, which he gave gratis or exchanged for bad books which he gathered to burn. He gave, moreover, 83,500 holy pictures, 20,663 rosaries, and 8,931 medals. After the first visit, upon calculation, it was found that about one million of religious articles had been distributed in and outside of his diocese.

The sower went through the field, sowing good seed.

*   *   *

What does it matter that hate and slander set their serpentine teeth on him and wished to undo, with calumnies, the heroic enterprises of the missionary?

General Gemeri responded with these words:

"Yes, let the archbishop come to give Missions. The fire of the cannon cannot do anything with the insurgents! We shall see if the fire of hell can do anything with them!"

Father Claret preached the Gospel in its entirety. If he inculcated submission in subordinates, he asked for more justice and charity on the part of the higher classes and greater care for the Divine worship and for the clergy, who through their poverty and loss of prestige, were the mockery of the sects.

For this reason the holy Archbishop, under date of November 24, 1851, wrote to his former superior, the Bishop of Vich, these prophetic words which already had their bitter accomplishment:

"I am filled with indignation on seeing the criminal neglect on the part of the Spanish government in regard to divine worship and the clergy in the archdiocese. I am going to tell you a truth which perhaps may seem incredible. There are parishes in which no endowment has been provided, neither for worship nor for the clergy; and, at times, the poor parish priest has to go to the hut of the negro to be invited to partake of his yams and bananas, so as not to starve.

"God and you know that I am a Spaniard and as such I shall die, if it is necessary. But I tell you that, although the Spanish nation were guilty of no other sin than the great injustice that it is committing in these parishes of this metropolis, God will punish it terribly!" And thus God did punish it.

On the other hand, speaking of the simple people, he said in the same letter:

"When giving Missions and visiting the parishes of this archdiocese, I get great satisfaction on seeing the docility of the people and the abundant fruit produced here."

In another letter directed also to the Bishop of Vich, he wrote these words which, for the honor of that pious people, merit to be engraved on bronze in immortal remembrance:

"There are persons who have come one hundred and fifty-six leagues expressly to hear the divine word and to make their confessions."

Father Currius, writing of the spiritual fruits which the holy archbishop gathered at the first Mission which he gave in the cathedral of Santiago, in Lent, 1851, uses words, which are profoundly expressive in their detail:

"This has been very extraordinary! Suffice it to say that many young people asked to go to confession even on the streets; before this they did not even dare to go to the sacristy. The people came thirty and forty leagues to go to confession and ease their consciences."

A canon of the cathedral of Santiago alluding to this Mission, after weighing the triumphs of grace, concluded:

"The distribution of Holy Communion on the closing day lasted from six o'clock in the morning until one in the afternoon, three priests being actively engaged in the act during that time. It was ascertained that not one person in the city failed to receive Holy Communion."

As a magnificent synthesis of all these testimonies of the eagerness with which the Cuban people listened to the words of their Venerable Pastor, that very valuable declaration might serve which the illustrious Don Antonio Barjau made in the Informative Process:

"In Cuba I saw three thousand, four thousand, and even five thousand horsemen accompanying the saintly archbishop from one town to another."

A brilliant episode of popular enthusiasm, that recalls the

processions of the crowds following Jesus across the fields of Judea!

On beholding these people, the Archbishop Missionary said sorrowfully as did Our Lord:

"I have compassion on the multitude. Many have not eaten for days. Would that I could perform the miracle of the multiplication of the loaves! Well, since I cannot provide them with material bread, I shall not tire in giving them evangelical bread."

So he did. His sermons were long and varied. His Mission lasted from two weeks to a month. The people pleaded with him even to prolong his stay. Once Father Claret acceded to their insistence. It was in the city of Puerto Principe, in the parish of Our Lady of Mercy. The Mission lasted during the month of August and September.

On raising the net Blessed Anthony asked the aid of all the priests to help him bring it ashore, for like the nets of the Apostles, it broke on account of the abundance of fish.

LI

INSPIRATIONS OF ZEAL

THE SERVANTS OF THE GOSPEL—NEW WORKMEN
FOUNDATION OF A RELIGIOUS ORDER—ITS DEVELOP-
MENT AND TRANSFORMATION—PHILOSOPHY OF
LOVE OF NEIGHBOR—THE ARCHBISHOP'S
ROSARY

The servants of the Gospel presented themselves to the householder and said, "Sir, did you not sow good seed in this field; how comes it that there is so much cockle?"

And the Lord said to them: "An enemy hath done this."

In like manner the missionaries of Cuba presented themselves one day to Archbishop Claret and said to him: "Have we not sown good seed in the field of the diocese? And yet there is so much cockle?"

Father Claret answered: "An enemy hath done this! Let us work until the time of the harvest, for then the angels will separate the wheat from the cockle."

Thus it happened. The reality of the struggles and the dangers did not intimidate him in the enterprises of his zeal but increased his ardor.

The practical study of men and things and the knowledge of new weapons that the enemy would wield to destroy his apostolic work, inspired him with new strategy for combat—defensive and offensive at the same time, and that was the strategy of rapid consolidation.

His own hand planted much, but he needed other hands that would cultivate that immense nursery of souls. And who are to be the operators of that work of consolidation and perfection? The Religious.

*   *   *

Father Claret, therefore, with the authorization of the Queen and of the Government, called to Cuba, during his administration, various religious orders, assigning each a zone of action.

His plan embraced four points: the foundation of seminaries; the formation of seminarians; the education of youth; the direction of hospitals, and the work of the Missions.

He called the "Lazarists" for the direction of the seminaries; he asked the Franciscan Fathers and Capuchins to continue his favorite enterprise of the Missions; he recommended the establishment of charitable institutions to the Daughters of Charity; and he wished that the Fathers of the Society of Jesus and the sons of St. Joseph Calasanctus take charge of the education of the youth.

For the education of girls and young ladies, he did not require the aid of any existing congregation, for he founded a new religious order called "Instituto Apostolico de la Inmaculada Concepcion de Maria Santisima y de la Ensenanza," which was born into the Church on August 25, 1855, with solemn vows and papal approval, under the rule of St. Benedict, with proper modifications made by Blessed Father Claret.

This Order grew rapidly in spite of the hazardous circumstances of that time, thanks to the influence that the Holy Founder constantly lent it, and owing also to the enterprising spirit and ardent zeal of Maria Antonia Paris de San Pedro, who was born in Villamoll of Tarragona in 1813, and died in the odor of sanctity in 1884, in the convent of Reus.

This Order has two periods in its existence; both very holy and successful. To the first period, in which every community has its government independent from that of sister communities belong the Convents of Santiago de Cuba, (1854), of Tremp, (1860), of Reus, (1865), of Baracoa, (1875), of Velez-Rubio, (1880) and of Huercal-Overa, (1900). In the second epoch belong all the communities, excepting that of Carcagente that were united in 1920 to form one religious congregation of simple vows, under the direction of one general government, with new Constitutions approved in the year 1922, bearing the title of the Congregation of Religious Teachers of Mary Immaculate.

This congregation founded the houses of Vicalvaro (1921), that of Villena established already in 1900 by the Daughters of Calvary and incorporated later into the new Congregation (1921), that of Palma Soriano (1922), that of Orgaz (1925), that of Madrid (1925), that of Barcelona (1926), that of Leviana, (Asturias) (1929), and that of Mendoza (Argentina) (1934).

It cannot be denied that this latter Institute is one of the most brilliant glories of the holy Archbishop of Cuba, and as such, the sons of Blessed Father Claret direct and help it.

* * *

All these enterprises of the tireless archbishop had the identical propelling force and the same basis of agreement and of union. He possessed that most active and heroic zeal for the conversion of souls, which is the inner philosophy of his life.

Let us read, as proof, some words of the greatest tenderness with which Blessed Anthony reasons his love for his neighbor and his zeal for the conversion of souls. He writes thus in one of his personal works:

"Oh, my neighbor, I love thee.

"I love thee, because God wishes that I love thee.

"I love thee because God commands me to do so.

"I love thee, because God loves thee.

"I love thee, because thou hast been created by God according to His image and for heaven.

"I love thee, because thou hast been redeemed by the blood of Jesus Christ.

"I love thee, because God has done and suffered so much for thee; and as a proof of my love for thee, I will suffer for thee all pains and labors, even death itself, if it were necessary.

"I love thee because thou art loved by our Blessed Mother, my beloved Mother.

"I love thee, because thou art loved by the angels and saints of heaven.

"I love thee and for love of thee I will free thee from sin and the pains of hell.

"I love thee and for love of thee I will instruct thee, teaching thee the evil thou must avoid, and the virtues thou hast to practise, and I will accompany thee on the road of good works and to heaven."

For that reason he wished to carry to the heart of all his priests this sacred fire of the love of· one's neighbor. When he saw in his clergy, especially in his parish priests, some deficiency in the practice of zeal, or some remissness in the fulfillment of duty, he would correct it immediately in a supremely delicate way.

An eye-witness gave proof of the case.

*   *   *

The mandate had been issued that, at least on Sundays and feast-days, the rosary be recited publicly in church; this was one of the points that was closely inspected in the pastoral visitations.

He was preaching a Mission in company with two priests. During the afternoon it occurred to him to surprise the neighboring parish by a visit.

It was Sunday. The people, complying with the exhortations which the Holy Prelate had made in his sermons as well as in his pastoral letters, had gathered in the church to recite the rosary. The family was assembled, but the father, the parish priest, was absent.

The sacristan, after waiting in vain for the priest, knelt on the steps of the chancel and began to lead the rosary.

Soon an agreeable surprise came to the people. The Archbishop had entered the church. He ascended the chancel, and kneeling down next to the sacristan, personally led the rosary with edifying piety.

The parish priest was soon advised of the presence of the archbishop. He ran to the church, and, in consternation, he knelt down at his side.

"Pardon me, Your Excellency," the priest said as they entered the sacristy. "I was unable to come to lead the rosary, because I had a grave and urgent occupation."

"I thought so," answered the Archbishop. "For that reason I ask that you inform me when you are busy; for when I am giving a Mission in the neighboring towns, I will come personally to lead the rosary when you cannot do so."

The parish priest humbly took the advice, and when at nightfall the bell rang calling the people to church, he would say to his companions: "I will go lest the Archbishop take my place."

LII

THE WORKER OF WONDERS

God watched over the steps of this herald of his glory. For this reason he was called the "worker of wonders."

One day, as the archbishop went out, accompanied by the authorities and the most prominent persons of the town, an immense crowd followed and acclaimed him for a distance of four leagues. At the point where he was to take leave, they erected an arbor of palm branches, under which the venerable archbishop could rest a while.

"Where do you wish to pass the night?" Father Claret asked his companions.

"In the 'hacienda' of Altagracia," replied the most informed. "The house is large and commodious. The owners will be highly honored to have the archbishop as their guest, for they are religious people."

Father Claret said nothing, but word passed on through the crowd that they would pass the night in Altagracia.

Not all of those who accompanied the archbishop did so through motives of enthusiasm and affection. When they heard that it was planned to spend the night at Altagracia, they looked at each other and smiled scornfully. They then hurriedly separated themselves from the group.

"We have rested sufficiently," said the archbishop. "We have a long walk before us, and we must make use of the time."

They then took leave, expressing gratitude to the authorities and to the public. Accompanied by his missionaries he again started on the road toward the capital of Santiago.

On arriving at the ranch of Naranjo, it was twilight and they were rather tired. The archbishop addressing his companions said:

"You see it is already late, and we are still at a league's distance from Altagracia. Do you think that we could stay here at Naranjo for the night?"

They did so. Father Claret and the missionaries slept tranquilly, but the owners of the ranch heard, at day-break, cries and hurried footsteps of people rushing along and running precipitately to the ranch of Altagracia.

What had happened? The flames that illuminated all the penumbra of the morning indicated enough.

"They have killed the archbishop! They have burned him alive at Altagracia!" cried the people. "Let us look for the assassins who, at midnight, traitorously set fire to the house!"

They reached Altagracia. The farmhouse was an immense bonfire. Workmen and proprietors remained in the field all that night. Only a child, and at her side an old blind woman were seen weeping near the house which crackled and fell to pieces devoured by the fire!

"Where is the archbishop? What has become of the missionaries?" the strangers asked them in consternation.

"We have not seen anyone here! answered the boy.

"The fire awakened us," added the aged lady; "and we could only save ourselves. All the rest perished in the flames."

"What about the archbishop and the missionaries who came to spend the night here?"

"Not here. We were alone in the house."

Soon they saw several priests in the distance.

"Here they come!" all cried. "God protected them. It is they! The archbishop and the missionaries!" All ran joyfully to congratulate them.

"The ways of God!" exclaimed Father Claret. "The Blessed Virgin did not wish that we be killed as yet."

*   *   *

His hands raised to heaven, were the lightning-rods of divine vengeance; and these same hands, descending to earth caused the rapid cessation of the trembling of the earth. An eye witness gave testimony of this.

It was in the epoch of earthquakes that caused such ravages in Cuba. One day the archbishop was preaching in a public square, because the people were afraid to gather in the church, for at the hour least expected, it might collapse because of the violence of the quakes.

Soon the noise of distant thunder was heard accompanied by tremors. The people gave forth a cry of terror and began to flee.

"Do not fear; that is nothing!" the archbishop said to them. "Everything will soon pass!"

The crowd gathered again and became calm at the words of the archbishop. But repeated violent and persistent tremors were felt. The archbishop then had a sudden inspiration. He descended the pulpit, and kneeling down he touched the earth with his hands, causing the earthquake to cease.

"Be tranquil! The quakes will not molest you again today!"

He then continued his sermon. In the future, the people never believed themselves so well preserved from the dangers of earthquakes, as when they were listening to the sermons of their holy archbishop. Thus God surrounded the apostolic work of the holy missionary with fame and honor.

*   *   *

The missionary companions of Father Claret were accustomed to miracles. Thus, when anything contrary happened during the time of the sermons, they looked very hopefully at Father Claret with the presentiment that the hour of something wonderful would soon arrive.

Father Fernando de Agullana relates:

"One day, people from a neighboring town came out to seek our services to begin a Mission that very night. Some came in a two-wheeled cart, and others on horseback. The weather was good when we left the house, but suddenly a terrible storm arose. At nightfall, we found it impossible to reach our destination, because the river was carrying volumes of water and there was no possibility of wading it. All the people who accompanied us said it was impossible to cross the river.

" 'It does not matter!' answered Father Claret. 'It is necessary for us to begin the Mission this very day. Let us confide in God.'

"Soon we heard the sound of bells and we found ourselves with cart and horsemen, on the other side of the river.

" 'A miracle!' all cried. 'This is evidently a miracle.'

" 'Be silent! Do not speak of it!' Father Claret said to us.

"We arrived at the town. That very night the Mission began."

*   *   *

It seems that a cloud of glory surrounded Father Claret on his passage through the world. He truly represented in his person the actual religiousness of Spain during one-third of a century. The very storms of persecution, when they became calm or ceased, formed over him, like a triumphal arch, the rainbow of victory.

How did his heart feel in the midst of these plaudits of the world?

An intimate friend, on seeing Father Claret surrounded by so many honors, ventured to ask him:

"How do you manage to keep yourself humble in the midst of all the applause of the world? Do you not feel tempted to vain-glory?"

Father Claret replied: "God has given me a singular grace, that is, the larger the concourse that comes to hear me, the greater and more public sinners that approach my confessional, the more general the acclamations of the people, the more humble I feel; a sadness comes upon me and so profound a depression overwhelms me, that it serves as a counterweight to prevent the wind of vainglory from shipwrecking the bark of my soul.

"I owe to God," he wrote later, "the good there is in me; separated from Him I am incapable of any meritorious act.

"I am like a water-mill, no matter how well built it may be, it cannot move if the water does not put it into motion."

In one of his personal papers he wrote this rule of conduct:

"I shall imagine that I am a picture in which God has painted his image and likeness. I shall look attentively at the picture before me; and I shall give thanks to God, because the Allpowerful One is working such wonders in me.

"I shall look at the reverse side on which I find *my* picture, as the picture of God is shown on the front. Behind a picture one sees only cleats and tacks which hold fast the rough edges of the cloth; the cleats are my faults, the tacks my imperfections; the canvas is my life and the rough edges are my good works; for as God says, our good works are like loathsome tatters.

"I shall look upon everyone as pictures and photographs of God. I shall look upon the face of the picture and appreciate and venerate it, and on the reverse side I shall behold myself on which account I shall humble and depreciate myself. In others I shall always see their good qualities and in myself only such as are evil."

*　　*　　*

This was the practice of the most humble Father Claret. Could a soul be better disposed to receive extraordinary graces from God?

The ring in which the artist has set a diamond will not become vain. The canvas on which the painter has drawn a marvellous picture will not become conceited. Thus also could the Author of Grace engrave on the soul of Blessed Anthony the gem of His Divine gifts. He knew well what he had of himself—nothingness and sin: and what he had from God— gracious gifts of mercy. A struggle between the humility of the priest and the generosity of God ensued, and both triumphed in this spiritual controversy.

If it is true that the humility of the priest showed in the exterior of Father Claret, it is also true that other gifts of God illumined the world for the latter's glory. Listen in this regard to the proposition of Father Agullana:

"Father Claret went to preach a Mission. The people were very indifferent in religious matters.

"As was our custom, the two of us made an hour of prayer together in the morning before beginning our apostolic task. His presence alone abstracted me from worldly thoughts. What fortune to make an hour's prayer near the holy missionary. It seems as though a heat of great devotion emanated from his body.

"This time, above all others, I noticed an extraordinary fervor in Father Claret. He was on his knees, with his hands joined. His shining eyes were turned toward heaven; his face seemed to be on fire; his lips whispered ejaculatory prayers. I looked upon him in silence and absorption.

"Soon I saw that, little by little, he was leaving the earth and rising in ecstasy; more than two meters in height had been reached in slow ascension.

"I feared that he would rise higher and that he would run the risk of injuring himself and fall to the floor when coming out of his ecstasy. I declare frankly, that I tried to make all the noise possible to awaken him from his rapture.

"It lasted a long time. Then, with the same suavity with which he was raised, he descended again to earth and continued his prayers normally until the accustomed hour."

Sublime prayer and synthesis of all the grades of mysticism! There his soul found consolation; there his spirit was illuminated; there his heart was fortified.

Father Claret came forth from prayer crowned with rays, like Moses from his audience with God. Afterwards facing the world, he could say with the Psalmist:

'The Lord is my light and strength. Whom shall I fear? The Lord is the protection of my life. Before whom shall I tremble?'

'I know that the enemy goeth about seeking to devour my flesh. But all those who have tormented me have been dismayed and have fallen to the ground.'

LIII

THE WOUNDS OF HOLGUIN

Holguin—a city in Cuba, 52,000 inhabitants—fills our memory with tragic celebrity. Its name evokes two memories; the remembrance of an assassin and the remembrance of a victim. The assassin was Antonio Abad Torres, and the victim, Blessed Father Claret. Here is the story:

It was the first of February, 1856; Archbishop Claret in the capacity of metropolitan of Cuba was making his pastoral visit through the towns and cities of his archdiocese. Would he return to his archbishopric of Santiago?

Two groups organized the same plan of assassination. A masonic group which bought, in order to execute their projects, a forged document; and a satanical conspiracy which, by permission of God, sent a tempting demon from hell, who at the hour of the crime, appeared near the assassin, encouraging and goading him on; he was invisible to the public, but was seen by Father Claret, who called him the 'black one'.

It was Friday. Blessed Anthony has arrived at Holguin from Gibara and was guest at the house of the vicar.

A man rapped at the door.

"Is the archbishop here?"

"He is not," they replied. "But he will be our guest here during his stay."

A flash of infernal joy illumined the face of the stranger and he went away.

Where was Father Claret at the moment? He was making his three customary visits on arriving in a city, viz: a visit to the hospital, consoling the sick; a visit to the jail, chatting with the prisoners; and one to the cemetery, praying for the deceased of the town.

It was twilight, and the inhabitants of Holguin—mostly Catholics—were gathered in the parish church of San Isidro. A Novena to the Heart of Mary was about to begin. The preacher was to be His Excellency, the Archbishop. He ascended the pulpit and preached on the mystery of the Purification of Our Lady, whose feast was to be celebrated the following day. The sermon lasted an hour and a half. In a rapture of eloquence he pronounced these words:

"Why should I not love the Blessed Virgin when she has often saved me from imminent danger of losing my life!"

The expression was both a hymn of gratitude and a throb of hope. The people were moved, but not all of them. Some of the conspirators were in the church, and among them, one with a fierce look and a cruel instinct; it was the assassin.

It was already night when the services were over. The front door of the church opened and through it passed the archbishop, accompanied on one side by Father Llado and on the other by the chaplain, Father Llausas; a page, Betriu, walked behind him, and the sacristan, carrying a lantern, led. Before them, on the sidewalks and at the opening of the streets seethed an immense crowd of people, who struggled to approach the archbishop, to salute him and to kiss his ring.

They entered San Isidoro street which was dark and winding. Suddenly a man started out from the left sidewalk. He made an inclination, feigning to kiss the ring of the prelate; he arose hastily and wounded the face of Blessed Claret with a razor thrust.

Father Claret seeing the criminal and also the demon, in form of a black man, urging him on, cried out:

"Take them away from me."

It was too late. A long, deep wound, from the forehead to the left cheek and various cuts on the bones of the upper and lower jaws, causing the loss of an amount of blood from the face and the mouth, had been inflicted.

The assassin had aimed a blow at the neck of the archbishop, in order to cut it, but the latter, providentially, had inclined his head and with a handkerchief in his right hand, had covered his mouth so as to avoid a cold after preaching. He thus deflected the blow of the razor, which reached only the cheek and the right wrist.

Shouts and cries resounded in the street of San Isidoro; the multitude exclaimed amid sobs:

"They have wounded the archbishop. They have killed Father Claret."

They angrily clamoured for the head of the criminal.

Two guards held and guarded the sacrilegious assassin, defending him from the ire of the people.

* * *

In the meantime, Blessed Anthony was taken to a nearby pharmacy, that of a member of the town council of Holguin, Don Manuel Guerra. There he received first aid. The servant of God was gentle and serene, but pale and faint.

Soon the Governor, Don Jose Delsa, arrived, and, after saluting the archbishop he said to him:

"Your Excellency, we have already caught the criminal: he is in jail. We will soon sentence him."

Father Claret raised himself up rapidly and said:

"No, no, I pardon him. Give him liberty."

On saying this blood gushed from his mouth. At two o'clock in the morning four grenadiers of the Havana regiment carried him on a litter to his lodging, accompanied by all the authorities, the doctors, and distinguished persons of the city. When alone with the chaplain, he asked him:

"Did you see that big black man behind the assassin who incited him and impelled him to commit the the crime?"

"Your Excellency, I saw the criminal perfectly; but I did not see the one who urged him on at the hour of the crime."

"Well," concluded the archbishop, "I only wanted to know if you had seen him."

The doctors repeated their painstaking solicitude several days and dressed the wounds, but seeing at last that complications had set in in the wound of the cheek and that a malignant tumor formed in the mouth, they resolved to perform an operation on the illustrious patient.

And what happened? On a fixed day the doctors came with their instruments. The patient, however, was cured.

Father Claret was silent then on the matter; but years later the cause of the prodigy became known.

"On the night before the operation," we read in his Autobiography, "I recommended myself to the Blessed Virgin, and I offered myself resignedly to the will of God; and behold I was cured instantly. So complete was my cure that, when the doctors saw me on the following day, they declared it was a prodigy and were filled with astonishment."

What about the wound in his right hand?

The holy prelate was, one day, looking at his hand compassionately and said to his companions: "This wound, when it cures, will look like a bust of the Mater Dolorosa."

So it was in reality. One was able to distinguish the figure of Our Lady of Sorrows, marked on the wrist by a white and purple scar, in such a way that his domestic and provider. Don Dionysius Gonzales, used to end his letters, which he addressed to Father Claret, with these words:

"Pray for me to your Mother of Sorrows." Father Claret often said:

"God has put this image on my hand, so that I may think more of the Blessed Virgin."

*　　*　　*

Only one regret was left Blessed Claret after the criminal attempt, it was that his martyrdom had not been completed· that he had not given his life for Jesus Christ. He had so longed for it! He had frequently asked it of God. Let us read the following words in his Autobiography:

"I took the road to the city of Holguin. A few days before

I felt very fervent and wished to die for Jesus Christ. To my domestics and those who came to see me from without, I did not know how, nor did I attempt to speak of anything except Divine Love. I was hungry and thirsty to suffer labor and to shed my blood for Jesus and Mary; and even from the pulpit I said that I desired to seal, with the blood of my veins, the truths that I was preaching to them."

His cure and convalescence was pleasing to him for it was slow and had the sweetness of martyrdom. Let us translate his words:

"I cannot explain the pleasure, the joy and happiness which my soul felt on seeing that I had attained what I so much desired, which was to shed my blood for love of Jesus and Mary, and to be able to seal with it the evangelical truths. My contentment was supreme on thinking that this was a sign of what I would attain in time, that I would shed all my blood and consummate the sacrifice with my death.

"It seemed to me that these wounds must be like the circumcision of Jesus Christ and the wounds to come in time would be like those He received on Calvary, that I would also die on the cross of the scaffold or from a dagger-thrust of an assassin, or from some other cause."

And, furthermore, remembering the spiritual delights that he enjoyed in Holguin, he said:

"In order to enjoy the felicity of those days even in the smallest degree, one could permit himself to receive knife-thrusts frequently."

In a letter directed to the missionaries of Vich, referring to the criminal attempt, he wrote these words:

"I hope that all of you will help me give thanks to God for the inexpressible favor of having been able to shed a little blood—five pounds—for love of Him who gave all His blood for me and to seal with it the truths of the holy Gospel, which I preach with so much pleasure.

"Ah, dear brethren! How sweet it is to shed one's blood for Jesus and Mary.

"I can assure you that in all this happening I have not suffered anything and have enjoyed it much, very much. Only in heaven can one enjoy more, but here on earth no greater spiritual pleasure is possible. I have become so fond of it that I would wish to try it a second time, and that the blow would hit the mark better than the first time.

"Nevertheless, I have made the deed known to the Holy Father, and shall do what he may tell me. In the meantime, help me to give thanks to God and to Mary, His sweet Mother. Cheer up and confide in God and in the Blessed Virgin, our dear Mother. Ah, how much she loves us!"

*   *   *

All these expressions of sweet rapture over the good fortune of having shed his blood for Christ prove that the victim suffered, but rejoiced.

And what was the fate of the assassin?

On the first of March, the Archbishop received a visit from the Captain General, Don Jose de la Concha.

"Your Excellency," he said, after saluting the archbishop. "The assassin of Holguin has been condemned to death."

"Very well," replied the archbishop, profoundly saddened. "I ask for an indult for him. I ask that he be given absolute liberty. Moreover, I wish that he return to his country, and I will pay the expense of his trip myself."

The Captain General, on hearing these words was profoundly edified at the spirit of charity and at the simple magnanimity of the prelate. At the repeated requests of the venerable archbishop, he obtained from Madrid, in favor of the criminal, pardon from the death penalty.

Later, Blessed Anthony Claret received a letter dated in the prison at Ceuta and signed by the assassin of Holguin.

"I will reveal to you," the latter said in a letter, "all the plot that was laid against the life of Your Excellency, and, besides, the names of all the accomplices."

Blessed Anthony replied:

"I do not want to know anything, neither about the plot, nor the accomplices. I only wish to seize the opportunity to tell the prisoner to prepare for a happy death, for he will have to present himself before the tribunal of God very soon."

In a short time the news circulated through Holguin, Gibara, Puerto Principe, and Santiago, that Antonio Abad Torres, the assassin of Father Claret, was dead.

LIV

THE PROPHESIES OF CUBA

The Prophecy of the Earthquake—The Prophecy of the Cholera—The Prophecy of War—The Prophecy of the Schism

We read in the Apocalypse:

"I, John, your brother, and your partner in tribulation, and in the kingdom, and patience in Christ Jesus, was in the island, which is called Patmos, for the word of God, and for the testimony of Jesus.

"I was in the spirit on the Lord's day, and heard behind me a great voice, as of a trumpet saying, 'What thou seest, write in a book'."

So also Father Claret, Apostle of God, "the least brother of the brothers of Christ," as he called himself, the man of sorrows and the martyr of the Gospel, was on an island—the island of Cuba—to preach the word of God and to give testimony of Jesus Christ.

And he like St. John, was carried away in spirit and made known the four great prophecies of Cuba, and he heard behind him a great voice, like a trumpet, that said:

"What thou seest, write in a book."

And what did he see? And what did he write? His Autobiography.

In it he announces, with words that are lightning and thunder, great revelations that God made to him on the island of Cuba, the new Patmos of the Missionary Archbishop.

*　　*　　*

It was August 20, 1852. Archbishop Claret was preaching a Mission in Bayamo, a town more than thirty leagues from the capital. One night the people noticed something extraordinary in the holy missionary. This strangeness was reflected in the pallor of his face and in the tremor of his voice. He began his sermon as was his custom, with full force, but at the most ardent and stirring point of his eloquence, he suddenly became silent; then directing himself to his audience, who looked at him in consternation, he pronounced these prophetic words:

"Let us pray to God for our brethren, residents of Santiago de Cuba, because they are in great tribulation. Tomorrow we shall go to console them."

When the religious function was over, the audience gathered in groups, in an attitude of surprise and alarm, and asked each other anxiously:

"What did the archbishop mean? What will take place in Santiago?"

In a short time a quake was felt in Bayamo, and amid tears and sighs the people said:

"The earthquake! Surely the earthquake has caused ruin in Santiago and he knew it by God's inspiration. But what will happen to us if a like disaster befalls us?"

The people, alarmed at the threatening catastrophe, came weeping to the holy archbishop that he might delay his leaving Bayamo.

"What will become of us?" they exclaimed. "We are also your children!"

Father Claret consoled them saying:

"Be calm. Nothing will happen here. But my presence is necessary in Santiago. I am going to console my brethren who have had a great misfortune."

"But what happened in Santiago?"

An eye-witness writes in detail. He says:

"A subterranean noise of thunder was heard, and from that moment everything moved; buildings vibrated; furniture in the rooms moved; window-panes and doors creaked; houses and churches tottered and walls and roofs fell to pieces; the inhabitants were terror stricken, and not feeling secure within their homes they went out into the patios, streets, and plazas. A glacial terror froze the blood in their veins. They stood still

and remained silent, looking at each other without being able
to explain what was happening. With a terrified voice they
cried:

"Mercy! Mercy!" The Archbishop arrived. On seeing thou-
stands of his children dispersed through the fields, the streets
covered with debris, houses in ruins, the episcopal palace torn
down, the churches crumbled, the Cathedral rent and the altars
broken, moved to profound pity by the tragic sight of the
catastrophe, he wept as Jesus wept over the ruins of Jerusalem.

The domestics and the missionaries wished to console the
archbishop; they wished to cheer him by telling him that the
punishment of the earthquake would not be repeated. But he
replied:

"They will return. It is useless to construct the cathedral
and the houses. The earthquake will return soon. God wishes
it. They are the great missionaries that God sends so that
obstinate hearts, who do not wish to listen to words of love,
may be converted."

One day, when the sun was setting, extending the pallor
of its rays over the heap of ruins, he said to his beloved
missionaries:

"My soul is sad, with the sadness of death."

Raising his face and directing his glance, full of profound
melancholy, to the city of Santiago, he said:

"Jerusalem, Jerusalem, thou that killest the prophets and
stonest them that are sent unto thee, how often would I have
gathered together thy children, as the hen doth gather her
chickens under her wings, and thou wouldst not?

"Behold, your house shall be left to you, desolate." (Matt.
XXIII, 37 and 38.)

*   *   *

It was in the city of Santiago. The churches were still filled
with debris. The stricken families had raised tents on the
shores of the sea. They had also improvised a chapel under

an immense covering. The pulpit was a platform and from it the holy archbishop preached a Mission.

Thousands of persons listened to him. His voice was sweet and sincere, threatening and terrifying, announcing simple Gospel truths and striking prophecy.

One day he made the following comparison:

"God does with many of us as a mother does to a lazy sleeping child, she shakes the cot or bed so as to awaken him and cause him to arise. If that does not suffice, she whips him.

"God does the same with many of his children, lethargic sinners. He shakes their beds, that is, their houses, by means of earthquakes, saving their bodies and their lives. If that does not awaken them and they do not arise, He will give them blows, sending them the cholera and the pest. God has made that known to me."

These last words, pronounced with prophetic accent, frightened and moved the public, so that, amid sobs, they begged mercy and pardon of God.

There was, nevertheless, among the hearers, one who grossly protested, calling them pulpit expedients, anathemas from beyond the grave, which only served to terrify simple people. But such was not the case. The announcements of the servant of God proved to be sadly true.

"Only one month had passed," said an eye-witness, "since the archbishop had spoken inspired by heaven, of the punishment of the cholera-morbus which threatened the city, when the terrible infirmity already raised its empire of terror and death.

"Santiago was an immense hospital, where only groans of pain and anguish were heard. But in a few days it looked like a vast cemetery, whose tragic silence was sadly interrupted by the echo of funeral cars carrying heaps of corpses, or by the priest's rapid footsteps, hastening to a death-bed."

That great, hardened and corrupted city disregarded the voice of the prophet, and today the prophet, on contemplating the terrible ravages of the epidemic, pronounced over it, the lamentation of Jeremiah:

"How doth the city sit solitary that was full of people! How is the mistress of the Gentiles becomes as a widow. The princes of the provinces made tributary."

*   *   *

This announcement of the prophecies and their speedy realization profoundly moved many hearts, and thousands of persons took part in those public rogations and devoted themselves to exercises of penance.

Father Claret loved all his children who were obedient to the Church and faithful to the law of God. On seeing among the wayward and fantastic many representatives of the distant homeland, his Spanish heart was saddened. He uttered, principally against his racial brethren, a third prophecy, which produced consternation in his audience.

He was preaching at the Marina. Suddenly he changed the subject of his sermon. His voice assumed a solemn tone and he spoke the following words:

"I have come to announce three great chastisements, which God has reserved to move many obstinate hearts to repentance.

The first, the earthquake, has already been fulfilled.

The second will soon come to pass; it will be the cholera morbus. And the third . . . ." Here he paused and exclaimed:

"Do penance for your sins and for those of the people, so that God may stay the arm ready to strike."

He publicly made the prophecy of the three chastisements also in the towns of Vicario and of Mazanilla. When Father Currius asked him later what the third chastisement would be the servant of God replied:

"The punishment is a great war in which the Europeans, especially the Spaniards, will be pursued to death like hares in the forest."

He said the same publicly to a group of Spaniards, who

scorned the preaching of the holy prelate at a solemn Mission that was given in the town of Sara:

"You," he said, "are planning obstacles to the words of your archbishop who esteems you and interests himself in your spiritual health, as an affectionate father. I pray God that the terrible punishment that is threatening you may not fall upon you, for here you will be pursued like hares; and these fields will be watered with Spanish blood."

Thus it happened. On September 11, 1868, in that same place—Sara—more than three thousand peasants, on horseback, with guns and chopping knives, gathered by Don Carlos Manuel Cespedes, sent forth the cry of Independence against Spain, and surprising the unarmed troops of the town, gave knife-thrusts to the Europeans. Two of the Spaniards, before being assassinated exclaimed:

"This is a punishment of God! We have heard Father Claret's prophecy of this insurrection. My God, have mercy!"

*   *   *

There was in Cuba a stubborn generation: intellectuals, proud manufacturers, lovers of money, emigrants, concubines, traffickers in slaves, miners, soldiers and citizens, the incredulous and corrupt. All of them worked strenuously to discredit the Missions, prohibiting their servants and farmers from assisting at them.

They feared the Gospel truths; they did not want the people to know of their injustices. For that reason, one day, when the holy archbishop was giving a Mission in Datel, one of those cruel masters ordered his steward to give forty lashes to any slave who might attend the Mission.

It was, then, evident that neither the Mission of Father Claret, nor the mission of the earthquake, were sufficient to convert these proud spirits. But God rends rock and causes the mountains to emit smoke.

Thus it is also in the vast topography of the spirit. The organizations of human pride reach their heights like a challenge. But God crushes them as simply as He does great things. And the arrogances of man are like a mountain chain of smoke.

It was God's design to humiliate the enemies of Father Claret who obstinately resisted the grace of the Missions. It was this same servant of God who would predict to his people a new chastisement, as it was the prophets who communicated to Israel the message of sorrow.

*   *   *

Some time passed. Soon the lips of Father Claret were to open again to send forth over Cuba a fourth prophecy. His face was pale. His deep look was lost in the mystery of vague distance. He spoke little and prayed much. Amid his brief conversations burst forth, from time to time, sighs, as an echo of interior sufferings.

"What can be the matter with the archbishop? For some nine days he has been going about sad and preoccupied." So said the intimate associates of Father Claret, but no one dared to inquire about the cause, nor dared to ask the holy prelate himself.

On a certain day, one of them—the rector of the Seminary, said to him:

"Your Excellency, do you wish us to call a doctor? We notice that Your Excellency must be suffering much."

"No, do not be worried," the archbishop responded. "A physician cannot relieve me of my sufferings; they are moral sufferings."

After a brief silence he exclaimed:

"Let us beg God to avoid a terrible punishment which threatens this archbishopric. If it does not destroy the entire fruit of our apostolic works, it will carry away a great part of it."

He then changed the course of the conversation, touching upon indifferent things. But soon, as though overtaken by a sudden vision, he repeated the same words:

"Let us pray God that this may not happen!"

Father Claret did not clarify the mystery of his veiled prediction, but all who heard it later remembered it when the schism of Llorent, an ambitious clergyman, who declared he had obtained from the liberal Minister of the Interior, Ruiz Zorrilla, the nomination of Archbishop of Santiago. Although he was rejected by Pope Pius IX and excommunicated for being immoral and rebellious, he, nevertheless, succeeded in drawing into the schism a part of the Cathedral Chapter and separating from the Church many of the faithful whom the apostolic word of Father Claret had converted.

That was the cause of the archbishop's sadness. He had contemplated the spectacle of the ruins that the earthquake had caused in his beloved city.

He had witnessed the funeral procession of thousands of corpses that the cholera morbus had carried to the cemeteries. He had seen, on a horizon of blood and of crime, the war of the insurgents, that would wave the flag of independence over the fields of death, where lay, in heaps, the palpitating victims.

Among the shadows of the future, in a not far-distant date, he saw all the horror of a spiritual mortality which the schism was to cause in that archbishopric, which, with so much love and sacrifice, he had watered with the sweat of his brow, with tears in his eyes and with the blood of his wounds.

With the combined vision of these panoramas of mourning, how could the heart of the saintly archbishop be other than desolate and sad?

He was right, when on the Saturday before Septuagesima, on contemplating the Island of Cuba from the boat, he said to his missionaries as he closed his breviary: "We have recited the last Alleluia."

LV

THE RETURN FROM CUBA

THE THREE IDEALS—THE CALL OF THE QUEEN—IN THE COLLEGE OF BELEN—MARKS OF EDIFICATION—TAKING LEAVE OF HAVANA—THE INTERVIEW WITH THE QUEEN—THE THREE CONDITIONS—THE ARCHBISHOP OF TOLEDO

One day the missionaries of Cuba were gathered in the archiepiscopal palace. In the course of their conversation the following question was asked:

"What is the ideal of Archbishop Claret?"

"The ideal of Archbishop Claret," responded some, "is martyrdom. Remember the desire he always manifested to shed his blood for Jesus Christ. Remember how he rejoiced at the attempt on his life at Holguin, and the noble pride with which he showed the scars of the wounds. Remember that sentence from his notes upon the episcopal duties which read:

'A bishop must be prepared for one of three things: to be poisoned, to be persecuted, or to be condemned.'

"If he fulfills his obligations, men will poison him or persecute him as they persecuted Jesus Christ and his Apostles. If he does not fulfill them, God will condemn him, as He has threatened in Holy Scripture.

"He has fulfilled his pastoral ministry, for that reason, he ardently desires, as a recompense, the crown of martyrdom."

"The ideal of Father Claret," said others, "is to leave the honors of the episcopate. Remember the resistance with which he opposed his nomination as archbishop, and how, only by command of obedience, did he conform to the election. Remember the words he spoke on that memorable occasion.

'The day on which I can renounce the mitre I will leap to the clouds.'

"The ideal of Father Claret," the rest concluded. "is to dedicate himself to the missions.

"Remember his projects on joining the Propagation of the Faith, and his apostolate in Catalonia, in the Canaries, and in Cuba. The Missions had always been the great enterprise of his vocation!"

Thus the various opinions of this familiar inquiry were exposed. But, who was right? Which of these ideals did Archbishop Claret attain?

* * *

A distant scene: Madrid, the metropolis of the kingdom; and in Madrid, the Royal Palace, a poem in stone that sings of the power of the nation; and in the Royal Palace a Queen, sad and disheartened, hiding, in the midst of the splendors of the court, the grief of spiritual destitution.

Suddenly the Queen recalled a memory, the memory of a missionary, of an archbishop, of a saint, of whose prodigies she had heard many times, and whom she had once seen in the Palace while on an official visit of gratitude and leave-taking. She then said resolutely and joyfully: "He shall be the successor to Cardinal Bonel, in directing my conscience. He shall be my confessor!"

Father Claret was preaching a Mission. A communication was brought to him from the Captain General. The message read:

"Her Majesty, the Queen, desires that Your Excellency come to Madrid immediately. I believe she wishes to make you Archbishop of Toledo. Tomorrow she will send the order and will place a boat at your disposal."

Mysterious destiny! Which of the ideals was realized by his return to the peninsula? History testifies that all three ideals were realized.

First of all, the glory of martyrdom, of a slow and profound martyrdom, because he was the victim of the persecution of the sects, of impious calumnies, and of the ire of the revolution, dying in exile because he loved justice and hated iniquity.

He renounces his archbishopric, moreover, because as soon

as he accepted the nomination of confessor to the Queen, he asked His Holiness, Pope Pius IX, to loosen the bonds that tied him to his archbishopric, a desire which His Holiness satisfied by naming him titular Archbishop of Trajanopolis on June 13, 1860, after continuing, during three years, while in Madrid, Apostolic Administrator of the Metropolitan See of Santiago de Cuba.

Finally his third ideal—the exercise of the Missions, was realized. At the close of the 1857, Father Claret was the archbishop-missionary of Spain, of all Spain, because his apostolic word resounded with the echoes of eternity, in the principal pulpits of the cathedrals, churches and chapels of the entire peninsula.

Thus appears the historic personality of Blessed Father Claret in bold relief and in all its details.

It was February 22, 1857, a day of sadness and loneliness for all of the island! An immense crowd filled the port of Santiago. Tears and sobs, vivas and acclamations were the language of overflowing emotion. They were rendering just homage. All could repeat here the word of Jesus Christ: "If these were silent, the very stones would speak.' '

How much Cuba owed to the sacrifices of the archbishop-missionary! The boat weighed anchor. The holy archbishop was deeply moved on casting a last look on his beloved island. On looking into the future, he saw with prophetic light, the ravages of war, which was to inundate the fields with blood, and cover the city with ruins. He remembered the prediction of Jesus Christ:

"Days will come over thee! Then thy enemies will draw near, will oppress thee! They will cast thee upon the earth and they will overthrow thy children. There shall not be left a stone upon a stone, and all because thou hast not known the time of thy visitation!"

The travellers arrived at the capital of the island on the 28th. Archbishop Claret remained in Havana two weeks, awaiting the boat for the peninsula, and during his stay he was guest at the episcopal palace!

There were two weeks of work and of Missions, of direction of consciences and of examples of edification! He spent Holy Week in the Jesuit College of Belen.

On Tuesday of Holy Week, in the act of placing a monument, a workman fell headlong from the top of the scaffolding onto a stone ladder. All believed that he could only live a few hours. Father Claret, however, visited him in the infirmary, blessed him, and from that moment he began to improve rapidly and soon was completely restored to health.

Father Claret received numberless visits from the fathers of the community and from seculars, who brought thousands of pictures for the Servant of God to bless and to autograph so that they might preserve them as relics.

After dinner on Good Friday, he knelt in the refectory and kissed the feet of the fathers and brothers of the community, an act which edified and excessively moved all at seeing the profound humility of the prelate.

On another day he visited the Fathers of the Society of Jesus in the same College. Arriving at meal time he called the Father Rector apart and said to him:

"Father, I am going to ask you a favor."

"Your Excellency, command what you may wish."

"Permit me to serve your holy community at table."

"Ah, that cannot be. Neither I nor the Fathers could permit it. Ask something else, Your Excellency."

He entered the community refectory and again begged, on bended knees, that the Father Rector would permit him to serve them at dinner, as the least of the brothers.

Father Rector, moved by the repeated entreaties, permitted him to practice this act of humility. On that day the fathers and brothers received their meal, graciously served by Archbishop Claret.

Archbishop Claret preached in various churches of the

capital. The last words he pronounced on taking leave of the people of Havana were these:

"Good-bye, children. Until we meet in heaven."

The authorities and the prominent persons of the city came down to the port to wish him "God-speed", and in the name of the city, delivered the following document to him.

"Most Excellent and illustrious Lord Archbishop of Cuba:

"The devoted people of Havana, by means of their signatures affixed herewith, wish to give evidence in the most solemn manner, of the profound respect and love which your Excellency has inspired in the short time that we have had the pleasure of having you in our midst.

"Yes, venerable Apostle of Jesus Christ, permit us to beg you, prostrate at your feet, to offer your acceptable prayers to God, for your people, especially for those who are humbly addressing you, so that Heaven's blessings may descend upon each and every one.

"Now that you are parting, perhaps forever, benignly receive, as a loved Father, the vows of your affectionate children grouped about you, and who, amid tears, offer you their hearts, praying Heaven that you may arrive safely at the shores of your country, and fill you with infinite mercies during your precious life.

Havana, April 12, 1857."

Among the signatures were: the Marquis of Royal Proclamation, the Count of Penalver, the Dowager Countess of Villanueva, Countess de O'Relly, the Marchioness of the Royal Company, the Ruler of the Town-Council and the Royal Literary University. Such was the interim spent in Havana. Two weeks of great spiritual attraction!

* * *

He arrived in Madrid on May 26, and took lodging in a very humble house. Before two hours had elapsed, the chief steward of her Majesty, in the official coach of the Royal Palace, awaited him at the door of his humble abode.

The august sovereign anxiously awaited him, in order to

speak to him and to unburden her heart which was crushed with serious family and governmental troubles.

"I wish you to be my confessor," she said to him. "I wish you to direct my soul and that of the princess; to impart lessons in religion and moral law to the Infanta Isabel. I wish you to tell me the truth with sincerity and frankness, because I have resolved to fulfill the holy will of God in all things."

The Archbishop was surprised on hearing these words, because he had not been sufficiently informed of the reason of his coming to Spain. Although he encouraged and consoled the Queen in her efforts towards perfection, he asked for time to consider the matter.

He consulted his confessor, the Papal Nuncio, and His Holiness, Pope Pius IX. When he received the three replies, which all said, as by common agreement, that it was the will of God that he accept the new charge of Confessor to the Queen, he went to the Palace to communicate with her Majesty, assuring her of his acceptance, but only on three conditions:

That he was not to live in the Palace, and that he was not to be called there except to fulfill his ministerial duties.

That he was to enjoy full liberty to preach and to visit hospitals and charitable institutions.

That he would not be obligated to go through formalities when, for any reason whatever, he would have to see the Queen.

Noble independence of the saints, which the world does not understand nor practise!

"I accept all your conditions," the Queen replied.

The Archbishop then left the Palace.

* * *

Something else, however, entered into the plans of the Queen. She wished Father Claret to be her confessor, and, moreover, Archbishop of Toledo and Cardinal of the Holy Roman Church, as was her former confessor, Cardinal Bonel y Orbe.

The Government, on the other hand, made rude opposition to the appointment of Father Claret as confessor of the Queen as well as to his being Primate of the See of Toledo. The same opposition was manifested in the Palace. But the Queen sent her reply to the Minister with opportune grace:

"The confessor and the doctor must be left to the choice of the penitent and the patient."

The Government then, frustrated in its first attempt, artfully proposed as candidate for the Archbishopric of Toledo the bishop of Burgos, Fray Cirilo de Alameda.

It is evident from various documents that the Queen wished to propose Father Claret for the Primatial See of Toledo. But a letter, dated June 5, 1857, from Father Claret to Don Antonio Barjou, proves that he opposed this matter.

The letter says:

"Her Majesty wished that I become Archbishop of Toledo, but thank God, I have escaped. God grant that I may escape all the other points also.

"My intention is to be Archbishop 'in partibus,' and thus I shall be free to execute my plans, which are to remain in one house, living with priest companions, in order to dedicate myself entirely to the Missions and Spiritual Exercises throughout Spain."

Father Claret attained, in part, what he decided in the Lord for the salvation of souls, namely, to be titular archbishop without the obligation of residence, so that he might freely dedicate himself to preaching, an ideal which the realization of his new charge—confessor of the Queen—did not impede. Thus the Providential designs of the archbishop-missionary were fulfilled!

The torch of the nation was placed in the candelabra; a torch that shone and burned, like a Biblical torch, with brightness in the direction of consciences and with the sacred fire of apostolic zeal, which would extend its flames, like a blazing fire through all the provinces of Spain.

LVI
CONFESSOR OF THE QUEEN
No Politics—Plan of Life—Customs of the Palace Two Forces—The Grand Cross of Carlos III—Testimony of the Queen—The Brightness of the Mass

Two contradictory judgments were formed regarding the influence of Father Claret on the spirit of the Queen. The impious and sectarians called him the arbiter of politics, thinkthat his advice would orientate the decisions of the Queen regarding the formation of government.

And, on the other hand, there were Catholics who hoped that on account of his position, he would be able to change certain political situations, condemning his restraint in public matters.

Father Claret replied to both parties always with the same motto:

"No politics, only matters pertaining to God!" Thus he always maintained that prestige at court which even his enemies recognized in hours of sincerity.

Thus he was able to transform the Palace, which had previously been a museum of vanities, into an oratory of piety and into a place of activity.

Father Claret began the spiritual direction of the Queen by suggesting a plan of life. And the first thing he commanded her to do was to make a Spiritual Retreat, together with the ladies of the Palace, a practice of perfection which was to be repeated each year.

In order to increase the desire for virtue of the royal penitent, and of the waiting-maids and the court ladies, he composed his admirable book, "Spiritual Exercises," which, during the days of Retreat became the text of the meditations and readings, while "The Right Road" became the prayer-book of the Court, which the author, Father Claret, presented to the Queen and the court ladies, as a souvenir of the Retreat.

Let us listen to some of the references to the holy customs introduced in the palace. Blessed Claret says in some of his notes in 1862:

"At present the Queen and her attendants act in an edifying manner. They hear Holy Mass daily, read the Lives of the Saints, recite the Rosary, and frequent the Sacraments.

"The Queen and her daughter confess to me, as do also many of the attendants. All are constantly occupied.

"The Queen, besides her devotions and her attending to governmental duties and giving audiences to many persons each day, occupies herself in manual labor, in painting pictures and in embroidery; generally, however, she occupies herself in embroidery.

"Last year she embroidered a cushion for my prie-dieu. It has beautiful flowers worked on it. At times she also makes quilts.

"The princess is also busy. Besides her devotions and pious reading which she performs daily, she spends much time in the preparation of the lessons that are given her.

"During the recreations she plays masculine games rather than games for girls. During the five years that I have been dealing with her, I have never seen her play with a girl's toy, but always with such as boys use.

"Sometimes she would string beads with pliers and wire, although she also sewed and embroidered very well.

"The queen's and the princess' maids are always occupied either in the performance of their respective duties, or in reading some good book, or in making needle lace, or other things.

"Notwithstanding that the Queen is admirable in her morality, her piety, her charity and other virtues, and that all the other inmates of the Palace follow her example, I cannot adapt myself or be at ease by remaining in Madrid.

*   *   *

Father Claret frequently repeated, in his personal writings, a double idea, one of appreciation of the sanctity of the

Queen and of her Court, and another of the weariness and loathsomeness he experienced in being in Madrid. Thus he says in one of his autobiographical notes:

"What reason have you to feel such disgust for being in Madrid? Everyone in the palace respects you. All the royal family appreciates and honors you. Her Majesty, the Queen, loves you even to the extreme. Then, what motives are there for being so insistent?

"None. I myself do not know the reason. I can only explain the enigma by saying that this repugnance which I feel is a grace of God given me, so that I may not place my affection on the grandeur, honors and riches of the world. I recognize clearly that a continuous feeling of repugnance to courtly things, and this perennial desire to escape them, preserves me from envy and from placing my heart on the things that are appreciated in the world.

"I see that the Lord has effected in me what I behold in the planets; in them I observe two forces, the centrifugal and the centripetal. The centrifugal inclines them to flee, the centripetal draws them to the center. Their orbit results from the equilibrium of these two forces.

"The centrifugal force in me is my horror of the grandeur of the Court, and the centripetal force is the will of God."

*   *   *

The Queen, on her part, took advantage of every occasion to manifest practically the veneration she felt for her holy confessor.

Pope Pius IX presented the Queen of Spain with the "Golden Rose," and she asked earnestly that her venerated confessor be the pontifical delegate to make the presentation. Thus it was resolved by a Brief of January 28, 1868, and was carried out on February 12 in the Royal Chapel.

The Queen wishing to prove her gratitude, in some way, for the services which Father Claret rendered her, said to him one day:

"Ask for something, ask me for something; because you never ask for anything."

Father Claret responded:

"Yes, Your Majesty, I am going to ask one thing . . . that I may retire from the Court."

"Not that, not that!" replied the Queen.

So as not to give further heed to this petition, she gave him gifts and honors on several occasions, but without soliciting either his opinion or consent.

A solemn event occurred. The Prince of Asturias—later Alfonso XII—was born, November 28, 1857. On that happy occasion the King and Queen wished to honor Blessed Claret with the Grand Cross of Charles III.

They foresaw his resistance, and for that reason proceeded in an unaccustomed manner. Let us read Blessed Anthony's own words:

"After the birth of the Prince of Asturias, the very day that their Majesties went to Atocha, they told me to come to the Palace. As soon as I was there the King and Queen came forth from the room in which they had been awaiting me. Without saying a word they both placed the cross upon me.

"I did not say a word for I was in the royal presence. Since the King did not then inspire in me the same confidence as now, although he esteemed me, I was silent. Interiorly, however, I suffered great pain.

"On another day when I was alone with the Queen, I could not help but express my appreciation of the kind affection which had prompted my decoration with the Cross of Charles III, but, on my part, it had caused me pain.

"In proof of the pain it had caused me, I did not wear it for a long time, and even now I wear it only on days of rigorous uniformity and etiquette."

Thus lived Father Claret in the midst of grandeur, but grandeur did not live in his heart.

The veneration which the Queen had at this time for her saintly confessor was continually increasing, for each day she discovered in him additional supernatural lights.

There is on hand concerning this a document of immeasureable value. It is the sworn declaration that the Queen sent to the "Proceso Informativo" from her exile in Paris. The six points of the regal testimony read thus:

"Confirming the deeds and virtues of His Excellency, the illustrious Don Antonio Maria Claret, Archbishop of Trajanopolis, (of whom relation is made in the articles of Chapter VI of the Process of Introduction to the Cause of Beatification presented by the Postulator, Rev. P. Villaro), during the time that he was my confessor, viz: from 1857 to 1869, I must add:

"1. When my confessor accepted the charge, he did so reluctantly for the fear he felt at being at court, and because his humility caused him to wish to live far from honors. I chose him for my confessor, because I knew his virtues which gave evidence of his sanctity, and because I knew of the miracles he performed while a missionary. I thanked Providence for having placed so holy a prelate at my side. How great a consolation he afforded me on many occasions, and how clearly I understood the power of his prayers with God and our Blessed Mother, to whom he was greatly devoted!

"2. He was never taken up with politics, nor did he ever wish to advise me in political matters, except to express his opinion on such subjects as might concern the interests of the Church and the Sovereign Pontiff, as happened when circumstances obliged me to recognize the kingdom of Italy against my will. For the same reason Father Claret wished to absent himself from the Court and to leave me in the greatest distress concerning this affair. I could not be consoled until I received a letter from Rome, in which I was told that my confessor would return with the blessing of His Holiness.

"3. He continued to be my spiritual director until 1869, in which year, anxious to die, as he often said, either as a martyr or in extreme poverty, he went to the monastery of Fontfroide. Here he died in the greatest poverty, but very rich in holiness and virtue.

"4. For all the good which he has done me, as well as my family, I shall never, in all my life, find words to express my gratitude. I am persuaded that he will protect us from heaven where he is enjoying the happiness he so earnestly desired and to which we must all aspire.

"5. It is evident that Father Claret was all charity. He used every means to practice it, depriving himself of everything he had.

"6. In regard to his sanctity, I can assure you that one day I saw him saying Holy Mass in my oratory, surrounded by splendor, and that I have seen his predictions fulfilled. Thus, my conscience obliges me to consign it to writing, adding that while I had the good fortune of having Father Claret as confessor, I saw nothing but prudence, humility, abnegation and all the other virtues found in a real saint.

"From heaven, where he undoubtedly protects me, he shall see that I am fulfilling the duty that my respect, affection and gratitude inspire me in writing these lines, so that they may count in the process of the Beatification of the said Most Rev. Archbishop Claret."

QUEEN ISABEL II OF SPAIN.

LVII

THE MISSIONARY OF SPAIN

His Eloquence—Comparisons—Four Thousand Men and
Six Thousand Women—The Surprise of the Coach
His Journeys Throughout Spain—Christmas
Eve—The Virgin and the Child Jesus

The press of the epoch devoted long articles to the eloquence of Father Claret. It analyzed minutely the literary value and power of his word. The official Bulletin of the Conference of St. Vincent de Paul gave a synthesis expressive of all the human characteristics of his sermons.

"The object of Father Claret's sermons" it said, "is only the good of souls.

"His preaching, simple, cordial, and effusive, is the reflection of a father who loves his sons, or the counsels of religious experience with which an older brother proposes to guide his helpless, orphaned brothers.

"His resistance and strength bear no comparison. We have seen him standing for two hours in the morning and two hours in the afternoon, addressing apostolic exhortation and counsels to the people of Madrid with vigorous intonations and sustained energy. Not for a moment did he seem to be fatigued, nor did his voice weaken. He was not seen to wipe his brow, nor moisten his lips with water. It seemed as though all the weakness of human nature respected him in those blessed hours, anxious to concede to him a truce of moral triumph and inexplicable contentment of soul, and to grant the greatest of benefits to the troubled mortals who listened to him."

*   *   *

"The eloquence of Father Claret ranks highest in purely Biblical comparisons, valuable because they augment the persuasive power of his doctrine. These comparisons are so many, so appropriate and selected, that one can be assured that he has no rival, nor competitor in this phase of eloquence which for us is the most difficult.

"The best known proverbs, the most familiar objects, the exterior agents, the relations of man with nature and its innumerable creatures, and with art and its very vast creations, furnished the archbishop-missionary with an inexhaustible arsenal of comparisons, of most ingenious arguments, of extremely opportune phrases, of words that absorb the attention and interest in terms that, far from fatiguing the audience, make them regret that his discourses are not longer, notwithstanding the fact that they are unusually long.

"We shall cite here a few of the many beautiful, opportune and interesting comparisons, whose reproduction would fill volumes.

"One Sunday night he made a comparison which made a deep impression on his audience. He compared a Christian youth who lives in intimate contact with the world and the occasions of sin to a soldier of wax, perfectly armed and placed near a flame of fire. The archbishop called attention to the effect of the fire which heated and melted the wax. At first it caused the sword to fall, then the shield, afterward the breast plate, and the helmet, all symbols of valor, of strength, of faith and of the other virtues until the entire figure is destroyed and falls to the ground, and is completely consumed by the flames.

"The application of this simile to the Christian youth who placed himself near the blaze of burning passions and mundane concupiscence, and his picture of the first hesitation of this youth, of the power of temptation, of his defeat and of his fall into the flames of impurity made a deep impression on his hearers.

"Heaven grant that, as the impelling force of ignited powder throws a bomb of enormous weight to a great distance, according to the comparison of the archbishop, so our hearts, im-

pelled by the holy fire of charity may lead us to great enterprises and sacrifices, for the good of society."

Such were the expressions found in the news-papers and
Catholic reviews that published, at that time, the accounts of
the religious functions at which Archbishop Claret preached.

*   *   *

A summary impression of his apostolic works was given
briefly in a Catholic Review, "La Regeneracion," referring to
some months only of the year 1857.

"In addition to the ordinary sermons which he gave two or
three times daily, he, in the summer, preached a Novena in
the Italian Church and a series of sermons from September
until Christmas. These were followed by a Retreat to five
hundred priests, and another for one hundred fifty priests, with
abundant fruit and great edification.

"After that he gave the celebrated Spiritual Exercises to
four thousand men in the church of St. Thomas. This church,
in spite of its vast proportions, was unable to contain the crowd.
These Spiritual Exercises frustrated a revolution which, according to public rumors, was brewing against the altar and
the throne.

"Following immediately was a Retreat given to six thousand women, among whom were seen those of the aristocracy."

While giving a Mission to all classes of people, he alter-
nated this task with a Retreat for prisoners and also a Retreat
to forty French religious women who were gathered in their
boarding school.

"What eloquence Archbishop Claret possesses!" continues
"La Regeneracion." "He speaks two hours and a half in the
morning and two hours and a half in the afternoon. It does
not matter. The multitude does not tire. They besiege him
on all sides.

"When he descends the pulpit, his path is blocked by those
who kneel and ask to kiss his ring, or the hem of his garment,
or the fringe of his episcopal sash."

One afternoon during the Retreat for men, public enthusiasm prepared a surprise for him.

A part of the audience guarded the door of the sacristy and surrounded the portico of the church to take the archbishop upon their shoulders, place him in a coach ready for him, and in this vehicle drawn by men, they wished to carry him triumphant to his home.

The Archbishop knew of this, so he ascended to the rooms of the parish priest by means of an interior stairway and descending by another way, he was able to cross the street without being seen.

*   *   *

These triumphs, however, did not fill Father Claret's heart. His vision embraced wider horizons. He wished to cross the whole of Spain and to carry his apostolic word, like a torch of eternity, through all the provinces.

Her Majesty, the Queen, knew the desires of her confessor very well. In order to fulfill them in some way, a genial idea came into her mind, namely, to give a double Mission; a patriotic Mission and a religious Mission; one for love of country, and the other for love of Religion, both having grown cold and died in many hearts.

For that reason, she, in agreement with the government, organized those celebrated regal trips through all the regions of the peninsula. Archbishop Claret joined the royal retinue. The fire of his ardent, apostolic zeal developed along the way by means of talks and sermons. Thus his sublime ideal of being a missionary to all of Spain was realized in an unforeseen manner.

He preached in all the provinces, in all the cities and even in the most insignificant towns.

Everywhere his word was what it had been in Catalonia, in the Canaries, in Cuba, and in Madrid: the voice of the Angel of the Apocalypse, which, with the sound of trumpet awakened lethargic consciences. At the same time, his voice was like the rays of the lighthouse, which from the coasts of life illumined the road to eternity.

God sustained his power of resistance in a supernatural manner. His iron will, installed in his spirit, like a motor, impelled and turned everything in the cardinal direction of his missionary vocation.

"Your Excellency, you must be very tired with so much work in the pulpit and in the confessional," Don Pedro Carrascosa one day ventured to say to him. But Father Claret replied immediately with a deprecating gesture. "Look here, my son, look. I beg of you, never ask me if I am tired, because that is what irritates me. How can I tire, my son, serving God and souls? This cannot tire a missionary; such labor is to live and to reign."

*   *   *

But God took account of the sweat of the brow of His apostle; while the angels gathered those drops in order to set them, like diamonds, in the crown of glory, He wished to reward the sacrifices of His servant even in life. He did so as only God can do.

It was in Madrid, in the year 1864, in the month of December, on Christmas Night, during the thanksgiving after the Midnight Mass, in the Convent of the Sisters of Perpetual Adoration.

At his side, in the sanctuary, was the chaplain, Don Carmelo Sala, and in the chapel, the community of the Sisters of Perpetual Adoration, at their head the foundress and the spiritual daughter of Father Claret, who had been the Viscountess of Jorbalan in the world, and was now Mother Mary of the Blessed Sacrament (in religion), and who is known as St. Michaela Desmaisieres in the universal Church, since March 4, 1934.

Christmas Eve! Never was the night so holy as at that time for the servant of God.

Every year he celebrated the three Masses on Christmas in

the chapel of the "Adoratrices," and spent six hours hearing confessions, preaching and praying.

Before the Masses he gave a talk, and presided at the meditation of the religious and of the students. He celebrated the first Mass at midnight. At the Communion he again addressed the students. The second and third Masses followed in succession. At five o'clock in the morning he went to the church at Montserrat to hear confessions and remained there until mid-day.

After his first Mass, while he was making his thanksgiving in the sanctuary, a silence of adoration reigned in the chapel.

A mellow ray, the ray of the moon, which seemed to rock itself in the flight of the clouds, fell, at intervals, through the stained glass windows. The wind whistled. The last echoes of dissipation were dying out on the streets.

Soon a sigh, deeper than usual, burst from the breast of Blessed Anthony. This sigh was deeper, more ardent and more prolonged than usual. His face was burning; his bright eyes fixed and ecstatic. He smiled and wept at the same time.

Words of amorous delight came in fragments from his lips.

Kneeling on the bishop's prie-dieu, his extended arms looked like lilies resting upon a cushion. Folding his arms gently he seemed to press something tender and soft to his heart.

Celestial moments! The scene passed. Don Carmelo Sala, chaplain of Blessed Anthony and, moreover, a friend of his and his confessor, afterward addressed him:

"Your Excellency; Holy Christmas!"

"Ah, yes. Holy Christmas, Holy Christmas," exclaimed Blessed Anthony.

"Your Excellency: Had you some gift from God? Some Christmas gift?"

Blessed Anthony was silent, and his confessor, filled with veneration was silent too. A little later, Father Claret, in intimate confidence, said these solemn words to his friend, words which history has gathered and art has glorified:

"The holy Virgin placed the Child Jesus in my arms tonight."

Some privileged soul among the Religious of Perpetual Adoration must have seen the apparition of the Blessed Virgin placing the Child Jesus in the arms of Father Claret, for soon the community knew of the favor from Heaven.

A letter preserved by Sister Angelica, a religious of Perpetual Adoration, is proof of this fact.

"That Christmas night," it says, "the five hours we remained in the chapel listening to and seeing Father Claret, seemed but brief moments to us. No one tired. We felt as though we were in a region of happiness.

"The Sisters said that during his thanksgiving Father was in ecstasy and had received the Child Jesus in his arms. The Blessed Virgin had given the Child to him."

All his biographers refer lovingly to this act. Thousands of pictures showing the apparition have been circulated throughout the world.

The large stained glass windows in our churches recall the vision. It is one of the Claretian episodes that has been received with the greatest piety and devotion by the faithful.

LVIII

THE ROSARY OF VIRTUES

God erected a statue over the golden mountain of the Spanish capital, the statue of Father Claret, and the titular angel of Spain addressing bishops, priests, religious and seculars, spoke the following words from the sacred Book of Exodus. "Look at and imitate the model that I have placed on the mountain."

Spain contemplated the great missionary, and on seeing his examples and his prowess, exclaimed with astonishment:

"How admirable is God in His saints."

Spain drew near the hero because the hero drew near to Spain, descending from the heights and lavishing sacrifices in favor of souls, in the enterprise of his missions. On seeing him among the splendors of the world, humble and great, simple and wonderful, she said in a burst of enthusiasm, with the people of Israel: "A prophet has arisen in our midst! Blessed is he who cometh in the name of the Lord!"

This Biblical preamble could be a formula of expression for the national admiration that the multiple missionary activities of Father Claret produced.

But the historian must study the root of the causes by the exterior of the deeds. If Father Claret moved the machinery of his apostolate with such harmony and fecundity, it was because he bore within himself a creating power, the power of the interior life, which is the power of God.

* * *

And so it was one day, during a retreat in Madrid, he formulated anew his resolutions of sacrifice, mortification, of humility, of love of God, of zeal for the conversion of souls and exteriorly conformed his acts to the following program:

"For all that pertains to my person, food, bed and clothing, I shall be like a miser, close and niggardly, but I will be generous to my friends and companions, lavish to the poor and needy.

"I will visit the hospitals, prisons and other houses and establishments of charity frequently, and shall procure for them all the spiritual and temporal favors I can.

"I shall do all the good I can for ecclesiastics by means of literary and spiritual conferences, and, moreover, by giving books."

*   *   *

Through the testimony of his servants, we know the details of his order of the day in his private and public life, and how he fulfilled his resolutions.

He often spent whole nights in prayer and study. This was observed by his hosts and their servants, who through curiosity peeped through the key-hole, or who saw the reflection of the light. For that reason, his bed remained intact at dawn. When, however, he rested after the toil of the day, he did so for the space of three hours, from midnight until three o'clock in the morning.

He rang the corridor bell at exactly four o'clock in the morning to awaken his servants; and with them he then made an hour's meditation. He celebrated the Holy Sacrifice of the Mass after a long preparation, and spent a long time in thanksgiving. Until eleven o'clock he heard confessions. Crowds of people from Madrid, as well as from the towns, drew near his confessional.

One hour was dedicated to audiences, "lost-time audiences" as he called them, because all of them began and ended by asking for a recommendation, in the belief that he had influence at court and with the Ministers.

He daily received an average of a hundred letters. Although the answers were generally brief, his correspondence consumed the first hours of the afternoon. He then, accompanied by his domestics, went to preach in some church or convent—an almost daily practice. He next assisted some sick person or visited the prisons and hospitals. The latter exercise of charity was his favorite act.

"What a pity," he used to say to himself, "to have to walk through the streets with these garments of a bishop and assisted by domestics. How much more could I do if I were alone, without calling the attention of the people who come to kiss my ring and make me lose my time. Then, without being known, I could work more in those districts where so many souls have strayed away!"

He was very moderate at his meals, and it was evident that he did not drink wine, nor taste meat nor fish. Only on Sunday he ate a soft-boiled egg. A few vegetables constituted his daily food.

One year, at Christmas, his friends obliged him, after much insistence, to taste a little chicken. That afternoon he said: "You see how badly I feel? It is clear that my stomach cannot stand such luxurious food."

*   *   *

And why was Blessed Anthony so abstemious?

"For three reasons," he said. "First, in imitation of Jesus Christ; secondly, to mortify my flesh; thirdly, to save for my poor. Thus I can give more alms!"

When he was given a dish of sweets he felt great joy, and exclaimed: "Oh, what an exquisite dish of sweets my poor will have to-day!"

He often had to attend official banquets, but the servants and valets soon understood his manner of life, so, without attracting attention, he followed his normal frugality. He then had recourse to conversation with the guests that were at his side.

Blessed Anthony affirms that sometimes, at the end of these conversations, they asked him to set the place and hour when they could make their confession on the following day.

His mortification at table was accompanied by penances and acts of self-abnegation.

His feet were generally sore, for he had placed pebbles in his shoes which caused him great pain when walking.

One day a domestic entered his room unexpectedly. There he saw recently used bloody instruments of corporal penance, haircloths, little chains and disciplines.

It was in a church in Madrid. A leper wished to go to confession to Blessed Anthony. The people withdrew from the sick man. They felt repugnance at his wounds and feared contagion.

The leper finally approached the confessional. Father Claret tenderly placed his arms around his neck and pressed the head of the sick man to his heart. He gave him a long exhortation, and thus the penitent left consoled and fortified.

His confessional was assailed and surrounded by all classes of persons, men and women, young and old, poor and rich.

It happened that several times it was necessary to place two guards near his confessional, to maintain order and to give each penitent his turn. Some had taken their place in line since the previous night, waiting long hours in the church.

An aristocratic lady approached the grill of the confessional while a humble servant, whose turn it was to confess, waited on the other side.

Father Claret, addressing the lady, said to her:

"Madam, worldly titles do not serve here, nor do money and palaces. I am father of the rich and the poor. Please wait until this penitent has confessed."

The lady waited. She was confused, but edified.

*   *   *

His presence everywhere awakened sympathy and attraction. The people considered themselves fortunate to be able to kiss his ring or the mantelleta of his episcopal robes.

Wherever he preached there was sure to be a crowd. During the period in which the sermons were to be given, it was necessary to defend him, in some way, from the crowding and from the curiosity of the people who surrounded him, by means of a quadrilateral formed of four boards, and to carry him through the middle of the streets and plazas until he reached the church or entered his house. Such was the popular enthusiasms awakened by his apostolic word.

His modesty, as well in private as in large public gatherings, was exemplary. Many persons, on beholding him, awaited his exit at the doors of the church, or stopped him on the sidewalks of the street, or looked upon him with edification from the balconies and windows.

"I have observed," said Blessed Anthony, "that one forms a poor impression of the priest who does not keep his eyes cast down. Jesus Christ always did so. The Evangelists count the times that He raised His eyes as an extraordinary and unaccustomed action."

"During the six years and two months that I remained in Cuba, I confirmed more than three hundred thousand persons, mostly women, the greater part of whom were young. But if after each Confirmation I would have been asked about the type, figure or color of the one confirmed, I would not have known, because when anointing the forehead, I raised and lowered my eyes rapidly."

Those who visited him for the first time, attracted by his fame for sanctity, or by the hope of his influence, soon received two agreeable impressions, caused by the simplicity of his bearing and the poverty of his house.

The revolution in September attacked his dwelling, believing it to be a depository of treasures. It was ascertained however that the value of his furniture and the utensils of his kitchen did not amount to fifty pesetas.

His historian, His Excellency, Most Rev. Aguilar, Bishop of Segorbe, says on the subject:

"In spite of the fact that I knew the house of Archbishop Father Claret almost as well as my own, I never went into it without feeling a deep impression, comparing the poverty of its furniture with the dignity and position of the one who inhabited it, and with what one sees in other houses."

The Bishop of Tarazona, Don Cosme Marrodan, came to visit him one day, and on leaving his own house, exclaimed:

"I am going to visit a saint."

As soon as he returned to his episcopal palace, he ordered his furniture to be exchanged for a simpler kind, more like that found in the home of Blessed Anthony. When people were surprised at the poverty of his furnishings he responded:

"I wish to imitate the saintly Father Claret."

In the writings of Blessed Anthony we find two expressions which are a graphic resumé of the tendency of his spirit. The first is this: "I wish to die on the scaffold or in a hospital. On the scaffold as a martyr of the faith, or in the hospital as a martyr of poverty."

And the second phrase of laconic eloquence: "I would wish that at my death I may be found without three things, namely: without sins, without money and without debts."

Poor in spirit for the love of Jesus Christ, he loved, by preference, the poor of Jesus Christ. His house seemed to be a branch establishment of hospitals and asylums.

"No one ever visited him," says a witness, "without seeing at his door, or in his corridors, some sick or needy person."

"Such was his generosity to the poor," writes one of his domestics, "that in spite of having a revenue of 45,000 pesetas annually, he suffered want in attending to his few ordinary necessities.

One day a priest approached him on the street, and after kissing his ring, said to him: "Lord Archbishop, I am in misery. This is the only cassock I have."

"Go to a tailor immediately," said Father Claret to him, "let him make you a cassock and a cape, and charge it to my account."

The priest did so.

He ordered his porter and his steward never to send a poor

person from his door without giving him an alms, even though his visits were repeated.

"If they return, he said, "it is because the first alms did not suffice."

One day, after receiving his salary, he had the following conversation with his chief steward:

"Let us make the distribution. So much for divine worship, so much for the poor, so much for the spread of good books."

"Hold on, Your Excellency," his steward said, "What about us? What will be left for us?"

"Ah! the best is left for us: God's Providence."

"Very well, Archbishop, but do not forget how scanty our provisions are for each day."

"That does not matter. God will provide."

Thus the dialogue ended. It is a pity that his detractors did not witness this scene.

*   *   *

There is still a golden bead to be strung on the rosary of edifying anecdotes. The deed has all the guarantees of truth, because it is supported by the best historical proofs. It was on the fifth of July, 1866. A poor man called at the door. The porter went out and gave him an alms.

"No, that is not sufficient. I wish to speak to the Archbishop."

"The Archbishop does not receive at this hour; he is busy. If you have some message, I will deliver it."

"No, I wish to speak to him personally. I shall await his audience hour."

So he did. The porter told the chaplain of the insistence of that unknown man who, though poor and all, showed in his manner that he had received a good education. The chaplain, in turn, referred the request to the Archbishop.

"Let him come in," said Father Claret. The poor man reverently kissed his ring and said to him:

"Lord Archbishop, I am a poor and sick man. The doctor

prescribed baths to cure my infirmity. I do not have the necessary resources for either the journey nor the baths. I beg an alms for God's sake!"

Father Claret immediately called the steward and said to him: "Give this poor man the money he needs to pay for his trip and the baths."

"Pardon me, Your Excellency," the steward replied. "All our monthly allowance has been spent in alms and for gift books. It is impossible, Your Excellency."

Father Claret then took the archiepiscopal cross from his neck and said to the steward: "Never permit a poor man to leave my door without the alms he needs. Take this cross to the silversmith, Don Victor Perez on Lope de Vega Street. Bring its purchase price and help this poor man." He did so. The jeweler bought Father Claret's archiepiscopal cross for 1,314 reales and 29 maravedises, and this sufficed for the sick man's needs.

Later, the Bishop of Segorbe wished to prove personally the authenticity of the deed. He visited the jewelry shop of Don Victor Perez. On looking over the account book he found this note:

"July 5th, 1866. An archepiscopal cross, belonging to His Excellency, Father Claret: 1,314 reales and 29 maravedises. With its price he wished to pay for a poor man's trip."

We leave this deed in its historic simplicity. It would lose its force in a commentary. It is an integral touch of character, a concentrated poem of Christian charity.

LIX

ECHOES FROM THE PULPIT

Counsels on Sermons—She Will Be Lost—The Ulcered
Tongue—Sermon on Death—A Picture of
Conscience—The Conversion of Magdalen

God blessed the sweat of the missionary's brow. His passing through the world raised behind him a cloud of luminous dust—the great prodigies of grace. But Father Claret did not count his triumphs. His look was fixed on new horizons of exploration and vast territories of souls whom he desired to conquer.

He thought that his deeds of charity and the history of such heroism, forgotten by him, would also be forgotten by the world. But it was not thus. His life simple and hidden, was like a violet, which announces its presence by the intensity of its aroma.

He always sought humility; but the glory of his virtues and the clamor of his prodigies placed him, to his regret, on the plane of popularity and in the zone of the greatest religious reality.

For that reason, in all the publications of the churches and the announcements of the Missions, novenas, and spiritual retreats his name constituted the best inducement and the greatest guarantee of good attendance on the part of the people at the solemnities. This was the assurance given by the rectors of parishes and presidents of confraternities.

The testimony of his domestics proves that Father Claret preached nine and even ten sermons a day.

In Madrid there is scarcely a church, convent, or hospital of that epoch which does not preserve some recollection of the apostolic word of that archbishop-missionary. But the centers of his religious activity were, principally, the parishes of San Jose, San Cayetano and San Isidro; the churches of Montserrat, of the Italians and of the Knights of Grace; the convents of the

Adorers, of the Carmelites, and the novitiate of the Daughters of Charity, and all the asylums and charitable institutions, particularly the Hospital of St. John of God.

* * *

What the orators of the day most admired in Father Claret was his consistency in preaching his sermons.

One day, Don Hermenegildo Coll de Valdemia preached a brilliant and animated sermon. Father Claret assisted at the function. Don Hermenegildo received congratulations for his discourse. Father Claret, however, retired silently. On the following day, early in the morning, the celebrated orator visited Father Claret; greatly disturbed he said to him:

"Your Excellency, pardon me for troubling you with this inopportune visit. I need to unburden my heart to Your Excellency. I have not been able to sleep all night. Tell me, archbishop, did my sermon not please you yesterday? Your silence has been a warning and a reproof for me!"

Then Father Claret consoled and encouraged him, but at the same time gave him this salutary advice:

"Tell me, Don Hermenegildo, have you ever preached on the salvation of the soul or on the terrible misfortune of the damned?"

"No, Your Excellency, I have not yet preached on those subjects."

"Have you preached on death, on judgment, on hell, on the necessity of conversion, on avoiding sin and doing penance?"

"I have not preached directly on these subjects either."

"Well then, my friend, I am going to speak to you with all sincerity, since you have asked me to do so. It did not please me, nor can I approve the procedure of those who in their sermons omit these great truths of Christianity and only touch upon such subjects as serve but little to convert souls. I do not think that such sermons are either agreeable to or shall be approved by Our Lord, Jesus Christ."

Don Hermenegildo listened and was silent.

A few days later the people of Madrid saw a radical change in the oratory of that famous preacher. Formerly, they applauded his discourses, but now they wept at the unction of his sermons.

*   *   *

Who could give advice with such authority as Father Claret, who bore in his word the virtue of God, and who could move his audience with such apostrophes of a seer and such lights of a prophet?

One day he preached in the novitiate of the Daughters of Charity. He spoke on religious vocation and of the misfortunes of those, called by God, but who do not hearken to His voice.

Suddenly his face became animated, his eyes sparkled, and with accents of profound sorrow he said:

"At this moment there is one among you who is thinking of leaving her Congregation. I now tell her that, if she leaves, she will be lost."

His audience trembled.

A few days later one of the religious abandoned the Institute. The echo of the words of Father Claret, "She will be lost," resounded in the heart of the community.

One day, while he was speaking to the women of ill repute at the Hospital of St. John of God, two of them protested.

"We do not want sermons." Rising up, they began to walk about and to distract the audience.

"My daughters," Father Claret said to them, "listen to the word of God; for, perhaps, you may never hear it again. It may be the last time for some of you. God has made it known to me!"

Then one of them cried insolently: "I will neither listen now nor ever. I have been living this life for twenty years, and I have never yet repented of it."

"My daughter, it may be that you will never say another word. . . ."

Blessed Anthony continued preaching. This was at nightfall. That very night the unfortunate woman became seriously ill. Her tongue swelled and soon fell to pieces, corroded and ulcerated.

She died blaspheming and cursing.

* * *

It was in the church of Montserrat that Father Claret exercised his apostolic ministry most continuously. Owing to the great prodigies that took place there, the people gave it the name of "Church of Miracles."

One afternoon the church was filled with people. Father Claret preached with apostolic vehemence. Suddenly he became silent; he changed his discourse. As though speaking to an invisible person, he began to reproach him, saying:

"Hush, unhappy one. Do not think thus. Do you not know, miserable man, that one should not jest with God? Do you not know that death is certain, and that it may surprise you at this very moment?"

The audience was in consternation.

"With whom was Father Claret speaking?" each one asked himself. The lips of all present formulated the same prayer: "Lord, have mercy and pardon us."

An instant passed. In the middle of the church a man fell to the ground. All hastened to aid him, but he was already a corpse. I must add that his body emitted an unbearable stench. Father Claret was silent. The sermon could not have been more eloquent.

* * *

The Bishop of Plasencia, Don Bernardino Conde, ardently wished to listen to a sermon given by Father Claret. He took advantage of a memorable assembly at which the Nuncio, the Archbishop of Toledo and other high dignitaries of the Church presided.

The multitude was moved and more than all others the Bishop of Plasencia, who not being able to restrain his enthusiasm, exclaimed:

"He is a saint! He is a great saint! In order to speak of God as Father Claret speaks it is necessary to belong entirely to God, in imitation of Father Claret."

Testimony of a marvelous synthesis. For that reason God made the word of the apostle his triumphal vehicle in which He entered the dominion of souls to take possession of them, by means of conversions.

It was in the autumn of 1867, on a rainy afternoon. Father Claret was preaching in a church. A number of people entered it to get out of the storm. One of the refugees was a young perverse and vicious man. He looked at the multitude scornfully, while his lips uttered this expression:

"Father Claret! Deceiver of the people! Listen to the follies this man utters!"

Just at the time, Father Claret was speaking of the wonderful fruits of the Divine Word:

"Do you wish to have an actual example?" he exclaimed with accents of vehement persuasion. "Well, on this very day, this very afternoon, a sinner has entered this temple. He has despised the word of God. He has insulted the preacher with depreciating phrases. The word of God has, nevertheless, fallen upon his heart like a drop of redeeming blood and he has been converted. He is weeping over his errors. He will soon confess all the iniquities of his life."

The sermon ended. Father Claret immediately seated himself in the confessional. A contrite and weeping man fell at his feet. It was that arrogant and quarrelsome young man.

* * *

On another day, Father Claret was preaching in the church of Montserrat. Chairs, pews, aisles, and sanctuary were filled with people. In the vicinity lived two friends; one, Doña Balbina Gonzalez de Bravo and the other Doña Dominga Egurbide de Jimeno. Both were young and wealthy; the former, mundane, and the latter, very pious.

"Balbina, have you not heard the sermons of Father Claret?"

"No, nor do I intend ever to hear them. I have been told that he is a preacher who threatens and who frightens."

"No, my dear. Come with me this afternoon."

"I cannot. I have an appointment. I am expecting a visitor, and then, you see, I have theatre tickets."

The visitor arrived. The conversation ran thus:

"It is true. They tell marvellous things of this Father Claret. He is an archbishop, and, moreover, confessor of the Queen. Let's all three of us go to hear him this afternoon?"

"And what about the theatre tickets?"

"Never mind. You may use them tomorrow."

A little later, three ladies were riding in a coach to church.

Father Claret ascended the pulpit. The theme of his sermon could not have been more opportune. It was on the conversion of Magdalen. Nothing frightening, nothing terrifying. All was tenderness and mercy.

Doña Balbina was in front of the pulpit, seated in a luxurious pew. She was deeply impressed. She bent her haughty head upon her breast, tears streamed from her eyes.

"Balbina, we are going, the service is over."

"No; I cannot leave. I need to speak to that priest. I wish to make my confession right now."

They went to the sacristy, but Father Claret had left quickly to preach in another church.

That night, in the opulent home of the Gonzalez family, the servants noticed the restlessness, the sadness, the preoccupation of the troubled soul of their mistress.

On the following day, early in the morning, Doña Balbina entered the church at Montserrat. Father Claret awaited her in the confessional.

This worldly person, now converted, bitterly wept over her follies. She wished to give herself entirely to God. She wished to break the alabaster box of her heart at the feet of Christ, and there spread the perfume of a new love.

It was truly the conversion of Magdalen.

LX
THE VICTIM OF THE LODGES
Fourteen Attempts

There were in Madrid in the year 1866—according to statistics published in "Le Monde"—forty-nine lodges and one thousand Masons. It is certain that they formed a great conspiracy to impede the apostolate of Father Claret and make attempts on his life.

This persecution by the enemies of the Church was one of the greatest glories of the holy missionary. He thereby proved the greatness of his moral personality and the triumphs of his ministry, something which the Masonic organizations abhorred.

The words which he himself wrote to encourage those who suffer persecution for justice' sake, may be applied to the servant of God.

"Have you ever seen a fig-tree laden with figs, and many birds coming to eat them? Do you wish to know which are the best figs? The birds will tell you. The best ones are those that have been picked at most. This agrees with the Gospel. Our Divine Master, Jesus Christ, has said:

"If you were of the world, the world would love you. But since you are not of the world, the world abhors you."

The life of Blessed Anthony is interwoven with persecutions, intrigues, and threats. The world laid snares of death in his path, and God frustrated them from Heaven's heights. This is the historical truth.

How many attempts were made? Fourteen.

Fourteen attempts, like fourteen crowns that impiety placed at the feet of Father Claret.

What kind of attempts were made? Poisonings, incendiaries, assaults, knife- and dagger-thrusts.

Where were these attempts made? In the house, on the streets, in fields, but above all in the church and the confessional.

What was the result of these attempts? Defeat: the inefficacy of the poisons; the deviation of the knifethrusts; the discovery of the dagger; and, in regard to the assassins, there were either conversion or death.

What was Blessed Anthony's attitude toward all these persecutors? That of Jesus before his enemies,—silence.

"Let them alone," said Father Claret, "they are the builders of my soul. Let them alone. I know what is good for me. Poor creatures! If my enemies knew how much good they do me, they surely would not do it."

Thus spoke and acted Blessed Father Claret! What more have the great martyrs of Catholicsm done in presence of their executioners?

* * *

One day a large box arrived by special delivery. He opened it believing it contained books. What did he behold? A corpse, and on this corpse a paper bearing the following inscription:

"Within a few days you will be like this corpse."

His enemies had planned to do this, but God upset their plans.

His Excellency, Don Melchor Beltran, gentleman of the Royal Palace, sought spiritual direction from Father Claret.

"One day," he writes, "the holy archbishop was in the confessional. When I left it, a man in a blouse approached, apparently wishing to go to confession. The servant of God said to him:

"Throw that dagger away."

Immediately the man threw away the weapon which he had concealed. He apologized to Father Claret whom he had intended to assassinate.

We recall another case. The venerable archbishop was in a Hospital in Montserrat. An unknown man called at the door, asking an audience with the archbishop. It was granted him, and he went directly to the archbishop's room.

After the first salutations of courtesy, and before the man

had said a word which might have made him suspicious, Father Claret suddenly addressed him thus in an energetic tone:

"Throw away the dagger which you carry concealed."

Full of confusion, the unknown man, on seeing himself discovered, said frankly that he was a Mason, and that it had fallen to his lot to assassinate His Excellency.

Then, repenting of his criminal attempt, and touched by the marvellous way in which God had made it known to Father Claret, he fell upon his knees and asked to go to confession. The servant of God heard him and absolved him from his sins. A miracle of God's grace.

*   *   *

The following happening is also very striking. Blessed Claret relates it himself in his Autobiography:

An unknown man, of low stature and with distinguished manners, one day called at the door.

"Is His Excellency, Archbishop Claret, at home?"

"No, sir; he is in the church at Montserrat preaching."

"Will he return soon?"

"I do not know; perhaps in an hour."

The man entered the church while Father Claret, in a burst of fervor and sudden inspiration, exclaimed:

"Ah, my brethren, do you wonder at the enthusiasm with which I speak of the glories of my Mother, the Blessed Virgin? And why should it not be so, for during my life she has averted many evils from me, and even at this moment, she is delivering me from a great danger that is threatening me."

After the sermon the aforementioned man, who had been struck, as if by lightning, by those inspired words, went to see Father Claret. He prostrated himself at the feet of the holy archbishop, who heard the general confession which the penitent made tearfully. He then declared to the priest that he had been commissioned to assassinate him with a dagger, for such a deed had fallen to his lot. The plot was instigated by the lodge of "carbonarios" to which he belonged, but having by chance heard the above words of the sermon, which caused him to understand that Father Claret read the evil designs of his heart, he felt himself suddenly changed into another man, and moved to repentance and to renounce this evil sect to which he belonged, although it would cost him his life. It was evident from that moment that more than a hundred hands would be raised against him.

The servant of God treated him affectionately, consoled and encouraged him, helped him disguise himself, secured a passport for him under another name, and advised him to go to a foreign country. His charity did not stop here. He gave him a pension from his own revenue which would help him defray his living expenses.

What does the world say on beholding these deeds of heroism? These are acts of the saints which the folly of the cross produces in their lives!

The biographers continue enumerating other attempts which he suffered at different periods of his apostolate, but there is one among others which resounded in all Spain and which merits to be placed in bold relief.

It was in the year 1866. Father Claret was preaching a Triduum of the Forty Hours in the parish church of St. Joseph. Like a golden star the Holy Eucharist shone on the Tabernacle. The holy archbishop, from the pulpit moved his audience with his characteristic sermons in which he united love and terror, conviction and unction, flashes of prophecy and the prodigies of a spiritual thaumaturgus.

One afternoon, at the hour for the sermon a woman entered the church. She was passing through the street. On seeing so great a multitude congregated in the church, moved by curiosity, she entered it and there knelt among the devout public. The preacher spoke of the goodness of God and the ingratitude of men; words of deep tenderness and of strong threats. God put a secret force into those words. A few moments later, that young woman was praying and sobbing. The scandalous clothing she wore and her tearful eyes were a contrast that called the attention of the passers-by.

When the service was over, amid the bustle of the crowd, she went out into the streets. She was preoccupied and weeping.

On turning a corner, a young man appeared. He was the accomplice of her sins.

"What has happened? Where do you come from? Why are you weeping?" were the three darts of questions he rapidly thrust at her.

"Tell me quickly! Quickly! I wish to revenge those tears!"

She, overcome, did not know what to reply. But soon, in a firm and serene tone she said:

"I do not wish to hide the truth from you. I shall tell you all. I have been at church. I heard a sermon that moved me. I wish to change my life." The young woman wept as she said this.

"And who was the preacher?"

"I do not know him. I only know that they call him Father Claret. I wish that you also were to hear him for surely you would be converted, as I have been."

"Father Claret! I know who he is. *I* listen to that man's sermons? No, never. But I will go in search of him soon to thrust a dagger into his heart."

A little while later two youths, at the extreme ends of the districts of the "Inclusa," rented a room and there formed a plan for an assassination. Who could be the victim? The preacher at San Jose who, by his sermons, converted that lewd woman.

"I will remain here in this house," said he jestingly. "I will go to bed, feigning to be seriously ill. You must call Father Claret at the late hours of the night to come to attend me. This dagger will then pierce his heart. Do not fear. The crime will remain a secret, for we shall flee in the darkness."

*   *   *

One night an urgent call came to the archbishop's house.

Don Gabriel Sanchez Blasquez, the chaplain, came to the door.

"Are you Father Claret?"

"No, I am his chaplain."

"Have Father Claret come to a dying person at once. I will accompany him myself."

"No, no! I always accompany the archbishop when he goes on a night sick call."

A few minutes later all three were on the way to the house of the sick man. It was two o'clock in the morning. Darkness surrounded them. The streets were in silence. In the distance were heard the steps of a night wanderer. Overhead the stars sparkled. The moon, with the sky as its background, was the witness of so many crimes, and the confidant of so many secrets.

They arrived. The youth and the chaplain remained together at the door, and Father Claret entered.

It was a miserable room leading from a narrow passage. In the rear, a bedroom; in it a bed; on the bed lay a sick man; near the patient a candle light. Father Claret entered and saluted the sick man who did not answer. He took the candle in his hand and approached to see if he was sleeping. But no, he was not sleeping, he was dead. On his forehead stood a cold sweat. His eyes were rigid, a grimace on his lips, and in his clenched hand he had a dagger.

Father Claret gazed upon the spectacle for an instant, then left the room. Greatly moved, he said to the young man who waited at the door with the chaplain:

"But, sir, why did you not call me sooner? There is no sick man here, but a corpse. Go to see him and pray for the repose of his soul."

They entered. The dim candle light emitted rays and produced shadows which augmented the horror of the spectacle. On an improvised bed lay a corpse, that of the obstinate sinner, the accomplice of a mad pursuit, the criminal who wished to thrust his dagger into the bosom of the saint.

The young man gazed upon the scene. His body trembled with horror, a deathlike paleness came over his face. Then came a cry of sorrow. Bathed in tears he fell into the arms of Father Claret.

"Pardon me, Father," he exclaimed. "I am as great a criminal as he. This is a punishment from God. Pardon me, Father, but do not denounce me to the authorities. I wish to be converted. Hear my confession! Right now, right now!"

Sobs choked his voice.

A little later, a scene, which would immortalize an artist's brush and canvas, was enacted in that room. The body of a criminal stretched upon a bed. On his knees the accomplice of the dead man's crime, confessing his sins. The victim seated like a judge who listens and absolves. The chaplain, standing in the shadows, acting as witness. Above, the angels contemplating that picture of the justice and mercy of God.

Father Claret arose and with pathetic accents he pronounced these words:

"I shall not make this deed known to the authorities. I shall not reveal any names, but I shall reserve one right, the right to publish this punishment of God, which shall be for many a striking warning."

LXI
THE LIVING CIBORIUM
The Fact—Documentary Proof—Voice of Theology
Clauses of Fire—Monsignor Lafleche

Marvels of God! During nine years and two months, our Sacramental Lord wandered, really and truly, through Spain, France, and Italy, in the triumphal chariot of a saintly body and in the golden luna of a heart.

The people felt the "passing of God," but were unable to discover the Eucharistic mystery. A double key held it concealed; the key of the secret and that of humility.

But the day of revelation came. Biographers published it for the glory of God. The testimonies of the informative processes gave it official status. The Pontifical approbation of the heroicity of the virtues, of the gifts and of the Divine favors, placed upon it the seal of confirmation, and the piety of the faithful accepted, with veneration and joy, the historic reality of this extraordinary grace.

Its synthesis, in all sobriety of thought and word is this:

"Blessed Anthony Maria Claret preserved in his bosom uncorruptedly, from one Communion to the other, the sacramental species, from August 26th, 1861 until the date of his death, which occurred on October 24th, 1870."

A most singular favor which has scarcely ever occurred in the lives of the saints. Sublime privilege of the Most Holy Virgin, who thus lent her bosom to be the first tabernacle of the world to preserve in it the Incarnation of the God-man; thus he gave his heart for the first tabernacle of the church wherein the Eucharistic God would always be preserved.

But are there proofs that support and record this favor granted to Blessed Anthony Maria? There are, and very clear, repeated and weighty ones.

Let us consider Blessed Anthony's own testimony. The following are the words that on May 15, 1862, he wrote in his spiritual notes reserved for his director.

"On August 26, 1861, finding myself at prayer in the church of the Holy Rosary, at La Granja, at seven o'clock in the evening, the Lord granted me the great grace of conserving the Sacramental Species, and to have, day and night, the Blessed Sacrament within my heart. . . .

"Therefore, I must always be interiorly recollected and devout. Besides, I must pray and brave all the evils of Spain, as the Lord has told me. Effectually, I remember that without merit, talent, or without any interest from persons, He has raised me from the lowest depths to the highest place, at the side of the kings of earth. . . And now, He has placed me at the side of the King of Heaven! Glorificate et portate Deum in corpore vestro!"

Father Claret was very humble; the favor he received was extraordinary. Fearing to be the victim of illusion he attempted, the following year, to efface from his records what he related of this grace, but the Lord and the Blessed Virgin forbade him to do so.

Thus read his own words in his autobiography:

"On May 16, 1862, at a quarter past four, while I was at prayer, the same thing happened to me as had happened on the twenty-sixth of August of last year, regarding the Blessed Sacrament, which I have already quoted and written. I thought of erasing it yesterday and have the same thought today, but the Blessed Virgin told me not to erase it. . . . Later, during Holy Mass, Jesus Himself told me that He had granted me this grace of remaining in my heart sacramentally."

*   *   *

What other authorities confirm this benefit? The Most Illustrious Don Carmelo Sala was, during those years, the companion and confessor of Blessed Father Claret. Well, Don Carmelo gives three splendid testimonies.

The first document is a letter dated December 18, 1879, which read:

"It is true that Father Claret told me that the Blessed Virgin Mary obtained for him from her Divine Son, the grace of preserving in his heart the Sacramental Species from one Communion to the other."

The second document was addressed to His Excellency, the Archbishop of Tarragona, dated April 28, 1880, and gives us the following paragraph:

"Among other graces, Father Claret saw the Blessed Virgin several times and received, through her intercession, precious gifts, such as the gift of chastity, preservation from all dangers of the flesh, and the privilege of keeping within his heart the Sacramental Species from one Communion to the other, as he himself told me during one of the last years I spent with him."

The third document is the declaration he gave in the informative *Proceso* at Vich, for the beatification of the servant of God in which we read the following:

"As regards the preservation of the Sacramental Species, I have this to say: The servant of God had a spiritual book read during meals. At that time, "The Life of Our Lady" by Venerable Agreda was read. One day they read the chapter concerning the Blessed Mother, who preserved in her virginal heart, incorrupt, the Sacramental Species, from one Communion to the other, thus always enjoying the Sacramental presence of her Son. When the meal was over, and I was accompanying Father Claret to his room, the servant of God told me that the Blessed Virgin had obtained for him a similar grace."

Thus read the testimonies of Don Carmelo Sala. Now then, could one suspect an illusion of fervor or an hallucination of the imagination in Blessed Anthony's appreciation of this grace?

No, because Blessed Father Claret did not have an impressionable character; his faculties were ever governed by an unusual equilibrium, common sense, and clarity.

Blessed Anthony Claret did not receive this favor in the time of his youth, a time most exposed to misconception, but in the last years of his life, a time of maturity, of persecution, of interior martyrdom and of the highest state of supernatural contemplation.

For this reason, all the biographers that have treated the life and virtues of Blessed Anthony Claret critically, have proclaimed the historic reality of this Eucharistic prodigy.

For this reason, three very prudent men, contemporaries of Blessed Claret, Father Paladio Currius and the Reverend Fathers Jose Xifre and Clemente Serrat, have repeatedly affirmed it.

The tradition has been unceasingly transmitted among ourselves in the Congregation, and his spiritual director, Don Carmelo Sala, after admitting the above testimonies, added these words of confirmation:

"I did not have the least doubt that this grace was a reality, knowing as I did, the purity of soul of this servant of God, his heroic virtues, his very fervent devotion to the Holy Eucharist, the sincerity and uprightness of his spirit, his exemption from all illusion and pretense.

"It is certain that his presence, in spite of the simplicity of his manner, his cordiality and the confidence he always showed me, produced in me a sentiment of veneration, respect, and reserve that inspired me as did none other of the high dignitaries with whom I came in contact."

Who can calculate the effects of sanctity which this conservation of the Sacramental Species produced in the soul of Blessed Anthony?

In truth, what does Theology say of this grace?

It says, that, if the Holy Eucharist, by virtue of its real presence in a man, augments sanctifying grace during the time in which the said Species remain incorrupt, as grave theologians assert, among them, Cayetan, Suarez, Lugo and St. Alphonsus, how great must have been this treasure of divine grace in the heart of Blessed Anthony, when for the space of so many years he had Jesus, our Sacramental Lord, within himself.

And what does Asceticism say of this grace?

It says, that, if in the words of St. Theresa, one Communion suffices to make a saint, how very holy Blessed Anthony must have been, when he was receiving Holy Communion every instant, so to say, during the nine years and two months that he preserved the Sacramental Species incorrupt in his breast.

And, finally, what does Mysticism say of this grace?

It says that it is one of the most extraordinary supernatural favors known at the present time, to have been granted to any saint, although something similar is told of Venerable Inez de Beniganim, of Sister Gertrude of the Congregation of St. Charles, and of St. Rose of Lima; it is the highest of graces, because being similar to the state of contemplation and infused love, accompanied by the experimental, intimate, and constant presence of God in the spirit, it could well be called, in the classification of mystic stages, "spiritual nuptials," celebrated between God and the soul by means of the Eucharist.

This life of union chained his thought to God, and nothing could disturb him in the intimacy of his colloquies. As he himself wrote to his spiritual director, "In the streets and the plaza, in the midst of an agitated throng of people, I am as recollected as if I were at prayer."

Happy betrothal, which transfused into the heart of Blessed Claret a powerful attraction toward the Eucharist, and created in his soul, as a sublime necessity, the habit of passing long hours in contemplation before the Prisoner of the altar!

He once wrote in his "account of conscience" as follows:

"Before the Blessed Sacrament I feel an inexplicably lively faith. I almost become sensible of the wounds of Jesus and long to kiss them, and finally I feel myself embraced by Him. When the hour for leaving the Divine Presence comes, I must make every effort to resist the inclination of remaining there longer."

This furnace of love had as outlets some ardent phrases,

some burning exclamations, some flames of ejaculations, which issued like living fire from his heart and mouth.

Because these are burning darts of the saint's pen and the sudden radiations of the Eucharist in his heart, I wish to place them here in the integrity of his text which he placed in the hands of his spiritual director.

"After Mass," he says, "I am, for the space of half an hour, totally annihilated. I do not desire anything except the holy will of God. I then live through the life of Jesus. He, in the possession of me, possesses nothing. I possess everything in Him.

"I say to him: 'Oh, Lord, Thou art my hope, my refuge! Thou art my glory and my end! Oh, my love! Oh, my beatitude! Oh, my joy! Oh, my reformer! Oh, my master! Oh, my father! Oh, spouse of my life and soul!

"I neither seek, O Lord, nor wish to know anything except Thy holy will in order to fulfill it. I do not wish ought else but Thee; in Thee and only through Thee and for Thee do I desire other things. Thou art sufficient for me. I love Thee, my strength, my refuge, my consolation.

"Yes, Thou art my father, my Brother, my Spouse, my Friend, and my All. Make me love Thee as Thou lovest me, as Thou wishest that I love Thee.

"Oh, my father, consume my poor heart. Consume it as I do Thee for my nourishment, so that I am wholly converted into Thee.

"Through the words of consecration the substance of bread and wine is changed into Your Body and Blood. Oh, Omnipotent Lord, consecrate me, speak over me and change me into Thee."

Words of audacious sublimity which only love can inspire! Such was Father Claret, a light and flame, because he bore in his bosom the sun of the Eucharist.

Thus is presented the historical basis of the emblem used by the then future Claretian Order. Thus the distinctive sign on the pictures and statues of Father Claret is a resplendent consecrated host on his bosom.

And so the world has a key to the mystery of modesty, recollection, unction, and godliness which was so much admired in the holy archbishop. He was an angel of adoration, who in the midst of the world was far from the world; who lived an interior life joyfully in the Divine Presence because he had, day and night, as his sacramental guest, the God of the Holy Eucharist.

*   *   *

We shall conclude this outline with the words of a Most Serene Infanta of Spain and of an illustrious prelate of the Church.

"I must declare," says the Infanta Maria Isabel de Borbon, "that neither my august parents, nor the royal family, harbor the least doubt of the sanctity of Archbishop Claret.

"I remember very well that he often spoke of his desire to suffer martyrdom.

"I saw him in Rome when he was there for the Vatican Council. People were impressed, on seeing him pass through the streets of the Eternal City, by his modesty and attentive demeanor. He looked like a prelate in "capa magna" bearing the Blessed Sacrament!"

Let us listen to another authority.

One day, Monsignor Lafleche, Bishop of Canada, was conversing familiarly with his missionaries, and speaking of Blessed Father Claret, he said:

"I had no dealings with him, but I saw him sometimes. Whenever I saw him during the Vatican Council on the streets of Rome, I found myself tempted to genuflect before him as before the Tabernacle."

Later, Monsignor Lafleche read in the biographies of Blessed Anthony the relation of this extraordinary grace, and then he understood the cause of those divine radiations of Father Claret.

He was a living Ciborium!

He walked through the streets of Rome like a portable tabernacle of the Eucharist.

LXII

APOSTLE OF THE PEN

On the outline of the XIX century formed by dogmatic apostasies and moral prevarications, there shines in bold relief the triptych of Blessed Anthony Claret, which represents his triple historic personality of Missionary, Archbishop, and Founder.

Around the three panels there is a red, wide border which bears, as an index of life, the motto of his archiepiscopal escutcheon: "The charity of Christ presseth us."

And so it was. The charity of Christ impelled Father Claret, while a missionary, and traced the route of his apostolate on the map of Catalonia, of the Canaries, Cuba, Spain, France and Italy, and later hurled his 25,000 sermons like so many explosions of bombs. These sermons formed the sum total of his oral preachings.

The charity of Christ impelled him as Archbishop when he, traversed four times, mostly on foot, the hundreds of miles over which the archdiocese of Cuba then extended, and when he uttered over that island, like flashes of a seer, the four prophecies of "earthquake, cholera, war and schism." He later left Cuba, to fertilize the seed of his word with the dew of bloody martyrdom, for the knife of an assassin wounded his face in an attempt on his life at Holguin.

The charity of Christ finally inspired him when he became a founder, when he formed a Congregation—the Congregation of the Missionary Sons of the Heart of Mary,—which, in the Cenacle of Vich, felt "tongues of fire" like those that the Apostles felt descending upon them on the first Pentecost; when he divided the world into zones, so that his sons might plant in it, the bloody beam, the cross of Calvary. With the pressure of that lever he hoped to turn the heavy weight of the paganized world to God.

*   *   *

This triple personality of Father Claret—as Missionary, Archbishop, and Founder, has something of the apostolate besides preaching; namely, the apostolate of books.

No one can deny that the heart of Father Claret was an immense turbine which God installed in the electrical center of the Spanish Church.

If this force, on bursting from the lips of the preacher produces crashes of thunder, resounding in eternity, this same energy, on moving his pen to write cast over the paper thoughts like flashes of lightning that shine today, though imprisoned in the pages of his books.

When I was in Rome, I heard from the lips of Pope Pius XI that memorable discourse in which he proclaimed Father Claret an "Apostle of the Press" because he employed, together with preaching another ministry. Quoting His Holiness: "Father Claret employed this more extensive, more modern, more clear-seeing, more intense, more skillful, more popular ministry, that of the press, the book, the pamphlet." I then understood that from the heights of the Vatican descended, in memory of Father Claret, a vindication and a reparation: a vindication of the pseudo-scientific outrages and a reparation of the indifference of pseudo-Catholics.

*   *   *

Is there anyone who can deny Father Claret the glory of being a writer?

One day, the servant of God was at prayer. On contemplating the waves of impiety that were dragging along souls in their current, like debris of a moral shipwreck, he wished to dam the advances of corruption. Raising his eyes to an image of the Blessed Virgin he heard these words:

"Antonio, write."

Then looking up to the Crucifix, as though in a trustful consultation he heard a repetition of the same command: "Antonio, write."

From that time on, Blessed Antonio Maria Claret managed, with equal mastery, the two great professorships in the Catholic apostolate, the pulpit and the press.

Why do we not take a panoramic view of the literary productions of Father Claret as a whole? Because we prefer the eloquence of some figures which have all the documental precision of critical history. The catalog of his books enumerates 144 volumes under 120 titles of different works, with a total of 21,000 pages. It is one of the largest libraries of the world which one single author could form with a collection of his own complete works. What are the subjects of those 144 volumes? They are dogma, moral, asceticism, mysticism, law, apologetics, pedagogy, history, sociology, medicine, music, and agriculture.

The intelligence of Father Claret was like a polished diamond reflecting the rays of all sciences, and his pen on touching the paper left there numerous brilliant writings.

What was the editorial success of these many publications?

There are books written by Father Claret that have had 160 editions and the sum total copies of his published works until 1901, reaches the critically verified number of eleven million volumes with a total of 2.500,000,000 pages.

It is a constellation of books, thrown by one man into space, sown like a star to illumine the path of life amid the shadows.

*   *   *

What profit did he obtain from this surprisingly large diffusion of his works?

Father Claret did not look for pecuniary gain from his publications; he rejected it, depreciated it; he did not wish to adulterate the gold of his zeal with the base alloy of commercialism.

He who did not receive any renumeration for his thousands

of sermons, did not accept compensation for the numerous editions of the millions of copies of his published works.

He presented his original writings to the editors, and then gratuitiously distributed the printed book to the readers.

This is an art in commerce which business men of the world would assuredly reject, because no one could understand the mystery of this philosophy without a "key of heaven."

What pecuniary losses did this proceeding occasion?

Let us see some figures. In the years 1851 and 1852 alone —the first two years of his archiepiscopacy in Cuba—as many as 79,217 books left Barcelona for that Island at the express request of Father Claret.

It was documentally proved that during the six years which he remained in Cuba, he gave to the diocese the fabulous number of 200,000 books. What influence those booklets and pamphlets must have had!

He frequently travelled through the Peninsula accompanying the Queen in her official retinue. He then had the foresight to send ahead a box of books to every station at which they stopped, and in his railway compartments he always had a quantity of magazines, which he distributed at the station and even threw them along the road to passers-by; sometimes he left, as though through carelessness, booklets and pious leaflets on the seats in the train—to arouse the curiosity of the travelers and railroad men and to touch their souls with an impression of the truth.

There are details of propaganda which historians have gathered, such as the following:

"Father Claret crossed the greater part of Andalucia accompanying the Queen. In the towns along the way he distributed gratis 85 *arrobas* (a measure of 25 pounds) of literature in pamphlet form. This traveller was inspired with but one sublime idea and had but one ambition: God and souls!"

*   *   *

It is not strange that his steward informed him many

times that his monthly allowance was exhausted and that there was scarcely enough money left for the needs of the day. What did that matter to Father Claret. The sublime obsession for the spread of good books preoccupied his whole life, and he put all his money into this project with holy prodigality.

He gathered some alms for this purpose, but the principal contribution came from his allowance as Archbishop of Cuba and as confessor to the Queen. The sum total of what he spent during his life in buying books, in order to give them afterwards to the people at Novenas, Missions, Retreats, at visits, and on journeys, amounted to more than one million and a half of pesetas.

Wonderful record! There could be no better inscription that we could carve upon the pedestal of his statue than these glorious figures.

*   *   *

And when did Father Claret write, if he devoted the day to the pulpit, the confessional, visiting the jails and hospitals? He himself gives the answer:

"I write my books during the time that I snatch from my rest."

That time was the greater part of the night, because his rest generally did not exceed three hours, as his biographer declares.

He wrote his books in order to give them away later gratuitously, as spiritual alms. He said:

"I do not wish to give too much money. I prefer to give alms in the form of books. Money is quickly spent, but books are a continuous source of good."

He sent books and pamphlets to towns unsolicited and sometimes without a fixed address. He used to say:

"Since we cannot send missionaries everywhere, let us send good books, which are able to do as much good as missionaries themselves."

Thus thought Blessed Father Claret, thus he acted.

What was the source of that science which flowed so abundantly in his writings? He studied much and read constantly. But on seeing the disproportion between his scientific preparation and the merit of his books, some thought that Blessed Anthony's scientific knowledge was infused.

One day, Father Domingo Coma, a religious of the Dominican Order, who accompanied him sometimes on his Missions in Catalonia, marvelled at the torrents of doctrine that flowed from his lips, asked him whence he drew all this knowledge.

Blessed Anthony then presented him a diptych of the images of Jesus and Mary which he always carried with him, and then said: "This is my book."

He fixed his eyes upon these images as in fervent prayer, before he began to write. Upon them he directed his gaze, as an interrogator, when some doubt in his study assailed him. Upon them he pressed a kiss of gratitude and of love when he suspended his writing.

The compendium of libraries and universal specialization which Father Claret used was: the diptych of Jesus and Mary!

*　　*　　*

What were the general qualities of the writings of Blessed Anthony Claret?

We can say, expressing them synthetically, that they are: truth of concept; clarity of exposition; simplicity; plasticity of the image; unction of spirit; an abundance of comparisons; originality in titles, variety in the application of ascetic doctrine, and a general profound and sensible movement of apostolic zeal which actuates, with the unrest of conquest, the depth and form of all his literary production.

Father Claret always composed his books with a moral aim as a means of proselytism and an organ of apostolate and never as an aesthetic creation. He was a missionary of the pen and not a landscape painter who portrays, with no other aim than artistic contemplation, the panoramas of the spirit.

Balmes was surprised at the number and variety of the writings of his friend and seminary companion, Father Claret, and the great poet Verdaguer, wrote these words in "Aires de Montseny":

"Father Claret was the first, the most active and the most popular promoter which the Castilian language had in the XIX Century."

He gave his plans deep thought, his arguments were in order, he was choice in his comparisons and in the emotions of his heart, all of which were truly characteristic of him. The means he used were interrogations and exclamations and the strategic combination of exhortations and examples.

And then, moved by his humility, he frequently sent the originals to theologians and literary friends of his, such as Don Jose Caixal, Don Pedro Naudo, and Father Esteban Sala, to freely make the corrections they would deem opportune. He also submitted his rough drafts and the first proofs before printing them.

He only regretted being unable to supply sufficient material in writing for the voracity of the printing press and for the greater voracity of souls who hungered for God, for the truth, and for good.

For this reason he sought writers; contracted authors; assigned apologetic and pious material which would meet with editorial success; carefully followed the bibliography of foreign productions in order to have the best works translated into Spanish. Reviewing the three volumes of his letters, 320 in number, we see that he wrote to Balmes, to Don Jose Quintana, to Don Vicente Lafuente, Quadrado and many other literary men of his time, encouraging them to write much and well, each in their own way, to spread Catholic ideas and to better Christian morals.

When they made known their lack of pecuniary resources to have their writings printed, he himself made contracts with editors and booksellers and, moreover, guaranteed the sale, because, as his steward affirmed and his biographers repeated, he set aside 1,150 pesetas every month to buy books and to distribute them gratis.

What a holy obsession Father Claret had to promote good reading!

*　　*　　*

What do all the literary merits of his works amount to compared to the transcendental value of the spirit of God which agitates all their pages?

The writings of Father Claret are like holy sermons filled with unction. Even the most profane reader will soon observe that his words are a reliquary which preserves for veneration, through the centuries, the heart of the apostle.

God, who had preserved the life of Father Claret from so many attempts, defended his books from the fire of hate as well as from fiery flames. The following incident gives evidence of the fact:

It was in April, 1852. Dominicans, Jesuits, and secular priests conjointly gave a very solemn Mission in Balaguer. Father Serra, one of the missionaries, gave one of Father Claret's books entitled, "Advices to Maidens," to a young girl who had been to confession to him.

"They have made me a present of a book, a book of Father Claret," said the young girl joyfully, as she entered her home. She pressed it to her bosom like a treasure and a relic.

"Such things are for priests and friars," said disdainfully the master of the house, an infidel and a blasphemer.

A little later, the young girl opened the book and began to read it by candle-light in the kitchen. The man became infuriated and snatched the book out of her hands.

"Take this book which will please you more," he said to the young girl, giving her an obscene novel. The young girl rejected it with holy indignation.

The man then threw Father Claret's book into the fire, saying: "Thus I would do with the author, if I could."

God, however, wished to honor the author in his book. Instantly the live coals burst into flames which spread into the room burning the immoral book but left the book of Blessed Anthony intact amid the flames.

"A miracle, a great miracle!" exclaimed the young girl enthusiastically.

The man, filled with terror, left the house. He looked for his friends and told them what happened, saying these words that history has preserved:

"Either my servant and the missionaries are demons, or they have a special protection of God."

Night came on. But he could not sleep during the whole night.

"If the flames burn my kitchen thus, how will the flames of hell burn?"

That was the thought which penetrated his mind like a fiery dart.

Early in the morning, at dawn, he called a missionary priest. He wished to go to confession.

The sacristan saw him in the church. On remembering the deeds of that wicked man, he asked himself with uneasiness:

"Is it confession or a conspiracy?"

The new prodigal's tears of contrition proved his sincerity. His conversion was a miracle. A new prodigy of the flames. The cause of all of this was one of Father Claret's books.

*   *   *

How many silent conversions must the reading of Blessed Anthony's works have brought about!

His sermons were of surprising efficacy, but they ceased when his voice was hushed. His books, on the other hand, are sermons impressed upon innumerable pages, which crossing time and space, carry to souls, silently and constantly, the echoes of eternity. Thus they will continue converting and sanctifying, preserving and fortifying.

Surely theirs is the glory of fecundity, because they bear the blessing of God. Why should they not merit the predilection of souls, if several of the books can show, as a *visé* of supreme authority, the express approbation of Jesus Christ and the Blessed Virgin.

The biographers of Blessed Anthony underscore particularly the five times Heaven approved some of his writings.

The first approbation was given while Father Claret was in Cuba. Our Holy Father, Pope Pius IX, had declared the dogma of the Immaculate Conception of the Blessed Virgin Mary. Joyfully and fervently Blessed Claret wrote, at that time, a magnificent Pastoral on the Immaculate Mother, extolling the mystery of her stainless conception.

This document was completed at half after five in the afternoon of July 12, 1855.

The servant of God then knelt down near the table and prayed before an image of Our Lady who presided over his study.

On raising his eyes in gratitude and love towards his loving Mother, he saw that she directed a look at him, while her lips, with gentle accents, pronounced these words:

"Thou hast written well."

The heart of Anthony trembled, and the lines of the Pastoral seemed to vibrate with emotion, like the strings of a harp, intoning a hymn to her purity, at the feet of the Virgin.

Later Our Lady gave him the sweet recompense of a second approbation. Don Carmelo Sala, his chaplain, relates the occurrence.

"Being at table with him," he says, "I observed in him a moment of suspension. He raised his eyes, as though looking at a person who was speaking to him, a smile playing upon his lips!

"Coming to himself he continued eating. Then, on accompanying him to his room, being his confessor at the time, he said to me:

"The Blessed Virgin told me that the little book I had

written on the mystery of the Immaculate Conception was well done."

Our Lord did him a similar favor. He gave him a third sign of approval, which encouraged him to still greater desires to exercise the apostleship of the pen.

We here copy the very words in which the servant of God expressed the details of that grace.

"At half after eleven on June 7, Corpus Christi Day of 1860, while in the Church of Santa Maria, in Madrid, praying with great fervor and devotion after Mass and before a procession over which I was to preside, suddenly Jesus said to me: 'Thou hast written well.'

"I understood that the book to which Christ referred was the first volume of: 'The Instructed Collegiate or Seminarian,' and I knew clearly that He spoke to me of that book."

Later Father Claret published the second volume of that classical work which has formed a large generation of priests in Spain and in America. Upon it fell another express approbation which Jesus formulated in these words:

"It is well."

The fifth and last approbation which Blessed Anthony declared he received from Heaven, was on March 2, 1865.

The Servant of God, wept while he was meditating on the Passion of Our Lord. He saw a cloud of human iniquities arising from the world seeking purification in the Heart of Jesus, wounded and bleeding.

"Enough," he then said. "I do not wish that my sweet Jesus should suffer more!"

Taking up his pen he immediately wrote a poem of love and reparation—a precious jewel—entitled: "The Passion of Jesus Christ."

He took the spirited pages into his hands and placed them as an offering at the foot of the crucifix.

Instantly the lifeless eyes of Christ seems to open. A smile spread over his livid lips and the following words fell like roses from them:

"Thou hast written well, Antonio."

Who can imagine the joy, the consolation, and the holy fortitude these five approbations of Our Lord and the Blessed Virgin infused into the spirit of Father Claret?

His pen was now sanctified. At the end of those works, so authentically approved, was seen the "rubrica" (peculiar mark or flourish added to one's name) of Jesus and Mary, and the most beautiful of all criticisms, the approval of heaven.

* * *

What did all the keen reproaches of the impious matter and the calumnies of intrigue and hatred that were raised against him in the press, in the lecture hall, in the academy and in parliament, organized *en masse* to wound his reputation with interpolated and adulterated texts, with phrases perversely interpreted intentionally and violently contrary to their originals? What impression could have been made upon him by those eternally severe censors of literature, those critics of microscopic vision, that were looking for some impropriety of spelling, some redundancy in words, some morphological incorrectness in his bi-lingual productions, and who did not see, on the other hand, the gigantic silhouette, that his long chain of books traces in the horizon, books mounting to millions of copies, eternal in worth, guarding his forceful ideas, and raising them like the oak and cedar with incorruptible strength, in the creative form of thought?

But these double tactics of the world—hate and depreciation—created about the historical figure of Blessed Anthony an atmosphere of hostility and of indifference, of prejudice and of ignorance.

One must here affirm, in a truly graphic phrase, that Father Claret was the "great calumniated one" of the XIX century and is today the great "unknown" of the XX century.

But the Church is the repairer of all injustices. On placing the image of Father Claret in the Vatican with the "Gloria de Bernini" she wishes to exalt her hero, proscribed by the revolution, and has made the newly Blessed a star in the Catholic firmament, so that he may take on in the world, like all the stars of the heavens, the character of internationality.

Truth triumphs sooner or later, in science as well as in art, in history as in life.

Blessed Anthony Claret who had overthrown impiety by ascending the altars is also conquering proud intelligences by his glory as a writer.

I believe that when historians and librarians investigate the field of ascetical literature of the XX Century, they will find themselves confronted by a pyramid, a pyramid of books counting 11,000,000 volumes.

And when they ask the name of the engineer who constructed this literary monument they will see a statue on the apex of this pyramid of books, the statue of Father Claret, who wields a pen in his hand, like a burning torch, illumining the path of generations on their way toward eternity.

LXIII
THE BLESSED AND THE SAINT
Parallelism—The First Interview—The Letter and the
Constitutions—The Trisagion of the Angels
Counsels of Perfection—The Five Vows and
Their Practise—The Sixth Vow—History
of a Portrait—Synthesis and
Conclusion

Two figures of sanctity, suggestive and heroic, shone forth
in the XIX century over the altar of the Spanish Church. These
were Antonio Claret and Micaela Desmaisieres.

God united them on earth; and the same Pope united them
in the glory of the altar!

She was born on the first of January, 1809, and died August 24, 1865; he was born on December 24, 1807 and died on
October 24, 1860.

She rejects the crown of a Viscountess in order to give herself up to works of charity; he wanted to renounce the archiepiscopal mitre to consecrate himself to works of zeal.

She is the Foundress of the Religious "Adoratrices;" he is
the Founder of the "Sons of the Heart of Mary."

She falls a victim in the act of performing a heroic act of
charity in Valencia; he dies in Fontfroide, a victim of his love
for justice.

She is a Saint since March 4, 1934; he is pronounced
Blessed since February 24, 1934.

She wears a monstrance on her breast as a symbol of her
love for the Holy Eucharist; he carries over his heart a host
in remembrance of the miracle of the Holy Eucharist.

They are two souls with the same spiritual features; purity
and sacrifice, apostolate and persecution, fortitude and triumph!

* * *

"When did they meet each other?"

It was in the year 1848. Blessed Anthony Claret came to

255

Madrid in company with His Excellency, Don Bonaventure Codina, Bishop of Canarias. He was going to the *Afortunadas* Islands as Missionary Apostolic.

A venerable priest, who had great prestige at court on account of his virtue, talent and rank, gave him hospitality in his home during the time he stayed in the capital. This was Don Jose Ramirez y Cotes, uncle of the Viscountess of Jorbalan.

Father Claret was acquainted with the heroic enterprise of the Viscountess; and the Viscountess admired the marvellous apostolate of Father Claret; yet the two illustrious founders had never met.

One day, Don Jose Ramirez received a visit from his niece, Micaela. With great joy he introduced her to Father Claret. It was then that those two souls who were to be so intimately united through life, understood each other in God. It was a formal introduction, but it was the moment chosen by Providence, a moment that left eternal memories in their spirit.

The Viscountess took leave. Don Jose Ramirez then addressed Father Claret, saying: "This is my niece, the Viscountess of Jorbalan. Some praise her virtue; others censure her projects. Many of the aristocracy and of the lower classes say that she is crazy."

"Crazy!" exclaimed Father Claret. "It is the folly of the Cross! These are the works of God! 'Unto the Jews indeed a stumbling block and unto the Gentiles, foolishness!'" (Cor. I, 23).

*　　*　　*

Later on, in the year 1850, Don Jose Ramirez remembering the illustrious personality of the guest of 1848, proposed to the Papal Nuncio the nomination of Father Claret as Archbishop of Cuba. The Papal Nuncio accepted the proposition. Blessed Anthony, having been consecrated in the same year—1850—came to Madrid, and on passing through the Court had a second interview with the Viscountess.

The two saints conversed at leisure and at length. Several intimate and important spiritual conferences followed.

And what was the fruit of these conferences? Great and transcendental.

The biographers have gathered a fact far-reaching in moral meaning. It is said that the Viscountess had a great repugnance to visiting hospitals. Her habits of education and delicacy opposed this tendency. She exposed this difficulty to Father Claret in one of these spiritual conversations. He said to her:

"It does not matter. Grace is above nature. This will be your great victory. Do not fear. God will give you courage, constancy, and consolation."

The Viscountess obeyed. She began to visit these refuges of misery and pain. At the beginning her health suffered from this violence and she soon fell ill. She did not, however, desist. Her moral strength overcame her natural repugnance. In spite of all, she seemed one day to turn from the stench of some sores. She did not hesitate, and in an act of self-conquest, she kissed the sores of the sufferer. Then, with an impulse of heroism, she sucked the putrid matter of the ulcers. This act was the decisive victory in her spiritual life.

This sublime act of the holy foundress was soon known to Father Claret. He gave thanks to God, full of joy, and with a hopeful heart he said to himself: "There are no more ties . . . The eagle has taken full flight."

* * *

Two years had passed since these two holy souls had their second interview. One day, the archbishop, Father Claret, received at Santiago de Cuba a letter and an insured package. The letter was an autograph of the Viscountess, and the package contained the rough draft of the Constitutions by which the new foundations of the Religious "Adoratrices" were to be governed. Blessed Anthony read the letter and the Constitutions with pleasant surprise, and wrote the following answer which we literally take from the "Letters" of Father Claret:

Santiago, May 13, 1853.

To the Viscountess of Jorbalan,

Esteemed Madam:

By to-day's mail I received the letter and Constitutions which you kindly sent me. I have read them and they please me very much. I have made known your message to Don Juan Lobo. Both of us will do something in favor of that House, although it will not be what I would like to do, because my revenues are not for the poor and needy of Madrid, but for those of Cuba, which needs are many after the earthquakes and epidemics. Saint Thomas of Villanova says that the Prelate has to think how he can help the poor of his diocese and not those of the diocese belonging to another because the Lord has given him charge of his own diocese and not of another's diocese. It is not right to take the bread away from the children to give it to others.

I have thought and spoken of you many times, of your House and of the good which is being done. How I wish you would be in my archbishopric! Take courage, then, the Lord will not abandon you; It is His work! If necessary He will work miracles as He did when the Hebrews were in the desert. He does the same every day for Christians who trust in Him and not in men.

Be so kind as to tell your poor charges to remember me in their prayers. Tell them that although they have been sinners, God will not reject them if they have truly contrite and humble hearts; even though they have sinned and are contrite, they will, by their fervor and devotion, deserve communication with God in preference to those souls who have never sinned, as we see in the example of Mary Magdalene, who saw the Risen Savior before the other Marys, and even before the Apostles; this is something for which the mercy of God is to be praised. I am

Yours affectionately,

The Archbishop of Cuba.

Contrasts of life! Eternal strife between the judgments of God and the judgments of the world! The year 1853 was the time of greatest contradictions and trials for the Viscountess. At the time when the work of the Founders was most censured by society, and her spirit was in great unrest there came into her hands this letter of Father Claret; it came as though it had been sent by Heaven. It was full of sweetness and radiant with prophetic brilliancy.

These are God's opportunities; but Providence wanted something more. The "rotation of souls" in the firmament of the Church sometimes has astronomical conjunctions, similar to the stars in the heaven. United in the same ideal, under the Eye of God, they revolve unseparatedly in the firmament of sanctity. This was verified in the case of the Viscountess and Archbishop Father Claret.

How did the Viscountess become aware of the future new interview?

The biographers of Blessed Anthony and of the Saint tell us briefly.

It was in the year 1857. One day the Viscountess went to visit her Majesty, Queen Elizabeth II.

"The august sovereign," says the historian, Don Vicente Lafuente, "affectionately and kindly received the visit of the humble religious, who, conquering her lofty character and aristocratic pride, presented herself, for the first time, at the palace, clothed in the habit of an "Adoratriz.""

The two spoke of the things of God. The Queen told her that she had called a simple and virtuous Archbishop to Spain, and that she would soon make to him a general confession of her whole life, in order to give herself more fully to the practices of piety.

"He is already in Havana," said the Queen, "and soon he will be in Madrid. He is Archbishop Father Claret."

"Father Claret! The Archbishop of Cuba!" replied Mother

Sacramento. "I know him well. He is a great protector of my work."

As she spoke a flash of joy lighted her countenance.

*   *   *

Father Claret, really, soon reached Madrid. He arrived on May 26, 1857. Soon after, two holy souls, Father Carasa and the Viscountess of Jorbalan, were admitted to his spiritual intimacy. God blessed the friendship of these three holy souls. An edifying anecdote proved it. So also did the stories of several religious "Adoratrices" in the Declaration which they made before the ordinary Tribunal, and they are reproduced by the biographers both of Blessed Anthony and of the Saint.

The marvellous event happened thus: The Viscountess, now Mother Sacramento, used to hear angels sing the *Trisagion*, every day at four-thirty in the afternoon, no matter where she would happen to be. The Viscountess communicated this favor, granted to her by our Lord, to Father Carsa in order to know its significance. He, in turn, gave an account of this extraordinary occurrence to Father Claret. Both agreed to ask Mother Sacramento to implore Our Lord to grant them also the favor of hearing the *Trisagion* sung by angels. The Viscountess obeyed. One day, a little before four-thirty, Father Claret and Father Carasa went into a room, next to the one in which the Viscountess was working. Exactly at half past four, they were also delighted with the angelic harmonies which repeated:

"Holy, Holy, Holy Lord God of hosts! The heavens and the earth are full of Thy glory! Glory be to the Father, glory be to the Son, glory be to the Holy Ghost!"

Henceforward, it became the pious custom of the Religious "Adoratrices" to say the *Trisagion* every day at half past four in the afternoon, no matter where this hour may find them.

This heavenly favor strengthened the traditional devotion which Father Claret had already cultivated—the daily recitation of the *Trisagion* in honor of the Most Holy Trinity. In order to spread this practice among the faithful, he composed a book of short pages, under the same title. It contained fervent prayers which found ready acceptance among the people, and which he used as the official text for this holy exercise. In this manner, Father Claret proved his gratitude for the hearing of that angelic concert.

*   *   *

At the death of Father Carasa, in the beginning of 1858, the Archbishop, Father Claret, took charge of the spiritual direction of the Viscountess and her House of Madrid.

"Even before the death of Father Carasa," says the historian Father Aguilar, "the Viscountess and her Daughters had consulted the Archbishop, Father Claret, on several affairs of importance, for Father Carasa's health was fast declining in the last months of his life, and he could not attend to the needs of the Viscountess. Father Carasa himself often consulted the servant of God on business concerning the direction of the Viscountess. It is said, that since Father Claret came to Madrid he was, together with Father Carasa, joint spiritual director of the illustrious Foundress."

For this reason, at the death of Father Carasa, the transition from one director to another was very easy and natural. Since that date—1858—the Viscountess placed herself unconditionally under the direction of Archbishop Claret.

The title of confessor to the Queen, and the fame of his virtues and miracles had surrounded him with an aureola of glory; this authority having been given the new Director, the Viscountess began to feel new courage; thus the goodness of her work was confirmed before the public. Her spirit and her work gave rise to many discussions at times. Sometimes they originated in the hatred of sectarians and at other times in the all too human judgment of many Catholics.

*   *   *

The Epistolary of Father Claret, as well as that of the Viscountess, is a permanent monument of this wise direction: prudence and wisdom, kindness and delicacy, inspiration and zeal, on the part of Father Claret; confidence and sincerity, humility and obedience, veneration and affection, on the part of the Viscountess.

By the text of the letter it can be inferred that Father Claret considered the Viscountess as a great saint, to whose prayers he recommended the fruit of his preaching and ministry: and that the Viscountess venerated Father Claret as a man of God, whose counsels she followed like messages from heaven.

In confirmation of this, Queen Elizabeth II said in the testimony which she presented at the Process of the Beatification of Mother Sacramento:

"Father Claret, my confessor, who also was Micaela's, used to tell me that she was a great saint; and he would command her to come to the Palace to visit me sometimes, for her visits benefited me greatly."

In folio 282 of the Apostolic Process, is added the following testimony of inestimable value:

"The confidence, which the Most Reverend Father Claret entertained for the kindness and virtue of Mother Sacramento, was so great that he communicated everything to her; he would tell her of the supernatural gifts and special favors which God granted to the said Father Claret."

Spiritual conferences, elevated and fervent! Those two hearts, like two stars communicated light and heat to each other; thus both augmented the central focus of the love of God in intensity and efficacy.

*   *   *

Father Claret used to write to her with the noble sincerity which is reflected in the following letter taken from the Epistolary of Blessed Anthony. The passage which refers to the direction of the Viscountess is quoted:

"Please give my regards to the 'Adoratrices' and to your pupils, without forgetting Mr. Gregory and Mr. Besalu.

"And what shall I tell you? What? Practise humility, patience, and charity. Besides, I command you, when you are afflicted, to go before the Blessed Sacrament. Tell our Lord that I sent you to Him. Ask Him to be with you in your sorrow, and with Jesus say:

" 'My Father and my Spouse! If it be possible, let this chalice pass from me. Nevertheless not as I will but as Thou wilt.' Repeat these words not only a second and a third time, but many times until you are satiated."

There is in the Epistolary of Blessed Anthony another document of spiritual direction given by Father Claret to Mother Sacramento; it is in answer to the consulations which she made with regard to spiritual matters.

The Viscountess had written to him how disgusted she felt over everything she did, as it seemed to her that she committed many imperfections in every way, and that she never performed a thing in the way she ought to have done.

The servant of God, after consoling her and telling her that the Lord permitted this in order to keep her humble, added:

"You ask for a remedy? The answer is: humble yourself and say: 'Lord, do not expect anything good from me. You must do everything. I do not know how you permit me to take part in your works. I am like small and mischievous children, who spoil everything on which they lay their hands. Lord, amend my errors! Pardon my faults!'

"In this manner you will go struggling on and advancing until death. You must be like those who weave tapestry. While they weave, they see their work on the wrong side, and after it is finished, they look on the right side and find it beautiful."

With this noble simplicity of style and holy liberty, Father Claret would write to the Viscountess.

If his letters were flames of fervor what must his spiritual conferences and his admonitions in the confessional have been?

*   *   *

Something of this is reflected in the copious Epistolary of the Viscountess:

One day, January 14, 1860, writing to one of her daughters, she said:

"Father Claret comes today to speak to us about Jesus. Can you imagine what he will say?"

"Yesterday Father Claret wept when he pronounced the name of Jesus."

Words of a saint qualifying another saint! How beautiful and profound! Let us repeat them with reverence and love: "Yesterday Father Claret wept when he pronounced the name of Jesus."

In another letter she says:

"It is a pleasure to see a saint as humble and congenial as Father Claret."

In another document she reveals the following:

"The Bishop of Avila, His Excellency, Fernando Blanco, asserts that among the most virtuous persons he ever knew, was Father Claret."

On August 7, 1860, she wrote to the same Bishop of Avila, who at that time was tortured with scruples and other troubles of conscience.

In this letter we read a sincere and expressive eulogy of Father Claret's art in spiritual direction.

"The desire to console you," says the Viscountess to His Excellency, the Bishop of Avila, "makes me write to you. I asked Our Lord the seemingly impossible, that is, to send you some one to calm you. How glad I am to know that the chosen one is Father Claret, and thus is made possible what seemed to me to be a hard petition to obtain. Open to him your heart, make known your doubts, your troubles, with all confidence. He is a saint from every point of view! You will see that what I tell you will come true. You will obtain peace of soul by believing and letting Father Claret guide you. What a consolation God gives me in this for you, as I regard you as belonging to me.

"This favor undoubtedly comes from God. I am not an

Andalusian. No; but fire like the mines is found after seeking for it a while, not under the earth, but in the heavens.

"A great fire will be set ablaze, for Father Claret is inflamed easily. My heart is already moved by his sayings:

" 'Let us love God! Yes; love him for me!' "

"He loves God vehemently. 'Prayer and the love of God,' he used to say, 'if these are given to me then I am a bishop.'

"Do you see, Your Excellency, how the love of God animates souls?"

After this letter of the Viscountess was read, the illustrious prelate of Avila waited anxiously for the visit of the archbishop, Father Claret.

What was his impression of this interview and the fruit of these spiritual conferences?

There is an unpublished letter of the same bishop of Avila, addressed to the Viscountess, dated August 28, 1860. In this letter we read the following words, which are a profound and grateful eulogy to the direction and virtues of Blessed Father Claret.

Among other things, this venerable prelate of the Order of St. Dominic said:

"Today is the feast of St. Augustine, the saint of penance and love. Father Claret departs tomorrow, but he leaves me encouraged, instructed, edified, confounded, inflamed, amazed. I do not know just how. See how many things he has left me." Words of enthusiasm and sincerity vividly reflect the state of his soul, which had been in trouble and is now consoled and serene. All due to the direction he had received from Father Claret.

The viscountess read this letter and was delighted with it. When she heard how her holy confessor was so solicitously attended in the episcopal palace, during his stay in Avila, she wrote immediately to the Bishop expressing her gratitude for the kind reception given to Father Claret, saying that she considered it as having been done to herself.

"I am pleased with the manner in which you and your domestics have entertained the saintly Father Claret."

The Viscountess, knowing that everything pertaining to Father Claret, as well as his counsels, always interested the virtuous Bishop of Avila, wrote thus in a letter dated January 27, 1861:

"Yesterday, Father Claret was here; he heard my confession with so much fervor that he left me encouraged. He gave a conference similar to a retreat-day conference. It was splendid. It was so direct that it was easily understood. He spoke so very well!"

When writing to the same prelate—February 15, 1861— and counseling him to have humility in the midst of his trouble and scruples, she recommended to him the following document of direction given her by her saintly confessor:

"If I confess my sins," says the Pilot—Father Claret— "I exaggerate them . . . He is glad if I accuse myself of some fault that humilates me."

In a letter dated December 22, 1859, to Sister Caridad, Superior of Valencia, who also knew Father, she said:

"Father Claret is leaving here at this time; he came to see me on account of the megrim from which I suffered and because he said he found me sad the last time he visited me.

"I cannot tell you all he suggested in order to encourage me, as he said."

Thus did the Viscountess express herself. These epistolary flashes reflect the noble friendship and the great spiritual intimacy between these two souls, Father Claret and the Viscountess of Jorbalan.

* * *

The counsels of Father Claret were held in so great esteem by the Viscountess that she even sometimes communicated these points of perfection to other souls, hoping that they too might benefit them.

One of the first confidants and depositories of the spiritual teachings of Father Claret, was always the Bishop of Avila, Fray Fernando Blanco.

Among other advices, the one which the Viscountess communicated to the bishop of Avila, in a letter dated from Valencia, July 7, 1860, merits particular mention:

"Two days ago I went to confession to Father Claret, and he said to me: 'Madam, write down all your faults on paper each day. Then do not trouble yourself if you do not know your faults.' That advice is what worries me today.

" 'Let God bear you whither He wills. Make yourself as small as a child, which is carried about without troubling itself where it is taken or where it is brought. The Lord wants the soul to be very small, that He may act freely towards it when and how He pleases.' "

Thus spoke Father Claret. And thus the Viscountess recorded the words of her sainted director.

"Let us become small, like children, in the presence of God, that He may carry us wherever He pleases."

This advice is ever ancient and ever new in the life of souls. It is the way of spiritual infancy, so much recommended by Father Claret in his ascetic direction. It is the echo always vibrating in the world of souls, an echo of the words of Jesus Christ:

"Unless you be converted and become as little children, you shall not enter into the kingdom of heaven." (Matt. XVIII, 14.)

*　　*　　*

The repugnance which Father Claret felt for directing consciences by letter is a pecularity, worthy of note, found in the epistolary of the Viscountess. The Viscountess regretted this repugnance very much, for she had to be absent from Madrid very often, and when she was at Court, Father Claret was perhaps engaged in the duties of his ministry or accom-

panying the Queen in her trips through Spain, or staying at the
Royal Summer Resort.

The Viscountess gives testimony of this in several of her
letters.

On July 6, 1860, she said to a Religious:

"Father Claret does not want me to write to him."

On October 16, 1862, and also on several other occasions,
she had recourse to the Queen that she might bring to Father
Claret the news of certain affairs. Thus she wrote to Elizabeth II:

"Father Claret does not want to be disturbed in the affairs
of his ministry; and thus I beg your Majesty to deign to give
him my message."

The answers which Father Claret gave to these consulta-
tions were very brief; they were general, and not written on
letter paper nor in letter form. He merely made use of cards
and slips of paper. He often used the letters the saint had sent
him and in the margin thereof he wrote a line, a counsel, an
advice, an insinuation, words of direction which the Viscountess understood in their fullest meaning, because they fitted the
actual state of her spirit.

One day he wrote only these words: "Read the 'Glories
of Mary' by Alphonsus Liguori, and continue following . . ."
on the letter that had been sent him. It was an answer to
another spiritual consultation.

"I want you to pray in one way or another. As for the
rest, I do not worry.

THE ARCHBISHOP."

And again, in the same form of marginal annotation he
dispelled the doubts of his penitent in the following words:

"There is nothing but your imagination. God has permitted this tribulation in order that you may be more meek
and humble of heart in the future; experience will prove to
you that more flies are caught with one drop of honey than
with a barrel of vinegar."

These notes of direction gave the Viscountess light and consolation, fortitude and courage. She followed them with courageous and constant efforts.

She writes as follows in one of her letters:

"I will submit to any sacrifice and obey at any cost, the counsels given me by Father Claret."

Resolute words, which bore fruit in her important works; words and works which bore the seal of a manly character.

* * *

Notwithstanding, the Viscountess of Jorbalan had such an exceptional and beautiful soul, and her flights towards perfection were so high and developed so rapidly that Father Claret, although he avoided, as a rule, the direction of souls by letter, had with this holy penitent some epistolary correspondence which is a source of interest and makes us appreciate the mutual influence of the two illustrious founders.

There is one among the letters that merits special remembrance. From the reading of this letter the director and the penitent came forth highly exalted.

At that time Blessed Anthony was in Madrid and the sainted foundress at Barcelona, founding the fourth house of her Institute.

The Viscountess always kept this letter as a relic of a saint. We will transcribe it here in its literal integrity. It reads as follows:

Madrid, November 19, 1861.

Reverend Mother Sacramento,
Barcelona.

Dear Mother in Our Lord Jesus Christ:

I received your letter of the seventeenth of the current month. Since you have asked me to answer it for God's sake, I shall do so. Let me assure you that I approve the three vows and also the two additional vows, five in all, in memory of the five wounds, which is, as you know, my favorite devotion. In order that you may practice them with greater merit, you will do so in the following manner.

Before the Blessed Sacrament, whether exposed or enclosed in the Tabernacle, contemplate Him nailed to the Cross. Saint Michael said one day to a devout soul (*and it is certain that Father Claret was that devout soul*) that in this manner Jesus wished to be honored in the Blessed Sacrament.

Take His right hand with reverence and devotion. Adore it; and recite slowly the Our Father and Hail Mary and offer him your vow of poverty. Then do the same with the left hand, and offer Him your vow of chastity. Then honor the right foot and offer Him your vow of obedience. Do the same in honor of the left foot and offer the vow to choose always the more perfect way of performing your actions.

Note well that I say: these last two vows correspond to the feet. As we use our feet in walking, so should every step be done through obedience, if we wish to obtain God's blessing. Besides, if you wish to obtain much merit in everything, go forward with a right intention always trying to do what is best. Finally, draw near to the wound in the side, which is the wound in the Heart. Tell Him that you truly love Him; that you would rather die a thousand deaths than commit one fault, even a small one, deliberately. Lastly, recite one Our Father and Hail Mary in addition to the five recited; these six Our Fathers constitute a *major station* (devotional visit to a church).

Then form a desire to go to Communion, and, in fact, make a spiritual communion. Then think that you do not live in yourself, but in Jesus; that you are like a metal bar plunged into the forge, which melts and is moulded at the will of the artisan. Thus you must heat yourself in the love of God and melt and mould yourself completely to the will of God. Do this and you will see what will happen. You will not be able to understand it, nor to explain it, but I know what will happen to you. It may not happen always, even though you do so many times!

I am very happy. Today we have had a Court celebration.

Their Majesties are all very well. I saw them last night and also today.

I am passing over my Madrilanean troubles. I am happy everywhere, except in Madrid. It is my Calvary; nevertheless I do not wish to descend from my cross until I am unfastened.

My chaplain, Don Carmelo, has been sick with smallpox, contracted from a patient whose confession he heard. He has been in bed for fifteen days, but yesterday he was able to sit up a while.

Please give my regards to the bishop, as we are great friends and I like him very much.

Regards to all the Sisters who are with you. Tell them to pray to God for me and you do so also. At your pleasure, command

Your affectionate servant and chaplain,

THE ARCHBISHOP OF TRAJANOPOLIS.

*   *   *

The effect which this letter had on the Viscountess and all those who heard it, especially the Religious Adoratrices, was one of great joy and edification. There is a document to prove this. In a letter, dated September 19, 1880, His Excellency, the Most Reverend Bishop Jose Pozuelo y Herrero, who was Bishop of Canaries and later of Segovia, wrote to the Superior General of our Congregation. The following are excerpts of that letter:

"At that time, and in the same city of Barcelona, I had the honor to deal with the Viscountess of Jorbalan, Foundress of the Religious Adoratrices.

"This lady received a letter from His Excellency, Father Claret, who was living as usual, in Madrid. She spoke of the contents of this letter to the Canon of the Cathedral of Barcelona and to me. He wrote to her in confidence of what he suffered in the Royal Palace and at Court; but with such humility, charity and prudence; with such an abnegation of himself, that the three of us, as if coming to an agreement beforehand, burst out at the same time with this exclamation:

" 'He is a saint! He is a saint!' "

* * *

Blessed Anthony, in the above letter, speaks of the five vows of his saintly penitent. Later the Viscountess made a new vow—a sixth vow—which news she communicated immediately to Father Claret.

What was this vow?

We have already guessed it by the reading of the intimate notes of the Viscountess.

It was the vow never to ask favors of the Queen.

Thus the Foundress expresses it in a letter dated February 27, 1862, written to Father Claret. From it we take the following words, which the biographers of the Viscountess should not forget.

"I do not ask you," she writes to Father Claret, "to talk to the Queen about the enlargement of the House, because I know that you do not like to bother her with petitions. I cannot do it, because of my vow not to ask her Majesty for anything. It is a sacrifice, but I do not regret having made it."

Precious document which proves the moral value and the social delicacy of this noble lady!

* * *

Rapid was the progress in virtue which the Viscountess made under the direction of His Excellency, Father Claret. The Lord was pleased to pour down upon this holy penitent the gift of contemplation. Among shadows and lights she was carried in a single flight to the pinnacles of sanctity. Proof of this is found in the following letter written by the Viscountess among others addressed to Father Claret. It reads thus:

Praised be the Most Holy Sacrament!

Madrid, January 1859.

Dear Father: A little while after beginning to pray, whether by day or by night, without knowing how, I fall asleep, as it were. It is not drowsiness, and I do not lose the presence of God; on the contrary, many things are presented to me which I neither hear nor see, and I understand them clearly and with certainty. I awaken so calmly and with such a peace that seems unnatural. Last night, I took great pains to avoid it, but to no purpose. On coming to myself, I was unable to explain what had happened.

Afterwards, I remained with a sweet sadness and a desire to suffer, and this is exactly what makes me fear that it may be deception on the part of the devil. For the reason that I do not have the courage to suffer gladly, it may be a snare which the demon lays for me. I now feel that I am not as strong as when I feel God's presence plainly. Today I did not pray.

Without consulting you, I do not dare to continue in this state, for I have spent days in great trials and tribulations and in working without ceasing.

Do not hesitate to tell me if I am doing wrong, as that would be natural for me.

M. SACRAMENTO.

*   *   *

The letters of the Viscountess reveal a blind faith and implicit confidence in the direction of Father Claret. It seems strange that Father Claret's answer sometimes consisted of only a line or two, and even these were written and signed by the archbishop on the same letter which the Viscountess had sent to him.

The key to this is that God granted to Father Claret and to the Viscountess a mutual spiritual understanding and a profound comprehension of their souls. This is recorded in folio 3864 of the Process of Beatification of Mother Sacramento.

"When Mother Sacramento knelt at the feet of Father Claret in the confessional both understood and comprehended each other, without uttering a word."

Sister Heart of Mary added in the same process:

"I asked Mother Sacramento how that could be? She answered:

" 'If you go out into the balcony you will see a car passing; perhaps also a woman carrying a basket on her head; a man riding a horse. You will clearly see one thing as well as the other. You will perceive everything, although they do not speak to you nor you to them; thus it happens in the present case.' "

Happy the Director who was able to see in the soul of his penitent the wonders of God; and happy the penitent who knew that her Director contemplated the panorama of her conscience in bold relief.

*   *   *

The same spiritual solicitude which Father Claret displayed in the affairs of the Viscountess he also had for the sanctification of the Religious Adoratrices and for the prosperity of their Houses and Colleges. That is why the Viscountess once wrote:

"We consider Father Claret as our own."

In another letter we read:

"Father Claret is the Superior of this House in Madrid." And as such it can be said that he acted effectively in the following case:

A certain pupil, for some time deceived the ladies who lent their support to the College by her pretense to virtue and her concealed hypocrisy.

"Dismiss her immediately; let it be done today rather than tomorrow," Father Claret said to the Viscountess.

"No; we cannot dismiss her," said a lady. "She is a model of observance and piety."

"She might have been bad," added another lady, "but leave her here, for God wants repentant souls."

The Viscountess observed her closely and was not long in following the advice of Father Claret. It soon came to her knowledge that the girl, besides being corrupt herself, had corrupted others. One day, in an excess of rage, the girl wanted to strangle one of the teachers.

* * *

Among the inmates there was even one who made an attempt upon the life of the holy Foundress. On a certain day, there was great alarm among the Religious and the pupils of the House of Madrid. What happened?

The Viscountess fell ill very suddenly and no one knew the cause of her suffering. Physicians came to examine her, but all in vain. An urgent call was sent to Father Claret. The holy archbishop came immediately. On seeing the illustrious patient in danger of death and that the physicians were unable to account for it, he said with an accent of certainty:

"She has been poisoned. This very day they have poisoned her, but do not fear," he said, "she will be cured in three days!"

And so it happened. That very morning one of the inmates, whom the Viscountess had brought out of the mire of ignominy, put poison into the Foundress' cup of coffee. The poison, however, mysteriously lost its destructive effects, and Father Claret's words were verified; before three days the Viscountess was cured.

* * *

There is another anecdote which deserves to be noted and remembered.

The Religious Adoratrices had a great veneration for their holy Foundress. They wished to possess a picture of their Mother; a picture that could be hung in all their Houses so that she could, as it were, preside at all the meetings of her Religious family; a picture that would console them during her absence, for she was compelled to leave them often—a picture of her whose heart imparted to them sweetness and encouragement; finally, they wanted a picture that, after the final separation and all through the years and centuries, would recall her bodily features in proportion as her Institute would reflect her spiritual features.

"No; I do not want my picture to be taken," the Viscountess would say: "Here is the picture which I leave you. It is our Constitutions."

With good reason the daughters insisted on securing a picture of their Mother, and they did not relent in their earnest desire to obtain one. One day they spoke of this to Father Claret.

"Your Excellency," they said, "we would like to have a picture of our Mother. Could Your Excellency command her to have her picture taken?"

"Hardly," answered Father Claret, and the conversation ended.

A few days later Father Claret was at the Royal Palace. He expressed the desire of the Religious to the Queen.

"Very well!" exclaimed the Queen. "I myself have been wishing for a picture of Micaela."

"Hardly!" answered Father Claret again. "The Viscountess wishes to be remembered only in prayer. Nevertheless, I shall try to secure it, because the Viscountess loves Your Majesty greatly."

One evening Father Claret went to the house of the Adoratrices to give a conference to the Religious and before leaving the house he spoke to the Mother Foundress.

"Mother, your daughters are asking a favor. They want a picture so that they may remember their Mother always."

"No; not my picture. Let them pray for me in life and after my death."

"But Mother, there is something else. Her Majesty, the Queen, wishes it."

The Viscountess was surprised and silent. Father Claret then added:

"Yes, Mother, the Queen deserves it, your daughters desire it, and I wish that the picture be taken."

The Viscountess obeyed. Soon the noted painter Luis Madrazo, enriched his collection of paintings with a masterpiece, full of life, spirituality and unction. It was the picture of Mother Sacramento!

*   *   *

The ministries which Father Claret exercised during his stay in Madrid as confessor to Queen Elizabeth II were many; yet, he always found time to give frequent conferences at the House of the Adoratrices. On this fact we have definite and authentic documents.

It is recorded that Father Claret was for a long time the extraordinary confessor of the Religious who came to him freely and confidently to discuss matters of confession and direction.

It is recorded that every year, in the month of October, Father Claret gave the Spiritual Exercises to the Community at Madrid. The saintly Foundress presided over the community almost always at the time of the retreat.

It is recorded that Father Claret celebrated the Midnight Mass on Christmas in the chapel of the Religious Adoratrices, hearing confessions both before and after Mass for more than six hours.

It is recorded that Father Claret preached the Monthly Retreat to the Religious and their pupils on the 25th of each month. This day was chosen for directing their consciences.

It is recorded, finally, that Father Claret visited the House of the Adoratrices almost every week to give a spiritual talk to the Religious and the pupils.

This being the case, was the Viscountess not right in saying that they regarded Father Claret as their own, and that they would obey him as if he were the Superior of the House?

*   *   *

Father Claret's solicitude for the sanctification of the Mother, for the perfection of her Daughters and the formation of the pupils extended also to the whole Institute. The consolidation and the prosperity of the Institute were his aim in Cuba as well as in Spain.

Fortunately, there are evident documents which should be remembered for the reintegration of historic truth.

It is recorded, first, that in the year 1850, when a state of indifference, slander and hostility prevailed in regard to the foundation of that great work of preservation and ransom which the Viscountess was planning, Father Claret had already been named Archbishop of Madrid. He encouraged her to develop her plans and strengthened her spirit for heroic acts of charity.

It is recorded, moreover, that in the year 1853, Archbishop Father Claret received, at Cuba, the Constitutions of the new Institute that he might examine and revise them and, if need be, retouch them before presenting them for Pontifical approbation. Such was the request of the Viscountess.

It is recorded, likewise, that Father Claret having been confessor to the Queen, exercised a powerful influence on the mind of her Majesty, the government and the prelates. When a new house was founded in Spain, the King and Queen accepted the title of protectors and patrons of all the churches of the Adoratrices.

It is recorded, also, that in the year 1858, the Viscountess sent to Father Claret, then at Gijon accompanying the Queen, the engraving for the design of their coat of arms and the device of the Institute, in order that her saintly Director might make any changes he might wish before giving it a definite and official character.

It is further recorded that, in the year 1864, the Viscountess, by command of Father Claret, sent an extensive report to the Holy See. The ends, organization and results of the Foundation, which constituted the matter of this report, made a very good impression on the Vatican Ecclesiastical Tribunal.

It is recorded, lastly, that, in the year 1866, Father Claret addressed to His Holiness, Pope Pius IX, a detailed and praiseworthy statement, asking final approbation of the Institute of the Adoratrices, servants of the Blessed Sacrament.

At the death of the saintly Foundress, in 1865, Father Claret did not abandon her daughters in their sorrow. Every year, until 1868, the year in which he left Spain, accompanying the dethroned Queen into exile—he would visit the Adoratrices on the anniversary of the death of their Mother, to console them and encourage them to follow the example of their illustrious Foundress. In one of the conferences delivered on the occasion of his annual visit, Father Claret pronounced these words which history has preserved as a proof of that miraculous fragrance which spread throughout the churches of the Adoratrices after the death of the saint:

"This sweet perfume which we breathe here comes from the spirit of your saintly Foundress. That blessed soul is in your midst."

The celestial fragrance which was perceived in that chapel by many religious and pupils is a historic fact which is corroborated by a declaration under oath. It figures in the Process of the Beatification of the saintly Viscountess.

* * *

God blessed the work of zeal which was developed in the Institute of holy Micaela by Father Claret.

And how?

By granting to His servant one of the most extraordinary graces in the very chapel in which his ministry of preaching and directing was so often greatly exercised. In 1864, on Christmas night, the Blessed Virgin appeared and placed the Child Jesus in his arms, radiant with glory. Thus were the labors of the Spiritual Director of the Viscountess of Jorbalan and Protector of the Institute of the Religious Adoratrices rewarded.

The Blessed one and the Saint! Two sublime souls! They passed through the world like two eagles in imperial flight, reflecting the clarity of heaven and carrying into eternity the prey of souls.

But in passing they did not die completely; the same as eagles, they have left their nest behind in the midst of the rocks, the nest of posterity.

Two Institutes, like two centers of spiritual generation, will ever preserve their remembrance and will prolong their race; two Institutes which love each other today as their Founders did of old.

God bless the children, as He blessed the Fathers. May these two Congregations be a quarry of apostles and saints.

LXIV

THE WORK OF THE FOUNDER

The Apostles and the Missionaries—Development—The
First Attempts—Scenes of the Foundation—Defini-
tion of the Missionary—The Five Prophecies—
The Voice of Statistics—Thanksgiving.

Twenty centuries ago, an event took place in the world,
which began humbly and silently, as all God's great things
begin. It was in Jerusalem. A small congregation—the congregation of the Apostles—gathered under the presidency of
the Blessed Virgin. This meeting had been called by Peter.
But this reunion of illiterate men had a strange vitality and
transcendency.

It was the "Council of Generals" on the eve of the battle!
It was an assembly of the "General Staff of Jesus Christ" who
studied the map of the world and traced the plan of operations,
for the conquest of the world.

A little later, the Apostles went forth from that common
center to the different nations, like eagles starting from the
same rock, flying in different directions through valleys and
over mountains.

* * *

Thus also the XIX Century witnessed a scene, inferior in
quality and transcendency, but in a strikingly similar manner.

It was in Spain, the nation of Faith, as Judea was then the
nation of God.

It was in Vich, the levitical city, as Jerusalem was then the
priestly city.

Father Claret convoked his elect in a cell, as St. Peter called
his Apostles in the Cenacle.

An image of the Blessed Virgin presided over the meeting
of Vich, like Our Lady presided, personally, at the meeting in
Jerusalem.

The preamble of the Spiritual Exercises was the beginning

of the missionary work, as days of retirement and prayer preceded the apostolic preaching.

The reunion of Vich was the first General Chapter of the Congregation.

The Apostles and the Missionaries had the same ideal and the same motto; the ideal and the motto of Jesus Christ:

"Go to all nations of the world . . . Teaching all peoples, baptizing them in the name of the Father, and of the Son, and of the Holy Ghost."

Both have fulfilled their historic mission, preaching and teaching and baptizing; the Apostles, like the vanguard of Jesus Christ, and the missionaries like the vanguard of the Church.

Extending themselves, like a conquering army, over the territory of souls, both were able to utter even in the very beginning, these words of Tertullian:

"We are but of yesterday, and we already fill your cities." We are citizens of all the nations; because our country for the present time is the world, and when the world passes, we still have heaven as our eternal country.

*   *   *

But God generally develops His programs through numerous ordinances and in measured advances.

What is the genesis and the development of the greatest work of Father Claret in the vast creation of foundations, in which was centered the plenitude of his spirit? It is called the History of the Congregation of Missionary Sons of the Immaculate Heart of Mary.

In the year 1812, Antonio, a child of five years, was weeping in his little bed thinking of the eternal pains which the damned would suffer. His heart, sensitive and kind—the heart of a missionary in the bud—wished to close the gates of hell and to ward off the perdition of souls.

This is the first stage of apostolic initiation!

In the year 1831, while studying philosophy in the seminary, he had a vision of the Blessed Virgin with the crown of roses, of the angels and saintly protectors, and of the infernal dragons, who curled around and bellowed at the foot of his bed. On gaining the victory over the temptations and gloriously wearing the crown of roses, he promises, in his heart, all his life to battle in order to destroy the empire of Satan in souls.

This was the second stage of apostolic initiation!

In the year 1834 he was ordained deacon. On reading, in the Roman Pontifical those words of the epistle of St. Paul to the Ephesians, which say: "Our struggle is not against men of flesh and blood, but against the powers of darkness of the world; against evil spirits, scattered in the air" he acquired— as Blessed Anthony says in his Autobiography—a clear knowledge of the meaning of those powers in the air, of those dragons seen in the vision he had in the seminary. These same words confirmed in his heart the resolution to snatch the prey of souls from those infernal powers.

This is the third stage of apostolic initiation!

In the year 1839, being Ecclesiastical Administrator in Sallent, having experienced the fruits of preaching, and reading in Holy Scripture the passages of Isaias and Ezechiel, he felt the flame of zeal bursting from his heart. Realizing that one man alone could do very little in the vast enterprise of the conversion of souls, he now wished to found a congregation of Missionaries.

This is the fourth stage of apostolic initiation, and the definite starting point for the selection, the working and placing of the corner stone of a Religious Institute.

The ardor of his zeal wished for prompt execution of his purpose. On seeing the impossibility of action at that moment, he felt that the charity of Christ urged him to the Foreign Missions.

In order to go to infidel countries the sooner, he entered

the Novitiate of the Society of Jesus, but a man of an enlightened spirit,—Father Roothan—said to him:

"It is the will of God that you return to Spain."

He returned to the peninsula immediately, and the hidden star of the vocation of a founder again shone in his spirit.

He made his first attempts towards preparations by forming missionaries in Vich chosen from among the priests of the Conference. With those whom he called "companions" he founded "the Choir of Nine Confreres of Carmen," in order better to conquer souls, by the ministry of the pulpit, the confessional, and familiar conversation.

Later, tracing the ideal in a more concrete profile, he formed, with those whom he called "his brothers," "The Apostolic Brotherhood," which is the most perfect experiment and final sketch of his future congregation.

This Brotherhood had, as functions of its apostolic zeal, four principal ministries which were:

1.   Missions, preached gratis in all the world.

2.   Retreats, to be given free of charge to priests and religious, men and women, to be organized periodically every month, in continuous rotation. The houses for retreats were to be proportionately large. At least one house was to be founded in each diocese.

3.   The press, in all its branches: periodicals, reviews, books, pamphlets and leaflets. And, finally,

4.   Teaching and the education of youth on the basis of brief and simple explanation of Christian doctrine and the progressive extension of religious studies.

These were the objectives of the Apostolic Brotherhood, a creation of Father Claret, assisted in this enterprise by his friend and counsellor and Brother of the Institution, Dr. Don Jose Caixal.

Thus, one sees, clearly and definitely, the architectural lines of the congregation, which was about to be founded.

July 16, of the year 1849, at three o'clock in the after-noon, six priests entered the Seminary of Vich.

"What were their names?"

Don Esteban Sala, Don Jose Xifre, Don Manuel Vilaro, Don Domingo Fabregas, Don Jaime Clotet and at the head of them, as leader and director, Don Antonio Claret.

"In what room did they meet?"

In a humble room of the seminary. It was furnished with a crucifix, a picture of the Blessed Virgin, a small table, a very modest chair for the President, and two benches without backs, for the small community.

"What was the text of the first conversation?" History has preserved the most salient points; words of assurance, of cheer, and of faith by Father Claret, phrases of humility, timidity and diffidence by his companions.

"Today we begin a great work," says Father Claret. He then continues to trace, in broad lines, the plan of the new foundation.

Father Vilaro looked at him smilingly, for he saw the dis-proportion between the magnitude of the program and the smallness of the executors. He then said:

"How can we perform such a great work? We are too young, and moreover, we are so few!" He became silent and then lowered his eyes sadly.

With greater force of voice and in prophetic accent Father Claret repeated:

"Today we begin a great work. It does not matter that we are young and few. Thus shall the power of God shine the more."

Father Fabregas as also Father Vilaro, exclaimed with faintheartedness:

"It is too great an enterprise! I do not believe that we are going to do anything."

Father Claret reflected a moment, then, animating his words as with a flash of lightning, he responded:

"Do you not believe it? Do you think that we will not realize this great work? Well, then, know that you yourself will see its development.

Thus it was, for Father Fabregas died in 1895, when the Congregation had extended through Europe, Africa, and America.

Father Sala, amiable and confident, was silent.

Father Xifre, energetic and nervous, with hand upon his chin, followed the progress of the conversation attentively.

Father Clotet, surprised in his simplicity that he should be called upon to collaborate in so great a project, said:

"It is a beautiful plan. I am not fit to work it out. What will you do with a man such as I with a weak constitution, of low stature, with a feeble voice, without oratorical gifts, of little ability?"

His accent was sincere, and his humble heart filled his words with a perfume like unto a violet.

"Enough!" replied Father Claret, "I am not asking for your qualfications. Answer only my question. Do you like the plan?

"I like it very well," said Father Clotet.

"Well, then," concluded Father Claret, "take courage, and have confidence in God and in the Blessed Virgin."

* * *

The first interview was over, and every one went to his own room.

History has recorded, as details of poverty, the number of pieces and the quality of the furniture of each room. It consisted of a bed, a small table, a chair, a wash basin and a small water jug. Nothing more.

Thus the Congregation began. But that great work needed great preparation.

The clock struck five in the afternoon. They again gathered in the conference room which also served as an oratory and they began the Spiritual Exercises. Assembled here were

Father Bach, Blessed Anthony's spiritual director, Dr. Pasa-rell, secretary to the Bishop, Dr. Soler, Bishop-elect of Teruel, and Dr. Naudo, although only to spend the days of the retreat under the direction of Father Claret.

That day, July 16, the Spanish Church celebrated the tri-umph of the Holy Cross through the miraculous victory at Navas, over the Moors, in the year 1212, and the Universal Church commemorated the Feast of Our Lady of Mt. Carmel.

Father Claret, uniting the two thoughts of the day into one text, took as his theme for his first spiritual conference these words of the Psalmist:

"Virga tua et baculus tuus ipsa me consolata sunt."

"Thy rod and thy staff, they have comforted me."

Around the central idea of that day, which was the founda-tion of a new Congregation of Missionaries, he explained and paraphrased the entire Psalm XXII during his sermon. This Psalm is one of confidence and courage, of joy and strength, of raptures of mysticism, and of the sweetness of the Euchar-ist; a Psalm which the Sons of the Heart of Mary ought to re-cite as a family prayer, because it is the Psalm of the founda-tion of their Institute.

*   *   *

Each time that Father Claret spoke, his words acquired more power to secure closer friendship, and more emotion, and in successive conferences he developed the substance of what was to be the asceticism of our Constitutions.

A fragment of these talks has reached us in its entirety. It is the Definition of a Son of the Heart of Mary, composed by a master hand, describing the ideal Missionary, in reality, the faithful picture of the spirit of the Founder. This is the definition:

"A son of the Immaculate Heart of Mary is a man who burns with charity, who casts fire wherever he passes; who desires efficaciously, and tries by all means to enkindle in all the world the fire of Divine love.

"Nothing terrifies him. He delights in privations. He accepts work. He embraces sacrifices. He takes delight in calumnies, and rejoices in torments. He thinks of naught else except to follow and imitate Jesus Christ in work, in suffering and in desiring always only the greater glory of God and the good of souls."

Who can estimate the results of those Spiritual Exercises, which were the first practiced by our humble Congregation?

We may say that this Retreat brought the fruit of the greatest transformation: from timidity to bravery; from mistrust to assurance; from dispersion of energy to solidarity of strength; from the localism of the town and of the region into the internationalism of the Catholic apostolate, which overlooked the panoramas of the whole universe, like zones of Christ.

A Dominican priest—Father Dominic Costa—who had observed these Missionaries when they left the Retreat, reflected his impression in these words:

"I saw them. It seemed as though these Fathers came out of the Cenacle. It was a representation of Pentecost."

The foundations of the edifice had now been laid and soon the structure would be raised.

The officers of the troops had now been formed and soon soldiers were to be recruited.

The nebulous ideal which, during so many years had revolved in the mind of Father Claret, now burst forth of itself, like circlets of light. The first attempt of preparatory institutions had now been definitely condensed, and a star appeared; the Congregation of Missionaries, Sons of the Immaculate Heart of Mary.

*   *   *

The Congregation! And how Father Claret loved it.

One day, on contemplating it with paternal emotion, he uttered five prophesies, some of which have already had an exact fulfillment. The first prophecy was on the apostolate of the Missionaries.

"Throughout all the parts of the world the seven claps of thunder of the Apocalypse will resound; their echoes will redound from century to century."

By the number seven, an indefinite Biblical number, he meant all the missionaries that are preaching the Gospel of Jesus Christ in the world.

The second prophecy was on the duration of the Institute:

"The Missionaries will struggle until the consummation of time, and in the agony of the generations they will fight in the last battle with Antichrist."

The third prophecy was on the protomartyr of the Congregation.

"Days of persecution will come. The blood of a martyr will water the tree of the Institute. I congratulate you. I regret not to have been the first member of the Congregation to shed the blood of my veins for Jesus Christ."

Thus it happened. On September 30, 1868, Pedro Francisco Crusats was assassinated in Selva del Campo by the Revolutionists through hatred toward Jesus Christ and the Church.

The fourth prophecy was on the propagation of the Institute.

"The Congregation will extend very rapidly over the world when it receives the baptism of blood of its first martyr."

It occurred exactly so.

The fifth and last prophecy was on the salvation of the Missionaries.

"All who die in the Congregation shall be saved."

Father Jose Xifre heard this prophecy. Filled with fear and joy, and anxious to receive some amplification on the prediction, he asked:

"Shall we understand this in the sense that all who die worthily in the Congregation shall be saved?"

Blessed Anthony replied:

"Our Blessed Lady did not lay down any conditions."

Two of the co-founders—Father Esteban Sala and Father

Dilaro died during the life of Father Claret and one day, speaking of them he affirmed:

"The two are now in heaven enjoying God and the reward of their apostolic labors, and are praying for their brethren."

These five prophecies of the Founder, which the Congregation preserves as a spiritual treasure in her archives, gave the newly created Institute throbs of hope interiorly and an aureola of providential destiny exteriorly.

For this reason, those missionaries in gratitude to God and to the Virgin Mary for the vocation received, exceeded all measure in their proofs of virtue, of abstinence, of mortification, of fervor and of zeal.

"These Fathers do not eat!" the Vice-rector of the seminary said one day. Blessed Anthony had to correct that excess of penance.

In all seasons, they rose at four o'clock in the morning, and devoted all the hours of the day to prayer, study, preaching, direction of the spiritual exercises, and in visits to asylums, hospitals and prisons.

The house was too small for the daily increasing number of retreatants who gathered there to place themselves under their direction. The missionaries, in the heroism of their abnegation and zeal, then withdrew all into one room and lay upon straw mats spread on the floor. Thus they passed the night quite satisfied and even joyful.

One day, Don Mariano Aguilar, who lived with the missionaries, became seriously ill. The doctor prescribed baths.

Blessed Anthony had already been preconized as Archbishop of Cuba, yet he personally wished to be the nurse of his suffering companion.

It is chronicled that both morning and evening he carried up buckets of water to his room so that the patient could take the prescribed baths.

The Congregation of Missionaries was the dream of Father Claret, even before it existed. Now that it was founded he centered all his affections and preoccupation upon it.

He suffered when his work was endangered in moments of persecution and intrigue. Turning then to Our Lady he said to her:

"Mother, guard them! It is your work! Do you not remember that you yourself inspired the foundation? It is your work!"

He always employed all his influence and his resources to make it prosper; within, by faithful observance, and without, by the exercise of the apostolate.

In his "Epistolario" we find 140 letters addressed to Reverend Father Jose Xifre, on matters relative to the Congregation. In one of them, dated August 20, 1862, he wrote the following lines which bear marks of his zeal, proofs of fraternal love:

"Tell my brothers, the missionaries, to take courage and work as much as they can; that I affectionately love the priests who dedicate themselves to the Missions; that I would give my blood and life for them; I would wash their feet, make up their beds for them; I would cook their meals, and I would deprive myself of food so that they might eat.

"I love them to such an extent as to grow distracted through love. I do not know what I would not do for them! When I consider that they work for God, so that He may be better known and loved and that souls may be saved, I cannot express my feelings. Just now, while writing this, I had to drop my pen in order to wipe my eyes.

"Sons of the Immaculate Heart of my beloved Mother, I wish to write to you, but I cannot, for my eyes are bathed in tears. Preach, and pray for me."

Thus spoke this Father to his sons! What a grand and noble heart palpitates in these words of tenderness and love!

The paternal solicitude, the enthusiasm and the intrepidity of the second General, Rev. Father Jose Xifre, also comforted the members of the new Institute of the Heart of Mary.

The civil authority gave the Institute its official recognition on July 8, 1859; the Holy See granted the "decretum laudis" on November 21, 1860, and definitive approbation on December 22, 1865. On February 11, 1870, the final approbation was given to the Constitutions of the Congregation, and after the publication of the New Code they were confirmed, with extensive eulogy, by the Pontifical Brief "Inter religiosas familias" on July 16, 1924.

The Claretian work grew rapidly. The humble plant which took root in Vich in surroundings of obscurity and poverty is today a gigantic tree that extends its branches to 24 nations, and its shade shelters its many sons of Europe, Asia, Africa, and America.

Today (1934) the Congregation counts 4,000 members, including priests and brothers, novices and postulants.

It possesses 14 Religious Provinces, with 210 Houses and Residences. It directs 7 Seminaries and 45 Colleges, with 5,000 students.

It publishes Reviews and Bulletins in 30 different languages.

Detailed statistics show that the Missionary Sons of the Immaculate Heart of Mary distributed—and that in one year only—10,000,000 Holy Communions and have administered 25,000 confirmations by delegation, 43,000 baptisms and assisted at 6,500 marriages.

The apostolic works also of only one year give the following sum total of our official statistics: 2,000 missions and Retreats; 90 Lenten Seasons; 350 Holy Week Services; 1,800 Novenas and Triduums; 3,000 days of Retreat; 40,000 talks and conferences; 20,000 panegyrics and 250 weekly catechism classes with 40,000 attendants.

And if this is the account of the works of one year, what will be the sum total of all the apostolic and cultural works performed in the 85 years of the existence of the Congregation?

And seeing this mountain of accumulated forces, who can deny that the Missionary Sons of the Immaculate Heart of Mary are continuing the Apostolic plentitude of their Saintly Founder in the Church?

*   *   *

It is true.   Our sublime patriarch was carried to heaven in a chariot of fire, symbolic of his charity, from the solitude of Fontfroide, but on ascending, he cast upon his sons, like Elias upon Eliseus, the mantle of his two-fold spirit.

"Obsecro ut fiat in me duplex spiritus tuus."

And the Congregation, conscious of its duty and the responsibility of its mission, develops, by means of its members spread throughout the world, the glorious ideal of our Father! "Et levavit pallium Eliae quod ceciderat ei."

On contemplating the great works of his apostolic zeal in all the courses of life, and seeing in these works the great likeness between the sons and their Father, the world, in hours of sincerity and holy envy, exclaims, as the prophets of Jericho: "Requievit spiritus Eliae super Eliseum."

People and nations and tribes and races, kissing the footprints of the evangelists of peace setting out on their triumphant career, like the disciples setting out to meet the prophet Eliseus, offer homage of affection and veneration, which is the treasured moral and scientific prestige of a religious Institution: "Et venientes in occursum ejus, adoraverunt eum proni in terram."

This is the account of history.   This is the eloquence of numbers, taken out of the pigeon-holes of official statistics.

For that reason, on seeing the present reality and the hopes for the future, and knowing that all is due to the mercy of Almighty God, I wish to close this picture with these words of the Apocalypse, which will be an homage of praise and gratitude to God our Lord.

"Blessing and glory, wisdom, thanksgiving, honor, virtue and strength be given to God for all eternity.   Amen."

LXV
THE EXILE OF THE REVOLUTION

Revolutions and Volcanoes—Dethronement of Isabel II
—Ministry in Paris—Words of Pius IX—The
Prophecies of the Americas—The Vatican
Council—Papal Infallibility—Illness.

Revolutions break out from within society as volcanoes break out from within the earth. And as volcanoes contain combustibles so do revolutions. These are the ideas, the systems, the theories, the passions and propagandas that disturb intellects, agitate hearts, enkindle the fire of discord, and raise the sudden blaze of hatred.

When these internal convulsions burst the armor plating of repression, then revolutions break out which are like the vents of a fiery volcano, flooding the nation, dragging along in its lava institutions and laws.

History has made the catalog of these revolutions, as geography has made the catalog of volcanoes.

If a revolution, in a period of activity, is a volcano in eruption, the great revolutions, on the other hand, appear in the midst of ages, dead, as extinct volcanoes appear in the mountains, which sometimes have had the sad celebrity of Vesuvius, which left, as a souvenir, the ruins of Pompeii and Herculanium.

* * *

Spain has, unfortunately, been in history one of the nations whose construction has been volcanic.

In the XIX Century it has seen many struggles, insurrections and wars. It has witnessed in Cadiz the revolt of a squadron and a few days later, the bloody battle of Alcolea; then the dethronement of Isabel II who had reigned as Queen of Spain for thirty-five years.

At last, that which Father Claret had foretold many years before was being fulfilled. In the extensive bay of Cadiz there gathered such warships as the Zaragoza, Teutuan, Villa de Madrid and Lealtad; the steamships Ferrol, Volcano, and Isabel II; the schooners Edetana, Santa Lucia, Concordia and Ligera, and transport ships Urca, Santa Maria and the Tornado. In command of the vessels were: Topete, Malcampo, Barcaizegui, Arias, the Guerras, Uriarte, Montojo, Pardo, Pilon Vial, Pastor y Landero and Oreiro and the distinguished Admiral of the "Zaragoza."

On September 18, 1868, General Prim presented himself to the squadron which was placed in battle array.

All recognized him; Topete delivered a speech to the crew; liberty was acclaimed, and with 21 cannon-shots the warship Zaragoza announced the dethronement of Isabel II.

At that time Father Claret had accompanied the Queen to San Sebastian. Her Majesty was spending the summer, with her court, at the beautiful capitol of Guipuzcoa.

The night of the 29th was one of intense distress for the royal family.

"Whom have you seen in my antechambers?" the Queen asked the deputies on the morning of September 30.

"No one," they replied.

"Well, then!" exclaimed the Queen with profound sorrow, "these deserted rooms tell you that I am not to expect help from any direction. . . ."

A little later the Queen was at the railway station. She was accompanied by her husband, Don Francisco de Asis, her uncle Don Sebastian, a doctor, a gentleman, two aides to the King, and two or three Spaniards.

And no one else? Yes, there was the best consolation of the Queen in all the bitterness of that hour, there was her confessor, the Archbishop Father Claret.

Noble gesture, magnanimous act on the part of the archbishop-missionary. Shortly before, when the false and mercenary political world flattered the Queen and wrested from her weak hand a signature to give an honest appearance to

the act and seemingly to applaude the plunder of the Pontifical
States, Father Claret left the Queen and fled from the court
to Rome as a virile and apostolic protest.   And if he returned
to his royal penitent, it was in obedience to the will of the Holy
Father.

But now the Queen was dethroned and was going into exile,
she saw her old flatterers silent, cowardly, involved in com-
plicity and treachery, while Father Claret, magnanimous and
serene, ascended the royal compartment of the train and with
the Queen and her family started on their march to ostracism.

The moments seemed long, because it was a time of concentrated sorrow and repressed tears.

When the exiles passed Bidasoa, history says that, as tears
fell upon the last spot of Spanish soil, a prayer ascended
heavenward.   As the Queen wept, her lips pronounced these
words:

"I cannot endure more."

Gazing sadly upon the horizon, Father Claret prayed:

"God pardon poor Spain!"

*   *   *

The nobility of the French emperor placed the historic
Royal Palace of Pau at the disposition of the Queen and her
family.   They remained there 36 days, at the end of which,
on November 6, at seven o'clock in the morning, they took
the express train for Paris.

What was Father Claret's occupation in the capital of
France?

He referred to it in a letter addressed to Don Jose Godino
on December 9:

"I am lodged," he said, "in a house belonging to the Sisters of St. Joseph.   The royal family now lives at the Hotel de
Rohan, at some distance fom my house.   Every Sunday morning they send the coach for me.   At half after ten we all go
to St. Germaine's Parish for High Mass.   It lasts until almost
twelve o'clock, for there is a sermon during Mass.

"Besides Sunday I go over every Monday and Thursday to teach the Prince and the Infantas. The rest of my time is taken up with ministerial duties, just as in Madrid.

"Her Majesty frequents the Holy Sacraments, for since she left Spain she is less occupied. Yesterday, being the Feast of the Immaculate Conception, her Majesty came to my chapel at the Community House to go to Confession and to receive Holy Communion, then took breakfast with me. The other members of the family came at ten o'clock, and all heard the second Mass, celebrated by Don Lorenzo, my chaplain.

"The people were edified to see the piety and the devotion of the Queen, but they were surprised at the calumnies that some Spaniards had raised against her, and said:

" 'Now the Spaniards are doing to the Queen what the French did to Marie Antoinette.' "

The Convent of the Josephite Religious offered Father Claret hospitality, but the presence of the illustrious exile enveloped that house with the aureola of the saint and with the social prestige of the confessor of the Queen.

Father Claret labored in Paris as he had done in Madrid. The pulpit, the confessional, asylums and hospitals were the centers of his apostolic activity.

Those who received the greatest benefits of these ministries were the many expatriated who had taken refuge there, and especially, the Hispanic-American colony. He gave religious conferences on the Thursdays of Lent, 1869, in the church of St. Nicholas de Beaujou.

The fame of his sanctity spread rapidly to the religious houses and to the devout public of Paris. Many pious persons solicited his spiritual direction.

Years after, the Sisters of St. Joseph kissed the pavement over which he had walked, and turned his cell into an oratory.

Great was the veneration that the virtue of their saintly guest had produced in them.

*   *   *

The residence of Doña Isabel was, however, soon converted into a political center, where all kinds of projects were formulated. Scarcely anything else was talked of there except Spanish politics and plans for restoration.

Blessed Anthony, always abhorrent of such business of the state, determined to leave as soon as the delicacy of the circumstances would permit. He could not abandon the Queen at once, and leave her in the midst of so great a misfortune as her dethronement.

Father Claret wished to flee from Paris, as he had before desired to leave Madrid. He was anxious to live either in Prades, near his missionaries, or in Rome near the Pope. This he manifested in a letter, dated March 3, 1869, written to Rev. Father Jose Xifre.

"In Paris," he say, "we are enjoying good health, are well situated and occupied in the holy ministry—preaching and hearing confessions. There is nothing to be desired on these points. Nevertheless, there is one thing that is annoying and abhorrent, and that is politics.

"You well know that I never wished to meddle in politics. But there are people who suppose that I mix in all these subjects. It has been so since I returned from Cuba. They will imagine it even more than ever, especially, now, that grave matters are to be treated of.

"Several times, on different occasions, I have spoken to her Majesty about my intended retirement, but she will not hear of it; she becomes sad and weeps, and the thought of it makes her ill. On seeing her thus, the inmates of the palace and even her physician came to me, asking me not to leave, charging me with her health and her life.

"Yesterday, however, I proposed the following plan, viz.; at the close of the Conferences or Mission that I am giving— preaching and hearing confessions—and at the same time preparing the Prince of Asturias for his First Communion, and the Infanta Pilar for her first confession, and the Queen for her

Paschal duties, all of which will keep me busy during the whole of Lent—I thought that as soon as Lent was over, that is on Easter Sunday I would leave Paris for Madrid. There I wish to speak to you at length on some very interesting subjects and then leave for Rome or some other place, until things settle down in Spain.

"I can forsee what is to come. Kindly think it over, commend it to God and discuss it with the consultors of the Congregation, and tell me what they propose. I wish to do the Will of God, nothing more!"

Everything seemed to indicate that it was the will of God that he leave at once for Rome.

He did so. He arrived in Rome on April 2nd. On the 11th he assisted at the Pontifical Mass with all the other bishops. On the 24th, he had a long and affectionate audience with Pope Pius IX, during which the Holy Father spoke as follows:

"My dear son: I am well informed in regard to your conduct. I heartily approve of your manner of procedure in the fulfillment of your apostolic ministry. I sanction your prudence and your dexterity in always leaving political matters alone. I bless you particularly because of the persecution that you have endured. Pray that the deliberations of the Vatican Council may have a successful issue."

Father Claret was filled with emotion at listening to these consoling and encouraging words spoken by the lips of the Sovereign Pontiff.

When he was taking leave, in order to return to France, to be near his beloved missionaries, the Holy Father said to him: "No, remain here in Rome, if your health permits, in order to work in the preparation of matters pertaining to the Council, and assist later at the sessions of the Assembly, with the other Bishops of the Catholic world."

Various Cardinals of the Roman Curia also pleaded with him to remain. Father Claret, obedient to the slightest intimation of his superiors in the Hierarchy, remained in Rome, a guest in the Convent of St. Adrian, the Generalate of the Fathers of Mercy.

The impiety which had persecuted him in Spain did not cease to torment him even in a foreign country.

One day, he received a package by mail, without postage; it had come from Spain.

"What can they be sending me from my beloved Spain?" he asked himself. On opening it he saw a collection of infamous caricatures, in which he was outraged and ridiculed. These caricatures were accompanied by newspaper articles replete with threats and calumnies.

One of the Fathers of Mercy, who was present at the time, affirms that Father Claret uttered only these words:

"May God be praised! This is but little to endure for God!"

Similar cases, with varying repugnant snares, were repeated several times. These parcels always came without postage, so that the recipient would have to endure a double molestation: that of offense and expense.

Father Claret immediately regulated his plan of life, subjecting it to the order of the day of the holy community of the Fathers of Mercy, except in regard to the time of rest, which, as usual, consisted of only three hours of sleep, in spite of his being ill and worn out by his continuous labors and penances.

He began to devote himself to apostolic works, the same as he had done in Spain. In order to become more versed in the use of the Italian language, he made a resolution which will serve as an example to every missionary.

"I have resolved," he said, "to speak Italian in all my private conversation while I am in Italy, so as to be prepared to fulfill the better my ministry among my sons in that country."

He practiced the language, as he had resolved.

A Roman, a penitent of his, a very intelligent and pious man once said to him:

"Your Excellency has not much facility in speaking Italian,

but, what difference does it make. Just to see you tells one that your heart is burning with love of God."

*   *   *

Father Claret as Archbishop of Santiago de Cuba was also Primate of the West Indies, so various documents affirm. This title of honor had for him a real and effective significance. It had long been the desire of his heart to go to the Missions in America.

During the time that he remained in Paris, the Spanish-American colony was his favorite audience, and while he was in Rome he often preached and heard confessions in the Latin American College, celebrating Mass and distributing Holy Communion to the students.

America was the noble preoccupation of his life, above all in his last years. In 1865, he had already thought of and re-solved to go to Mexico, to work in the territories of that immense Republic. Seeing, however, that he personally could not realize these ideals, he wished that his missionaries would take up, as a glory for their Institute, the apostolate of the Americas.

Relative to this there are words of consolation and en-couragement found in the letters of Blessed Anthony, words bearing prophetic light, which the heart of grateful America will ever guard as a relic.

One day, drawn by apostolic zeal, he wrote to Rev. Father Jose Xifre. After approving and blessing the project of the first expedition of the missionaries to the Republic of Chile, he added these words which America holds as a glorious prophecy:

"I tell you that America is a large and fertile field; that, in time, more souls will go to heaven from America than from Europe.

"This part of the world is like an old vineyard not bearing much fruit; America is a new vineyard.

"Bishops who have come to Rome from America—I have visited and treated with many of them—are learned and virtuous. They inspire me with hopes. I am old now, but if it were not for that, I would fly there. Since this is not possible, I go to the Latin American College. I have preached to them, given them Holy Communion. They are being well formed in virtue and science."

The above is only an epistolary fragment but of inestimable value in calculating the vastness of the apostolic heart of Father Claret. The evening of his life declined. Over the ruins of Europe, old and worn, he arose like a prophet of God.

Pointing in the distance, amid the foam of the ocean, rising out of the waters to be a new pedestal for the Cross, he said to the missionaries:

"The Americas! There they are! Go, and teach all these people, baptizing them in the name of the Father and of the Son and of the Holy Ghost."

His fore-finger like that of a general in command, fixed on the horizon, seemed like an arrow of light, that traced the route in the air. •

"It was the dream of Francis Xavier, who saw at a distance, like a golden beach, the red sky of the Far East." Father Claret also saw from the coasts of Europe the Americas gilded in the distance. But he was unable to go to evangelize them.

He then made one of the greatest sacrifices to God in his life, the sacrifice of a last apostolic ambition.

*   *   *

Eight months had elapsed since his arrival in Rome. The Vatican Council was most solemnly opened on December 8. It was the most important religious happening of the XIX Century, for the reason, that it was a gesture of doctrinal independence, an act of social value, and a proof of the universal discipline of the Hierarchy, all verified publicly, in an epoch of irreligion in the very heart of the Catholic Church.

Thus it was. A wall of bayonets and cannon threatened the temporal power of the Pontificate. Nevertheless, at the voice of the Vicar of Christ,—weak but eternal—eight hundred Prelates gathered from all over the world.

The great army of Catholicism surrounded the Major General to study the plans of a new military strategem.

It was the mystic realization of our Savior's words:

"Wherever the prey, there eagles will gather."

Cardinals, Patriarchs, Archbishops, Bishops, Prelates of all the dioceses—a large flight of eagles coming from all the mountains of the world to form the imperial court of the representative of Jesus Christ.

Father Claret had, as few others did, the personal experience of the needs of the faithful, because as an apostolic missionary and archbishop he had crossed Spain, the Canaries, Cuba, Italy and France. For that reason he was invited so insistently to form a part of the Vatican Council, collaborating first in the preparation of the subjects to be discussed, then assisting at the sessions of the Assembly; and, finally, intervening, with applause and efficacy, in one of the most critical and solemn moments in the discussion of the Council. "At the present," he says in a letter, "we are greatly occupied in the preparatory works of the Council, which, without doubt, will be for the greater glory of God and for the good of the Catholic world."

Later, in another letter, he wrote these words:

"We are assisting at the meetings of the Holy Council. It is going on well, thank God. I am hoping for great things as a result. We are praying much to God and to the Blessed Virgin, on whose day it began."

*   *   *

But a strange rumor circulated through Rome. Could it be true? It was said that a horrible attempt was being made against the lives of the Fathers while they were assembled in the Council chamber.

No one knew the source from which the notice had come, nor the precise details of the projected crime. But the precautions which were taken in the Vatican, and the rigorous inspection of the basement and halls, confirmed public alarm more and more.

The mystery was solved after years had passed, through notes Father Claret had preserved. They read thus:

"The lives of the Fathers were in great danger. Enemies of the Church had formed the wicked plan to blow up the chapel in which the sessions were held while the Fathers were assembled there.

"One of the criminals was converted and made a general confession when he fell ill. He admitted the attempt, saying to the priest that if he recovered, he himself would confess the deed, but in the case of his death he authorized the priest to reveal it.

"He died. The incident now being known, the basement of the Vatican was examined. Several barrels of powder were found."

The biographers of Blessed Claret, in annotating this manuscript, on examining the details of the story, and on following the steps of the saintly archbishop on his visits to the hospitals, declare that Father Claret himself had been depository of this secret, which he had to reveal, with absolute discretion, at the express and repeated wish of the deceased penitent.

Did the members of the Vatican Council know anything of this? There are no documents that give proof of it. It is only recorded that Archbishop Claret had the fame of sanctity in the Vatican Council. A circumstance came to corroborate this prestige.

One day, in one of the sessions, the dogmatic definition of the infallibility of the Pope was being discussed and prepared. Within and without the Council, above all, in France and Germany, rude opposition was being made as to the conception and form, as to the truth and opportuneness of the affirmative sentence. Inopportune suppositions, loud protests in the press, unjust exigencies in the States of the Church, scandalous publication of pamphlets and bulletins, and, moreover, the threats of interference of civil powers in the decisions of the Council; all of this was heating the atmosphere of the Assembly.

Then, on the thirty-first day, amid general expectation, the Archbishop of Trajanopolis, Antonio Maria Claret, asked to speak. Before the Fathers of Council, who listened to him attentively, he made a beautiful profession of Faith in the Infallibility of the Pope, and exhorted the opponents to raise their eyes above and to ennoble their intentions.

The venerable Assembly recognized the aureola of sanctity that surrounded the orator, the archbishop-missionary. They were deeply impressed when Father Claret in a burst of inspiration and eloquence, pointed to the scars of the wounds he had received at Holguin. Applying to himself the words of the Apostle St. Paul, he exclaimed:

"I bear in my body the wounds of Our Lord Jesus Christ. Would that it were granted me to shed my blood in the defense of the Infallibility of the Pope."

A respectful silence followed Father Claret's discourse. It is recorded that the Secretary of the Council pronounced these words:

"Truly, Monsignor Claret is a Confessor of the Faith."

*   *   *

The Archbishop of Trajanopolis spoke no more. It was his last praise in honor of the Pontificate.

An attack of apoplexy confined him to bed. Very Rev. Father Jose Xifre was promptly notified and prompted by the nobleness of his character, he immediately set out for Rome.

The General and the Founder embraced each other.

"Let us go to Prades. They take good care of their missionaries there. The Fathers and the Brothers are praying for the health of Your Excellency. We all wish to have you in our company always. Let us go to Prades."

Thus spoke Very Rev. Father Xifre. But the mind of Archbishop Father Claret was preoccupied with the thought of Papal Infallibility.

"I cannot go," he answered, "until the dogma of the Infallibility of the Roman Pontiff has been declared. I have offered my life for it. I wish to shed the last drop of my blood in its defense!"

A little later, Father Claret was on the road to Prades, accompanied by Rev. Father General. A flash of joy illumined his face. What had happened? His desires had been realized.

The Fathers in Council pronounced one word: "Placet." Pope Pius IX spoke definitely from the Apostolic Chair. Then appeared in the firmament of the Catholic Church, in the midst of a constellation of revealed truths, another dogma, that of Papal Infallibility.

This dogma always existed in revelation, although it was delayed for centuries in arriving at the splendors of definite declaration. Just so, there are stars in the spaces of creation that have existed since the beginning of the starry world, but which are seen on the horizon,—piercing the astronomical lenses with their light—only at the end of many centuries.

All had been providential. The fourth and last solemn session of the Council was held but a new conspiracy threatened the liberty of the Pope.

On the sea of Europe, ships of war appeared, focusing the mouths of their cannons on one point, the heart of the Church. At sight of this omen of the coming tragedy, the Pope suspended the deliberations of the Assembly.

The Fathers of the Council returned to their respective countries. Pope Pius IX, mild and strong, raised himself against the revolution like a wall of eternity.

A GLORIOUS DEATH

The Scene at Prades—Monastery of Fontfroide—Fall
of Napoleon—Revelation of Death—"Cupio
Dissolvi"—His Holy Death—A Star of
Light—Apotheosis

The revolution of 1868 passed through Spain like a wave of fire, of blood and of tears.

After having assassinated the amiable and angelical Father Crusats, in Selva del Campo, it tore a plant in bloom from the soil: the Congregation of the Missionary Sons of the Heart of Mary. But Father Xifre, like a solicitous gardener, took it up in time and transplanted it in another field, where it was sheltered from the winds. Prades of France! Memories of it are immortal in the history of our Institute. Forty Missionaries lived there in exile. Rev. Father General and his Council resided there. Here those great apostles of the Gospel had their truce of solitude and rest.

The College-Novitiate was situated here. It was like a nursery of youth, surrounding the family trunk with the power and glory of a crown of buds.

*　　*　　*

One day, a memorable scene developed in that retreat. It was twilight of a splendid evening in July, 1870. Above was the pallium of the blue sky. On the horizon the sun melted into gold. There was a house, arising in the center of the city, like an island of silence. Before it, a garden. In the shade of an arbor, the novices of Prades are having recreation.

Suddenly they see a venerable figure approaching; it is the Father Founder, Archbishop Antonio Maria Claret. He came along smiling, accompanied by the Very Rev. Father Xifre and the other Fathers and Brothers of the community.

The heart of the Father and the hearts of the sons beat with the same pulsations, with the same sentiment—love. The sons looked at their father, and saw in him the Saint of whose life and miracles they had often heard in the Novitiate. And the father looked at his sons, and saw in them a new generation of missionaries, who were to perpetuate his apostolate.

A chair was brought and the Father Founder, who had arrived fatigued from his trip to Rome, seated himself. Fathers and Brothers, Students and Novices surrounded him. At his signal they seated themselves—the same as on the afternoon of the foundation of the Institute—on benches without backs. It was a picture taken from Biblical scenes. Thus sat the Patriarchs in the midst of their descendants!

The religious vocation, the observance of the rules, the conversion of souls, the benefit of persecutions, the love of God, devotion to the Heart of Mary, all the cardinal points of the ascetic and missionary life, shone for the time being in that friendly conversation, now in the form of an exhortation and advice, now by way of anecdotes and edifying examples.

All them passed his Excellency to kiss his ring. Father Claret's look rested placidly on each of them; he asked their name, their diocese, hearing which he recalled with feelings of homesickness his apostolic excursions through Spain.

The community, on bended knee, awaited what all sons await from their father in solemn moments—a blessing.

Father Claret raised his trembling hand and made the sign of the Cross upon them, saying: "May the blessing of Almighty God, Father, Son, and Holy Ghost, descend upon you and remain with you forever. Amen."

Was this to be his last benediction? It proved to be so.

*   *   *

The enemies of Spain were not satisfied to see Father Claret exiled. They attempted to pursue him in a foreign country, and for this purpose, they published a calumny to the effect that he was found on the frontier organizing a political conspiracy for the restoration of the monarchy.

An intimate confidant told Father Xifre that on the following day an authorized agent would come and take the Archbishop prisoner.

The Father Founder on being notified of his intended capture, exclaimed with sweet serenity:

"God be praised! I thought so. At least I have had the pleasure of seeing you. Blessed be God! Jesus Christ says: 'When they persecute you in one city, go into another'."

He went to the oratory to make his confession, and then changed his episcopal robes for a priest's cassock. Accompanied only by Father Xifre he went to the Monastery of Fontfroide in a coach. The community of Prades was left sad and disconsolate. The novices began to pray. Seldom did their prayers arise to Heaven with greater fervor and tearful unction as on this occasion.

*   *   *

Fontfroide! What an archive of reminiscences for the Sons of the Heart of Mary! Its name shall ever live among us, like the red sky of glory, because the sun of our Institute set there—that star, sweet and luminous, Archbishop of the Catholic Church, but to us only one thing—our Father Founder.

It was September 2, 1870. The venerable archbishop was in his room. Father Ildephonse was with him. Suddenly Father Claret arose and went to the window. While gazing upon the horizon, he exclaimed with prophetic accent: "Today something extraordinary is happening in France."

Some hours passed by when news on the wings of the press was circulated through the world—the fall and imprisonment of Napoleon in Sedan.

When the Third Republic in France had been proclaimed, a new campaign of hatred and calumny against Father Claret was organized.

Inquiries were made about his place of residence. On learning that he had taken refuge in the Monastery of Fontfroide, Spaniards and French, urged by secret fury, resolved to attack the convent and to take the holy archbishop prisoner.

"They shall not take him," said the Prior of the Monastery. "We have given him hospitality among us, and we will not permit any one to take him from us."

"We are safe," added Father Amadeo, physician of the monastery. "They shall not enter here. I am responsible for his life. I shall not permit anybody to touch the archbishop. I would rather allow them to burn me."

When Father Claret became aware of the new attempt against his life, he said with his usual serenity:

"Poor creatures! They do not know what they are doing. Pardon them. For they know not what they do."

*   *   *

The news that the archbishop was seriously ill and that only a few days of life remained, according to the opinion of the doctors, seemed soon spread through the infuriated mob. The revolutionists believed it and they suspended the realization of their plans.

Was the news of the grave illness certain? It was; painfully so.

Physicians and nurses lavished upon him all the remedies science had to offer. But all definitely in vain.

Father Claret knew that he would soon die, because quite some time previously he had received a revelation from God regarding the day and hour of his death. This fore-knowledge he proved by numerous phrases and confidential intercourse.

It was in October 1867. He was giving a Spiritual Retreat at the Escorial. He chose as text for his talk a quotation from the Book of Tobias, to which he added words which will long be remembered by his hearers:

"These are, my sons, the words that the old Tobias said on taking leave of his son, when he believed that he was going to die. That is what I also wish to remind you of, on this occasion. For what are three years of life?"

During the Spiritual Exercises of 1868 and in October 1869 he wrote these mysterious words:

"I shall remember this truth! Two years and ten months."

That was exactly the time he was to live, after completing his sixtieth year.

Thoughts and affections on death were uppermost in the "Exercises," which he made in Rome the latter part of May 1870.

The first four outstanding points read:

"1. Earth will be a desert for me. My thoughts, my affections, and my sighs shall be directed toward Heaven.

"2. 'Our conversation is in Heaven.' I will not speak, nor listen to anything except things of God and such as lead to Heaven.

"3. I want to have to die, so as to go to heaven and be united with God. . . . Desiderium habens dissolvi et esse cum Christo. . . . Like my sweet Mother Mary.

"4. I must be like a candle, which burns until it dies, giving off light. . . . The members take pleasure in being united with the head; iron is attracted to the magnet. And I, I desire to be united to Jesus in the Blessed Sacrament and in heaven.

"One saint in heaven loves God more than a thousand souls here on earth, according to St. Bonaventure. Misericordias Domini in aeternum cantabo. . . .!"

* * *

On the eighth of October the Community feared that its illustrious guest had reached the end of his earthly journey.

They hastily called two doctors from Narbonne. When their coming was announced to Claret, he said, with a smile:

"Fathers, this means that I am in danger. In that case, we must first think of the soul. I would like to receive the Sacraments."

"Very well, your Excellency," answered the Prior. "We shall get things ready right away. In the meantime, would you like to see the doctors?"

"As they like, Father. But first of all, the soul. Afterwards, let the doctors do what they will with my body."

He began to pray.

"My God, I offer Thee my life for the Church, for the Congregation, for Spain. Take me soon, O my God! Woe is me, that my sojourn is prolonged."

One of the doctors, seeing his ardor and his unceasing prayer, said to him:

"Your Excellency, do not fatigue yourself too much. Moreover, it is not lawful to long for death."

Father Claret then raised himself in his bed and turning his eyes to Heaven, in a burst of profound emotion, which impressed the bystanders, exclaimed, repeating the words of St. Paul:

"Cupio dissolvi, et esse cum Christo! I wish to die; I wish my body to be destroyed in order to be with Christ."

Solemnly, and with all the majesty of the liturgy, the entire community assisted at the administration of Holy Viaticum. His eyes, radiant with light and devotion, looked at the Sacred Host.

Before receiving Holy Communion he wished to make two professions in the presence of Jesus in the Blessed Sacrament: the profession of faith as a believer, and the profession of his vows as a religious, a Missionary Son of the Heart of Mary. The Very Rev. Father Jose Xifre, Superior General of the Congregation, received the two professions of the illustrious dying man, amid the sobs and tears which emotion drew from the missionaries and religious that surrounded the bed.

He then received Holy Communion and remained as in ecstasy. A sigh, an exclamation of love, and from time to time, a favorite ejaculation was heard.

"Cupio dissolvi, et esse cum Christo! I wish to die to be always with Christ!"

*   *   *

Father Clotet, who could not separate himself from Blessed

Anthony, because of the great veneration and affection he had always felt toward him, relates very edifying details of this last illness.

"The charitable care," says the servant of God, Father Clotet, "of those sons of St. Bernard, was greater than we could have asked for: There was no lack of either spiritual or corporal aid such as may be desired in the most critical moments of the life of a man; and these services were rendered with such prudence and charity that all present were in admiration.

"The illustrious dying man enjoyed inexplicable peace and continued repeating the ejaculations which I suggested to him.

"At times, I began the versicle of a Psalm, and he continued it alone, adding the Gloria Patri.

"The doctor and the infirmarian, seeing him suffer so much said:

" 'Poor Father. He is enduring a veritable martyrdom.' The patient, however, always retained the same peace and fervor, and when replying it was always with a sweet smile upon his lips.

"The doctors gave him a choice between two medicines and he replied:

" 'I do not wish to do my will. I will take the medicine the doctors give me.'

"He did not cease repeating the ejaculations that were suggested. He held a small crucifix in his hand and kissing it frequently, said:

" 'Adoramus te, Christe, et benedicimus tibi. We adore Thee, O Christ, and we bless Thee.'

"When we were silent, at times, in order not to fatigue him with so many prayers and affections, he would immediately say:

" 'What else? What more must I say?'

" 'Rest a while, Your Excellency,' his doctor would say, and he responded obediently: 'Very well, very well.'

"A little later, opening his eyes sweetly and looking at his crucifix, he exclaimed:

" 'I am hungry, very hungry for God, for Heaven, for souls!'

Father Clotet, drawing near him, said:

"Let us recite this prayer: "My Jesus, I wish to die with Thee!"

"Ah, yes!" he replied. "My Jesus, I wish to die with Thee. Father, repeat this ejaculation many times for me, for it does me very much good."

Afterwards, in the delirium of the last hour, his parched lips sent forth, with an imperceptible echo, the same exclamation: "My Jesus! I wish to die with Thee!"

"How he suffers!" his doctors used to say. "His state is one of prolonged agony, and in the midst of his pains what resignation and serenity."

Father Clotet writes, "I have never in my life seen greater tranquility."

*   *   *

"As his condition grew worse and after having received the last absolution, he continued the ejaculations that were repeated to him until night came on.

"When no longer able to speak, he continued making fervent acts of piety, now signing himself with the sign of the cross, now striking his breast, now devoutly kissing, with the aid of others, the image of Jesus Crucified.

"An hour later, his strength failed, even for these acts of fervor.

"Clasping his crucifix he seemed to enter upon a new agony. All indications were that his last moments were near.

"Three religious of the monastery remained near him, one at each side and a third at the head of the bed. In their white habits they looked like three angels that the Lord had sent to comfort him in his last long and painful critical moments.

"Father Lorenzo Puig and I were with them.

"It was probably about eleven o'clock when it seemed that he was dying. We lit the candles before the image of Jesus Crucified, and recited the prayers for the recommendation of his soul. While the long terrible struggle continued, we could not help but admire the great peace he maintained and the great resignation with which he suffered his bitter pain. At eight o'clock in the morning of October 24, he was found covered with a cold sweat. He received the absolution for the last time. The room was filled with religious who came to say the prescribed prayers for the dying.

"While the hands of the clock pointed to a quarter of nine, and still holding the crucifix in his hand, he calmly gave his spirit to God, our Lord."

* * *

Dead: His Excellency, the Most Rev. Antonio Maria Claret y Clara was dead.

Dead: The Archbishop of Santiago de Cuba, Primate of the West Indies; Councillor of the Realm of her Royal Catholic Majesty; Knight of the Grand Cross of the Order of Isabel the Catholic, of Charles III and of the Conception of Villaviciosa of Portugal; Archbishop of Trajanopolis; confessor of Queen Isabel II; preceptor of the Prince of Asturias and of the Infantas; and Father of the Vatican Council.

Dead: The Apostle of the XIX Century, the missionary that surprised the world by preaching 25,000 sermons during his life, for the glory of God and the conversion of souls; the writer of 144 different works and of eleven million volumes (counting subsequent editions); the director of consciences; the martyr of Faith; the Wonderworker for bodies and souls; the prophet of great events; the Angel of the Apocalypse who bore in his hands the columns of the rainbow and in his mouth the noise of thunder.

Dead: The Founder of the Missionary Sons of the Immaculate Heart of Mary; the creator of three cultural institutions, the greatest the XIX century saw; namely, the establishment of Parochial and Popular libraries which, in its first year formed 47 centers and put 12,000 volumes into circulation; the Academy of San Miguel, which, in the first eight years of existence distributed gratuitiously 8,000,000 books, pamphlets and bulletins; and the Religious Library, which, in 18 years, had printed 2,811,100 books, 2,509,500 pamphlets and 4,249,200 leaflets; three gigantic publications in which "The propagandist of the Catholic Press" saw the immense power of books and newspapers, and, who in order to offset the influence of bad publications, wished to install a printing press in his Archiepiscopal Palace of Santiago de Cuba, where he himself worked as printer in behalf of culture and religion.

Dead: The Counsellor of saints; the protector of Religious Orders; the propagator of the Holy Rosary and of devotion to the Heart of Mary; the ecstatic adorer of the Holy Eucharist and the Living Ciborium of our Sacramental Lord; the transfigured priest who celebrated Holy Mass amid splendors and who received the Child Jesus in his arms on Christmas Eve.

*   *   *

Dead: Father Claret. At his death God illumined the sky with the prodigy of an extraordinary "arctic aurora borealis" which was a symbol of an aurora of glory which was dawning for him; an aurora of glory in this world by the acclamation of his virtues and the propagation of his work; and an aurora of glory in Heaven which seemed to open amid splendors, to receive his soul, the soul of Blessed Anthony.

Dead: At his death he wished to communicate his passage to eternity to his constant friend, Don Paladio Currius, who was then at Vals de Tarragona. He caused a bell to sound by itself, whose echoes were heard miraculously at several leagues' distance, announcing the passing of the evangelist of peace.

Dead: During the funeral and the Mass, a mysterious little bird appeared in the church. It fluttered over the remains of the archbishop and sang sweetly, joining its arpeggios to the psalmody of the monks. The little bird was silent while the celebrant officiated, but when the choir intoned the responses it gave full power to its voice. At the end of the obsequies it disappeared from the church in the same mysterious way in which it had made its appearance at the beginning of the funeral services.

Dead: On his tombstone the words of Pope St. Gregory VII —words that were a synthesis of his life—were carved:

"I have loved justice and hated iniquity, therefore, I die in exile."

His mortal remains were later removed with triumphant pomp, to the Mother House at Vich. Here they rest in the Church of Mercy, deposited in a magnificent tomb, his holy body being for the Congregation of the Missionaries and also for the Teaching Sisters a beating heart that sends through the arteries of the two Institutions as it were a wave of life filling them with his spirit of zeal, of sacrifice, of purity, of meekness, and of charity.

Dead: From all parts of Spain, Canada, Cuba, France and Italy sounded forth hymns of praise and homages of reparation. Monuments of glory called "Apostolic Processes" were raised for his exaltation in Madrid, Tarragona, and Vich, and before that the "Informative Processes" of Barcelona, Vich, Tarragona, Lerida, Carcasona consisting of 1994 folios and attestations and documents on the life and virtues of the illustrious exile.

Dead: A short time after, the Church authorized the opening of the Cause of Beatification and Canonization, critically examining his writings and approving them; the heroicity of his virtues was studied in detail and proclaimed; the truth of his miracles that had been proposed for Beatification was attested, stressed and countersigned with the seal of authority. Finally, on February 25, 1934, the one who had been calumniated in the XIX Century—Father Antonio Maria Claret —was raised to the honors of the altar.

He passed through the world doing good as a Missionary, an Archbishop and Founder, and as a reward he had received the cross of persecution.

But our Lord says: "Blessed are they that suffer persecution for justice' sake, for theirs is the kingdom of Heaven."

It is history repeating itself.

God makes the sepulchers of his saints glorious, and the Church gathers their names to spread them, like stars in the Catholic firmament, so that they may shine for all eternity.

THE END.

POSTSCRIPT: St. Anthony Mary Claret was canonized May 7, 1950.

Saint Anthony at five years of age, thinking about eternity.

The Blessed Virgin saves Anthony Claret from drowning.

St. Anthony Mary Claret converting robbers.

St. Anthony Mary stops an earthquake by touching the ground.

3 Great Books!!...

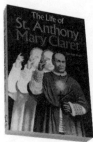

THE LIFE OF ST. ANTHONY MARY CLARET. Fanchon Royer. No. 1027. 302 Pp. PB. Impr. One of the best written, most captivating lives of a Saint we have ever seen. Here was zeal in a priest! Preached over 25,000 sermons and wrote 144 books in 35 years. In 6 years as a bishop, he confirmed over 300,000 and visited every parish in his diocese 4 times. Founded 3 orders. Worked countless miracles! Great!   **12.00**

THE AUTOBIOGRAPHY OF ST. ANTHONY MARY CLARET. St. Anthony Mary Claret. No. 1023. 227 Pp. PB. Impr. Does not duplicate the *Life*. Both books should be read together. Bares the soul of a saint and reveals the methods and techniques which were so successful for him! Both the *Life* and the *Autobiography* deliver an impact that is truly incredible!   **10.00**

THE MIRACLES OF SAINT ANTHONY MARY CLARET. Fr. Juan Echevarria. No. 1184. 318 Pp. PB. Impr. This book is full of true stories from the life of the great St. Anthony Mary Claret, telling how he healed souls and bodies, read hearts, foretold the future, was harassed by the devil, and much, much more! There is one great story after another recounted here!   **12.50**

THE SET OF ALL 3 ST. ANTHONY MARY CLARET BOOKS—*A $34.50 Value*—   Only 30.00!!